Postcolonial France

Race, Islam, and the Future of the Republic

Paul A. Silverstein

PLUTO PRESS

First published 2018 by Pluto Press
345 Archway Road, London N6 5AA

www.plutobooks.com

British Library Cataloguing in Publication Data
A catalogue record for this book is available from the British Library

ISBN   978 0 7453 3775 3   Hardback
ISBN   978 0 7453 3774 6   Paperback
ISBN   978 1 7868 0296 5   PDF eBook
ISBN   978 1 7868 0298 9   Kindle eBook
ISBN   978 1 7868 0297 2   EPUB eBook

This book is printed on paper suitable for recycling and made from fully
managed and sustained forest sources. Logging, pulping and manufacturing
processes are expected to conform to the environmental standards of the
country of origin.

Typeset by Stanford DTP Services, Northampton, England

Simultaneously printed in the United Kingdom and United States of America

Postcolonial France

Contents

Acknowledgments

I never intended to write another book about France, but events conspired otherwise. The seed was inadvertently sown by my mother-in-law, Tatiana Nikolaevna, who innocently asked me whether a short blog piece I was writing was "my book." The seed germinated over the next several years with the encouragement of many colleagues across several continents, and ultimately thanks to the unending enthusiasm, editorial wisdom, and especially patience of David Shulman. Gratitude as well to Philip Thomas for his meticulous copyediting, and to the entire team at Pluto Press, the perfect home for the kind of critical engagement to which I aspire.

I have tried out a number of the ideas and interpretations included in this book in departmental seminars, research colloquia, workshops, and conferences at universities across the globe over the past decade, including in Amsterdam, Ashdod, Berkeley, Bochum, Brussels, Chicago, Harvard, Hong Kong, Jerusalem, Leuven, Lille, Maastricht, Nijmegen, NYU, Pittsburgh, Prague, UCLA, and Utrecht, as well as here in Oregon. Colleagues and comrades across these institutions and beyond have at various points provided timely feedback, commentary, and inspiration. Indeed, in many ways, this book is very much the product of ongoing collaboration and collective reflection. I am particularly thankful for all the years of insight, encouragement, suggestions, and critique of Joel Beinin, Naor Ben-Yehoyada, Sarah Bracke, John Bunzl, Matti Bunzl, Azar Dakwar, Andrew Diamond, Laurent Dubois, Olivier Esteves, Nadia Fadil, Mayanthi Fernando, Steve Foster, Michael Frishkopf, Abdellali Hajjat, Abdellah Hammoudi, Michael Herzfeld, Elizabeth Hurd, Yolande Janssen, Rick Jobs, Jeanette Jouili, Ethan Katz, Julie Kleinman, Brian Klug, Anouk de Koning, Brian Larkin, Michel Laronde, André Levy, Françoise Lionnet, Ussama Makdisi, David McMurray, Nasar Meer, Annelies Moors, Susan Ossman, Esra Özyürek, Todd Shepard, Daniel Sherman, Ella Shohat, Andrew Shryock, Susan Slyomovics, Barbora Spalová, Federico Spinetti, Benjamin Stora, Tyler Stovall, Thijl Sunier, Ted Swedenburg, Susan Terrio, Miriam Ticktin, Anya Topolski, Kathrine van den Bogert, Lauren Wagner, Gary Wilder, and all my comrades within the MERIP collective. An especial shout out to Hisham Aidi and Chantal Tetreault for their eleventh-hour sanity check, as well as to the three anonymous reviewers who pushed me to clarify my intervention.

My long-term study of France was augmented by a generous Carnegie Scholar Fellowship from the Carnegie Corporation of New York. The chance to deepen the transatlantic conversation was enabled by a subsequent opportunity from the Fulbright Scholar program to spend a research sabbatical at the Interculturalism, Migration and Minorities Research Center (IMMRC) at the University of Leuven; I am grateful to Erica Lutes, Sofie De Rijck, and all my Leuven anthropology colleagues for welcoming an American stray.

Closer to home, the support I have received over the years from Reed College has always gone beyond all reasonable expectations. My colleagues and especially my students have provided a truly inspiring intellectual community. Special thanks to Malina Cheeneebash for help preparing the book's index. But of course the real source of unending support has been my dear friends and family. Anya and Nadya brought joy on a daily basis and patiently put up with my prolonged absences and derelictions of household duty. They may not have written the words which follow, but there would have been no words without them. I love you very much.

Chapter 3 draws on "The Fantasy and Violence of Religious Imagination: Islamophobia and Anti-Semitism in France and North Africa," in *Islamophobia/Islamophilia: Beyond the Politics of Enemy and Friend*, ed. Andrew Shryock (Bloomington: Indiana University Press, 2010, pp. 141–71). I am grateful to Indiana University Press for permission to draw on this earlier work.

An earlier version of Chapter 7 appeared as "Sounds of Love and Hate: Sufi Rap, Ghetto Patrimony, and the Concrete Politics of the French Urban Periphery," in *Music, Sound, and Architecture in Islam*, ed. Michael Frishkopf and Federico Spinetti (Austin: University of Texas Press, 2018, pp. 255–79). I am grateful to the University of Texas Press for permission to reprint the materials.

Abbreviations

AICP	Association of Islamic Charitable Projects
AQAP	Al-Qaeda in the Arabian Peninsula
BAC	Anti-Criminal Brigade
CCIF	Collective against Islamophobia in France
CFCM	French Councils on the Muslim Faith
CNHI	National Center for the History of Immigration
CRAN	Representative Council of Black Associations
CRIF	Representative Council of Jewish Institutions
FFF	French Football Federation
FIFA	Fédération Internationale de Football Association
FLN	National Liberation Front (Algeria)
GIA	Algerian Armed Islamic Group
ICI	Islamic Cultures Institute
INSEP	National Institute of Sport, Expertise, and Performance
LICRA	International League against Racism and Anti-Semitism
MIB	Mouvement Immigration Banlieue
MRAP	Movement Against Racism, Anti-Semitism, and for Peace
NPNS	Ni Putes Ni Soumises
PIR	Party of the Indigènes of the Republic
SONACOTRA	National Corporation for the Construction of Housing for Algerian Workers
UEJF	Union of Jewish Students of France
UOIF	Union of Islamic Organizations of France
ZUP	priority urbanization zone

Glossary

amicales (French)   Organizations established by North African states in the wake of independence to provide social and cultural services for its overseas population.

banlieue (French)   A suburb, often associated in the French media with those areas inhabited by those from a working-class or postcolonial immigrant background, but in fact socially and ethnically diverse.

beauf (French)   A slang term, short for *beau-frère* (brother-in-law), carrying the connotation of a "good ol' boy" or "cracker."

béké (Antillean Creole)   Descendents of the former plantation class of white slave owners, who still constitute a socioeconomic elite on the islands.

béton (French)   Literally "concrete," but metonymically used in reference to French public housing projects.

Beur (French)   A term for Franco-Maghrebis, derived from "Arab" (*arabe*); in popular usage in the 1980s but since disavowed.

bidonville (French)   A shantytown, often built on the outskirts of major cities, particularly in Parisian suburbs like Nanterre and Noisy-le-Grand, which housed Algerian immigrants and their families prior to their demolition in the 1970s.

caillera (French)   A French back-slang (*verlan*) term for "scum" (*racaille*), deployed in street and hip-hop argot to denote a gangsta.

cité/téci (French)   Terms for the public housing projects begun in the 1950s and built on the outskirts of French cities, often in close proximity to industrial zones, to rehouse the French working class, including immigrant laborers and their families.

communautarisme (French)   Sectarianism or communalism; a term deployed in media and political discourse to designate the supposed tendency of Muslim French and others from a postcolonial immigrant background to congregate in enclaves with their own internal moral and cultural values.

contrôle au faciès (French)   An identity check or police stop deployed as a security measure, particularly in the context of antiterrorism plans, disproportionately targeting non-white men.

convivencia (Spanish)   An imagined period of peaceful coexistence during the Islamic period of Al-Andalus, in which Christian and

Jewish populations lived among and alongside empowered Muslim inhabitants.

daʿwa (Arabic)   Literally "invitation," but referring to Islamic proselytizing practiced by a number of missionary groups.

dérive (French)   Literally "drifting" or "being adrift," referring to an ambulant practice developed by the Situationists in the 1950s to psychogeographically remap the city along lines no longer predetermined by capitalism and the state.

dhimmi (Arabic)   A shortening of *ahl al-dhimma*, a protected class of non-Muslims living in Islamic states who had delimited rights and were governed by their own civic law in exchange for an annual tribute (*jizya*); the term has entered the French language in reference to a particular status (*dhimmitude*) which is feared an encroaching Muslim majority would impose on Christians and Jews if given power.

droit à la différence (French)   "Right to difference," upheld by SOS-Racisme and other antiracist groups during the 1980s as a political message of multiculturalism and inclusivity.

émeute (French)   A "riot." A term deployed by the French media to refer to the anti-police violence in the *cités* that has periodically arisen since the 1980s, spectacularly so in October and November 2005.

état d'urgence (French)   A "state of emergency" legal provision deriving from colonial security regimes and recently enacted to quell the 2005 urban violence, and again following the November 2015 Islamic State attacks in Paris; as a security measure, it lowers the grounds for probable cause, extends the period of pre-trial detention, and allows for greater electronic surveillance.

étranger (French)   "Foreigner," generally extending to anyone of non-white French background, regardless of citizenship.

feuj (French)   A back-slang term for someone of Jewish background, often used in street argot.

Français de souche (French)   A reference to someone of French stock, literally referencing the trunk base or main root of a tree.

galère (French)   A slang term denoting despair or hopelessness, of being in a difficult or precarious situation.

grand ensemble (French)   A large-scale housing development built on the outskirts of French cities, bringing together public housing with educational, commercial, and administrative facilities, designed largely for the working and lower-middle class.

harkis (Arabic/French)   Originally an Arabic term for those serving in a *harka*, a "mobilization" of civilian men to fight for the state against an enemy. The term now refers to the those Muslims who fought on the side of the French colonial army during the French–Algerian war

(1954 to 1962), approximately 20,000 of whom were "repatriated" to France at the war's end; for many Algerians, the term is considered an insult, but those of *harki* descent have worked to gain official recognition for their ancestors' sacrifice.

harrag (Arabic)   Literally "burning," referring to the destruction of identity papers or homeland attachments in a desperate act of migration, generally across the Mediterranean, by North Africans hoping to reach Europe.

hejira (Arabic)   A reference to Muhammad's "migration" from Mecca to Medina, but deployed metaphorically to reference any spiritual journey.

hijab (Arabic)   A general Arabic term for a "cover" or "veil." In the context of France, the term is used in reference to the scarves used to cover pious Muslim women's heads and necks.

indigènes (French)   A colonial-era term used particularly in reference to (particularly Muslim) natives of North Africa, today reappropriated by activists – especially those associated with the Party of the Indigènes of the Republic (PIR) – to reference all those from a postcolonial immigrant background.

intégrisme (French)   Religious fundamentalism, originally referencing a movement in the Catholic Church that refused any evolution of doctrine or practice.

jma'a (pl. *jma'at*) (Arabic)   A local council in rural North Africa, particularly in Berber-speaking areas, consisting of male family elders and empowered to uphold customary law (*'urf* or *izerf*) and local decision-making; today its function is more symbolic than juridical.

khoroto (Maghrebi Arabic)   A pejorative term designating an uncultured country bumpkin.

laïcité (French)   A mode of secularism premised on the supersession of religion by liberal values of citizenship and on the relegation of religious practices to the private sphere.

les Bleus (French)   The French national football team, named as such for the primary color of their jerseys.

mission civilisatrice (French)   The "civilizing mission" upheld as a moral duty and justification for colonial intervention, and the resulting social and education policies developed for native populations.

négritude (French)   A literary and political movement developed by black colonial intellectuals Aimé Césaire, Léon Damas, and Léopold Senghor in the 1930s that worked to develop pan-African renewal, pride, and solidarity across the African diaspora.

niqab (Arabic)   A full-length veil worn by Muslim women, particularly in the Arabian Peninsula.

parcours du combatant (French)   A military obstacle course developed after World War I to train French soldiers; the term gives its name to the contemporary urban athletic practice of parkour.

pied-noir (French)   Literally "black foot," referring to colonial settlers in North Africa of European (French, Maltese, Spanish, Italian) descent, many of whom were "repatriated" to France in the wake of Algerian independence.

quartier populaire (French)   A "popular" or communal neighborhood, often lower-class and ethno-racially diverse, whether located in a suburban public housing project or within urban centers.

quenelle (French)   A "dumpling" or "suppository," the word also refers to an arm gesture developed by the black French shock-comic Dieudonné Mbala Mbala in 2005, criticized as an anti-Semitic version of a Nazi salute.

racaille (French)   "Riffraff" or "scum," famously deployed by then interior minister Nicolas Sarkozy in 2005 in a speech in Argenteuil to refer to local youth considered to be trouble-makers.

renoi (French)   Back-slang term for "black" (*noirs*), used in street argot to refer to Afro-French.

sans-culottes (French)   Literally those "without undergarments," a term used in reference to poor urbanites during the French Revolution.

seuil de tolérance (French)   A sociological term indicating a "tolerance threshold" beyond which an increase in the size of a minority population would be rejected by the majority group.

tariqa (pl. *tariqat*) (Arabic)   Literally a Sufi "path," but used to refer to the broader brotherhood of adepts.

tournante (French)   Gang rape; media reports of the victimization of young women in the *cités* to the sexual predations of men from post-colonial immigrant backgrounds provoked wide public anxiety in the mid-2000s.

traceur (French)   Literally a "drawer of lines," but referencing someone who practices parkour or freerunning.

Trente Glorieuses (French)   The "thirty glorious" years of relative economic prosperity in France following World War II.

'urf/izerf (Arabic/Tamazight)   Customary law, often associated with "tribal" or "Berber" constituencies in pre-independence North Africa.

verlan (French)   A form of word play by which the syllables of French words are reversed, often referred to as "back slang"; the term itself is a back-slang rendition of *l'envers* (inverse).

vivre ensemble (French)   Literally "living together," referring to an ethic of mutual accommodation across ethnic, racial, and religious lines.

zawiya (pl. *zawaya*) (Arabic) An "assembly" or "circle," referring to a Sufi lodge in North Africa, encapsulating both the group itself and the physical structure in which it gathers.

zone de non-droit (French) A "lawless zone" or "no-go area" imputed by French pundits to certain urban peripheries supposedly governed by local forms of street justice.

Introduction
Whither Postcolonial France?

In November 1934, in the midst of the interwar economic crises and far-right street riots that threatened to topple the elected French government, Leon Trotsky posed the pressing question of "whither France?" Would it descend into the violent fervor of fascist nationalism that marked its neighbors to the east and the south? Or would the working class and exploited peasantry rise up against the decades of bourgeois Bonapartism that had bankrupted French society economically, politically, and morally. "Will it be revolutionary socialism or Fascist reaction which will first ... demonstrat[e] in words and deeds its ability to smash every obstacle on the road to a better future?" he asked. "On this question," he argued, "depends the fate of France for many years to come" (Trotsky 1968: 14).

France's fate for many years to come would be one of fundamental division. France was literally torn asunder by the German invasion a few years after Trotsky posed his question, physically fragmented into a Nazi-controlled north, a nominally autonomous south governed from Vichy, and a Free French Forces government in exile under Charles de Gaulle. Moral, ideological, and tactical divides between "collaboration" and "resistance" continued to mark the French sociopolitical landscape long after the nominal "liberation" of 1944, morphing into extant rival national narratives of a rural, Catholic "true France" (see Lebovics 1994) and a secular, urbane Republic.[1] A shifting wartime geography of Allied and Axis military zones would give way to a new landscape outlined by a Cold War divide between East and West, and an emergent unified European zone into which De Gaulle would ambivalently position France as both within and without, jealously preserving national autonomy from American and German political-economic domination.

And such a postwar landscape was eminently an imperial one, with nominal distinctions between metropole and colony blurred in practice by the administrative incorporation of overseas territories, the granting of some level of citizenship to colonial subjects, and the circulation of African, Asian, and Caribbean students, soldiers, and workers who to a great extent carried the burden of the liberation and rebuilding of France during the so-called *Trente Glorieuses*, the 30 years of relative prosperity following the liberation. The debt owed for such lives and labors broadly animated anticolonial struggles for both national independence and alternative post-imperial federation arrangements, the latter envisioned by bicultural intellectuals like the *négritude* poet-politicians Aimé Césaire (Martinique) and Léopold Senghor (Senegal)—as historian Gary Wilder (2015) has recently traced. Most strikingly, on May 8, 1945, the very day Nazi Germany surrendered to Allied forces, French gendarmes fired on celebrating Muslim Algerians in Sétif and Guelma, northern Algeria, leading to a series of massacres that are often viewed as the opening salvoes in the long French–Algerian war of decolonization. While some critics like Ferhat Abbas, Albert Camus (2013), and Germaine Tillion (1958, 1961) continued to imagine for some years a future Algeria in which former colonizer and colonized could be reconciled,[2] most ultimately came to agree with Simone Weil's earlier assessment, echoing Trotsky, that "France will have to choose between attachment to its empire and the need once more to have a soul" (Weil 2003: 124). As Césaire (2000) and the Jewish-Tunisian intellectual Albert Memmi (1991) would attest, imperialism was but another form of fascism, and colonizing society was ultimately a diseased one that could only possibly be cured through its destruction.

National self-determination and the juridical separation of France from its African and Asian peripheries were of course not the inevitable outcomes of the anticolonial struggle, in spite of our methodological nationalist tendency today to take independent territorial nation-states for granted (see Wilder 2015). Decolonization had to be invented, as Todd Shepard (2006) has insisted. But the putative demise of France's overseas empire did not bring about the end of colonial relations or their entailments. The colonial situation remains written into the French landscape through the very structures and institutions forged in imperial times: in its present multiracial and multicultural demography, its architecture and urban plans, its fashions and customs, its security regimes and policing practices, its governmental mode of political liberalism.[3] Whether imperialism during its heyday was embraced as an ideology or massively contested by any given party, it ended up insinuating itself within France as a material condition and structuring structure, as a habitus and set of durable dispositions, as a structure of feeling and way of being-in-the-world.

To assert that France is *post*colonial is precisely not to claim that colonialism is over and done with. As postcolonial scholars have long emphasized, the work of the appellation "postcolonial" (hyphenated or not, with or without postmodern parentheses around the "post") is to underline that the present, the temporally post, is still, in some nontrivial ways, decidedly colonial (see Chakrabarty 2000; Prakash 1995; Spivak

1999).[4] But it equally should not imply that the French present is merely defined by a singular, static colonial "legacy," or that that "legacy" is all determining and mono-causal of the contemporary sociopolitical debates and dilemmas around citizenship and belonging. Not only must one take into account the heterogeneity of the colonial experience in and for different European subjects, but also recognize that the parameters and institutions with colonial genealogies have transformed over time, as have their coloniality in the process. Present structures of inequality may seem to recapitulate colonial ones, with barely reconfigured racialized subject positions, but they are situated in different contexts, and as such take on new forms and dynamics. Responding to their critics, French colonial historians Nicolas Bancel, Pascal Blanchard, and Sandrine Lemaire specify that their insistence on the "liveliness of colonial memories" in the French present does not in any way imply "a linear heritage, an identical reproduction of past practices." Rather, they continue, "thinking the postcolony is to necessarily understand how the phenomena engendered by the colonial fact have continued but also hybridized, transformed, retracted, reconfigured" (Blanchard et al. 2005: 13). Ann Laura Stoler has more recently drawn on the metaphor of "duress" to emphasize the "durability and distribution of colonial entailments that cling—vitally active and activated—to the present conditions of people's lives" (Stoler 2016: 25), a "past which is imagined to be over" (ibid.: 33) but which continues to exert force in transfigured and recursive forms. But, as she emphasizes, one must likewise take into account the "creative and critical—and sometimes costly—measures people take to defy these [forces and] constraints, to name that damage, or to become less entangled" (ibid.: 346). The challenge, she maintains, is not to flatly claim everything has a colonial genealogy, but to "track the tangibilities of empire as effective [and, I might add, affective] histories of the present" (ibid.: 378). This book takes up this challenge by showing how various, differently racialized men and women in contemporary France endure, express, engage, and ultimately enlist such postcolonial duress in charting a future beyond racist denials, assimilationist policies, discriminatory structures, and national frontiers.

COLONIAL LEGACIES?

Insisting on France's postcoloniality, and exploring how French subjects of color racially live and respond to it, is to enter fraught terrain. My first ethnographic field project conducted during the 1990s focused on young Franco-Algerian men and women in the outskirts of Paris who pushed back against the space-time of the French nation-state (see Silverstein 2004a). They commemorated their parents' lives as late-colonial immigrants, looked to the United States to make sense of the racial discrimination and police violence they regularly faced, and felt themselves viscerally connected to the Palestinian conflict and the violence in Algeria through family ties and a sense of a common struggle. I traced this contested field of belonging and suffering—what Michael Rothberg (2009) has since called "multidirectional memory"—to enduring tensions within French republican universalism, particularly as it developed in the colonial Algerian contexts: an ambivalence between the theoretical incorporation of indigenous Algerian populations as putatively equal subjects, and their slotting into new categories of racial, ethnic, and religious others in colonial law, policy, planning, and military administration. The state pressure on Franco-Algerian men and women to "integrate"—to relegate their cultural and religious beliefs and practices to the private sphere and subsume their public presentation to normative conventions of Frenchness—combined with the everyday popular racism and institutional discrimination they faced which made them feel like second-class citizens, seemed inseparable from these earlier colonial moments to both myself and many of those I interviewed.

Yet to make these connections was to run against the grain of mainstream French thought at the time, which broadly pigeonholed the study of "immigrants" (of whom those I worked with were classed as "second-generation") to the field of urban sociology and approached them as a "problem" of unemployment, inadequate housing, education failure and so on—of ultimately the failed social mobility of a former working-class population in a postindustrial context. The French republican social contract left no room for alternate identity diacritics, and French law prohibited the official collection of demographic data on race, ethnicity, or religion. For me to chronicle the racialized and ethnic dimensions of Franco-Algerian lives in peripheral Parisian neighborhoods and suburban housing projects (*les cités*), often experienced by my interlocutors as veritable "ghettos," in terms other than that of class was to import foreign categories of analysis and engage in a form of American academic imperialism (see Wacquant 2008: 135–62; cf. Bourdieu & Wacquant 1999). But as the sociologist Abdelmalek Sayad (2004)—himself an Algerian immigrant to France—brilliantly argued, mainstream French urban sociology tended to merely echo "state discourse" by treating Franco-Algerians as but objects of state projects and never subjects of their own destiny or the remaking of the French nation by cutting them off from the Algerian context of colonial and postcolonial emigration with which their lives remained deeply entwined. As I tried to connect French and Algerian sociopolitical and historical processes, I was accused of smuggling in alien postcolonial and diaspora theory more appropriate for the British or American (post)empire. Colonialism, for many of my white French interlocutors, was history, and colonial history was a separate field of study, broadly relegated to peripheral universities (Bancel 2005). My own work was of potential interest to them, not for what it had to say about France as a racialized postcolony, but for what it had to say about US obsessions with race and coloniality.

Since the mid-2000s, French academic and public discourse has decidedly shifted, resulting in what Bancel and Blanchard have called a "Paxtonization" of colonial history (Bancel & Blanchard 2005: 26), referencing the historiographic revolution that followed American historian Robert Paxton's study of the constitutive legacy of the Vichy regime for the postwar French republics (Paxton 1972).[5] The generalized amnesia surrounding the French–Algerian war—and the Algerian colonial past and present more broadly—tracked by Benjamin Stora (1991) had been ruptured during the new conflict in Algeria during the 1990s, with a proliferation of memory projects by differently situated actors (Berbers, *harkis*, *pied-noirs*) who demanded official recognition for their sacrifice for the French and Algerian nation-states.[6] On the one hand, Franco-Algerian artists, activists, and associations called attention to the suppressed violence of colonization and decolonization, the torture of Algerian revolutionaries, and the massacre of Algerian immigrant demonstrators in Paris on October 17, 1961. These efforts were emboldened by the 1997 trial of Maurice Papon, the chief of police responsible for the 1961 massacre, for his role in arresting and deporting Jews during World War II, as well as the later 2001 revelations by General Paul Aussaresses of the systematic use of torture during the French–Algerian war (implicated in the death of National Liberation Front militant Larbi Ben M'hidi), for which Aussaresses was subsequently indicted for "apology for war crimes." On the other hand, *pied-noir* groups insisted on national recognition of their respective sacrifices, planning several museums and monuments to commemorate the French colonial "presence" in Algeria and sponsoring a French parliamentary law of February 23, 2005, in which the "Nation expresses its appreciation (*reconnaissance*) for the men and women who participated in the work (*oeuvre*) accomplished by France in its former French departments of Algeria, Morocco, Tunisia, and Indochina" (Article 1). The law's fourth article caused particular public controversy for its specification that school curricula recognize the "positive role [of] the French presence overseas, notably in North Africa." French historians across the world denounced such an official imprimatur on what they decried as "colonial nostalgia," and while the

French Constitutional Council ultimately abrogated Article 4, the international outcry persisted.

Perhaps the most outspoken critics were a group of heterodox French scholars of colonialism and immigration associated with the Achac research group who would engage in a series of controversial publishing projects over the next decade tracing the "colonial heritage" within postcolonial France (see Bancel et al. 2010; Blanchard & Bancel 2005; Blanchard et al. 2005). This group included important Franco-Algerian scholars Ahmed Boubeker and Saïd Bouamama who had long been working on the fringes of French academia, as well as a new generation of historians, political scientists, and sociologists of color—including Nacira Guénif-Souilamas, Pap Ndiaye, and Françoise Vergès—with close ties to and training in American and British universities. Indeed, French universities had increasingly opened up to transatlantic postcolonial approaches in the wake of a Bologna process that had gradually harmonized higher education across Europe and resulted in a broadening of international graduate programs in France with instruction in English. In 2005, Ndiaye, author of a study on "the black condition" (Ndiaye 2008) co-founded the Representative Council of Black Associations (CRAN), the first French federation of Caribbean diasporic and French-African groups along the rubric of race, which, among other engagements, has led a campaign for reparations for victims of slavery and colonialism. Vergès, a feminist and antiracist activist from a politically engaged family of Réunion background, has served as president of the National Committee for the Memory and History of Slavery, which oversees the implementation of the 2001 Taubira Law that public recognized slavery as a crime against humanity. She and Guénif-Souilamas, a public intellectual in her own right, have been critical interlocutors of the Party of the Indigènes of the Republic (PIR) founded in 2005 by Franco-Algerian feminist activist Houria Bouteldja and Tunisian Marxist militant Sadri Khiari. Speaking on behalf of those "originating from the colonies, former or present, and from postcolonial immigration" who face discrimination, social exclusion, precarity, and "indigenization," the PIR's call to arms declared that "France remains a colonial state" and advocated for a "decolonization of the republic" (Bouteldja and Khiari 2012: 19–21).[7] These various efforts were catalyzed by the uprisings in October-November 2005 in suburban housing projects outside of Paris and other urban areas, in response to which the French government instituted a state of emergency (*état d'urgence*), originally formulated during the French-Algerian war, and applied overseas to suppress anticolonial insurrections in the intervening years.[8] In the wake of the Paris attacks attributed to the Islamic State of November 13, 2015, the extra-judicial policing powers enabled by the state of emergency legislation have been deployed as a mode of antiterrorism and adopted into permanent law.

MORAL PANICS

These palpable challenges to putatively color-blind policies and universalist ideologies have called forth a public reckoning that borders on a full-scale moral panic. On the one hand, a number of scholars, politicians, and pundits have mounted an ardent defense of the French Republic presented as under immediate, existential threat. Some have drawn on an Islamophobic "clash of civilizations" (*choc des civilisations*) rhetoric and identified the source of the threat as Islam, understood to be incompatible with French republican values of individual freedom and gender equality, or with norms of state secularism (*laïcité*), which ostensibly restrict religious expression to the private sphere. If the 2015 Paris attacks underlined for many the susceptibility of France to "Islamo-fascist" operations directed from abroad, others have pointed to the internal threat of born or converted Muslim-French populations who since the 1990s had been suspected of being seduced by jihad, training abroad and fighting in overseas Islamic wars, and re-importing the violence back home (see Pujadas & Salam 1995).[9] More insidiously, others, like prize-winning author Michel Houellebecq in his novel *La soumission* ("Submission") (2015), have portrayed liberal tendencies to tolerate and accommodate Muslim religious practices as ultimately complicit in the gradual (and willing) transformation of France into an Islamic republic. *Le Figaro* journalist Eric Zemmour (2014) characterized this as a veritable "suicide."

On the other hand, defenses of French republican universalism, particularly from mainstream socialist and feminist perspectives, have rejected the encroachment of particularist, sectarian tendencies that have arisen in the name of diversity. They accuse certain antiracist artists and activists, like those associated with the PIR, in their defense of black and Muslim lives, of promoting misogyny, anti-Semitism, and even anti-white racism.[10] They reject the postcolonial critique that posits colonial racism as immanent to political liberalism and, echoing the public defense of Nicolas Sarkozy, then interior minister, of the February 23, 2005 law, refuse to engage in overwrought apologies or "permanent repentance" for the past. Unimpeachably humanist scholars like political-scientist Jean-François Bayart (2010), historian Emmanuelle Saada (2006), and anthropologist Fanny Colonna (Colonna & Le Pape 2010) have criticized the historiographic simplifications of certain

French adaptations of postcolonial studies: the reduction of colonialism to mere violence (see Grandmaison 2005), the ignoring of hybrid identities and co-constitutive relations forged between colonizers and colonized, and the implication of an unaltered, linear colonial "legacy" in the present. For other scholars and pundits less outspokenly critical of past or present racial violence, the stakes tend to be more identitarian than historiographic, amounting to a defense of liberal ideals traceable back to the Revolution, to which colonialism and slavery are presented as regrettable exceptions (see Bruckner 2006; Gallo 2006; Lefeuvre 2006; Paoli 2006; Taguieff 2005). A postcolonial critique of the Republic, whether from a scholarly or activist perspective, calls into question their worldview, the "story they tell themselves about themselves," to use an expression of anthropologist Clifford Geertz (1973: 448).

From the perspective of what Bouteldja calls the "decolonial majority" (Bouteldja 2016: 139), the stakes are equally existential. Indeed, she presents her plea for solidarity and "revolutionary love," as a peace offering to a "dying Old World" (ibid.: 27). Meanwhile, Marwan Muhammad (2017), director of the Collective against Islamophobia in France (CCIF)—a key watchdog monitoring anti-Muslim hate crimes and advocating for Muslim-French rights more broadly—less polemically draws on economist Albert O. Hirschman's classic distinction between "exit," "voice," and "loyalty" (Hirschman 1970) to describe the choices that Muslim-French citizens face. Demanded by state policies and pundits to continually demonstrate their loyalty, these "children of Marianne, loved or not" (Muhammad 2017: 6), have grown increasingly frustrated by the barriers they face for success in France and opted for exit strategies, whether through adopting Salafi interpretations and identifying with the Islamic community (*umma*), or emigration to the Arabian Gulf, North America, or elsewhere in Europe seen as less Islamophobic. However, insofar as Muslim-French citizens "define this country, no more or less than any of our fellow citizens" (ibid.: 7), it is ultimately their decision whether to take voice or not that will help determine the future of France:

> On this ground depends the future of not only Muslims, but of the whole of French society, in its capacity to innovate and renew itself, to be true to what it wishes and pretends to be: a country where everyone can find their place, whatever their trajectory, their origin, their religion, or their beliefs. (ibid.: 232)

He offers his book, not as a "prayer for peace" (ibid.: 5), but as a plea against fatalism and as an "act of resistance" (ibid.: 7).

Journalist Edwy Plenel strikes a similar chord. Modeled on Emile Zola's famous 1896 article "For the Jews" in the French newspaper *Le Figaro*, Plenel calls his essay a "warning cry against indifference" and, moreover, an "appeal to forestall disaster … to avoid a *politique du pire* ['heartless politics']" (Plenel 2016: xii–xiii). Cautioning that Islamophobia rots French values from within and makes a "war of civilizations" a self-fulfilling prophecy, he warns of the rise of a reactionary right not only in the guise of the National Front, but also more mainstream political parties similarly anxious over the so-called "Muslim question." Such groups are but the "sorcerer's apprentices" of a "colonial past that has never really been closed" (ibid.: 12) but acts like a "ghost that continues to prowl, from the closet of unappeased memories" (ibid.: 29). The central dilemma of postcolonial France, for Plenel, is a choice "between identitarian retrenchment and national necrosis, on the one hand, or, as we wish on the other hand, the truth of history and reconciliation with historic memory" (ibid.: 29).

> Beneath the Muslim question, therefore, there lies the French question: our capacity to reinvent a France that instead of congealing into a fantasized and deadly sameness, launches itself toward the world by making its relationship to diversity the best key to every door. (ibid.: 51)

Plenel concludes that his book, entitled *For the Muslims*, could have equally been called *For France* (ibid.: 89).

While Plenel situates his historical narrative in the rise of fin-de-siècle anti-Semitic fascism, Trotsky and Weil's existential concerns over a different moment of anti-Semitism still ring strikingly prescient. Postcolonial France, as elsewhere across the Global North in the early decades of the twenty-first century, is facing new crises of capitalism and the rise of new demagogic populisms that similarly speak in the name of the nation against various internal and external others: immigrants, refugees, Muslims, Roma, or often some combination of these vulnerable targets. As in the 1930s, new EU-imposed austerity measures to stave off declining profits have rolled back social protections and dramatically sharpened the divide between rich and poor—a fracturing of the social compact that again is blamed on a cultural fracture of the nation. As in the 1930s, this has been accompanied by rising violence provoked by different groups who feel sidelined from social mobility, sometimes accomplished in the name of the nation-state, sometimes explicitly against it. As in the 1930s, some of these oppositional groups are organized transnationally, and such external organization is taken by some state actors and pundits as a form of treason. As in the 1930s, neo-nationalist groups threaten to turn populist rhetoric into electoral success and regressive, anti-humanist governmental policy (the *politique du pire* about which Plenel worried).

But as in the 1930s, the descent to further violence and fascism is not inevitable. As Trotsky repeatedly insisted, hope remains that various groups can come together in solidarity, fight back the demagogues, and create lasting social change. Such efforts necessarily require coordination beyond the nation-state, uniting movements for social justice both within and without France, with similar movements across Europe, and in the former colonial and presently neocolonial periphery. In this book, I explore the trajectories, works, and engagements of outspoken artists and activists like Marwan Muhammad or the PIR who are finding renewed inspiration in the late-colonial writings of Césaire, Frantz Fanon, Malcolm X, Amílcar Cabral, Audre Lorde, C.L.R. James, Stokely Carmichael, Kateb Yacine, James Baldwin, Angela Davis, and other theorists-*cum*-militants of race and revolution. These French men and women of color—whose families trace their migrant histories particularly to colonial North Africa, but also to West Africa, the Caribbean, Indochina, and the Indian Ocean—are insisting that they remain, in one way or the other, the oppressed "natives" (*les indigènes*) of a contemporary French Republic still subjected to and fighting against an even more insidious form of internal, racializing colonialism—that they are the new *sans-culottes* of a decolonizing revolution in the metropole still to come. They—like their racialized counterparts across Europe—look to the ongoing Palestinian struggle, to the Black Lives Matter movement in the United States, and to the successes and failures of the 2011 uprisings in North Africa and the Middle East not merely as sites of empathetic solidarity or instructive parallels, but as necessarily conjoined efforts for social justice whose outcomes are inevitably linked. And such an insistence—alongside their absolute refusal to apologize, remain quiet, or strive for invisibility as black or Muslim—has earned them further accusations of social treason, anti-Semitism, and reverse racism from self-appointed defenders of secularism, liberalism, and nationalism.

This book plumbs the dynamics and dilemmas of this present moment of crisis and hope. Through a set of interconnected chapters, I explore recent moral panics around urban racialized violence, female Islamic dress and male public prayer, anti-system gangsta rap, and various sporting performances in and around which seemingly sectarian politics have controversially appeared to arise. Inspired by courageous French artists, activists, and intellectuals of color, I trace these conflicts to the unresolved tensions of an imperial project, the present-day effects of which are still felt by many, if in certainly altered and renovated ways. And I try to provide a sense of how various individuals and groups have found ways to build flourishing lives within these racialized tensions, how they have responded to urban marginalization, police violence, and institutional discrimination in remarkably creative ways. The chapters which follow focus in particular on the modes of self-representation and popular cultural and embodied forms through which French men and women of color take voice, assert their presence, and seek to become the managers—and not merely the managed—of a multiracial, postcolonial France.[11] While not an ethnographic study as such, the book draws on prior fieldwork and archival projects in both France and North Africa, as well as several decades of regular visits and countless conversations and interactions with French men and women of color directly concerned with ongoing social transformations and political debates.

Addressing "French men and women of color" as the subjects of postcolonial France and the objects of this book's analysis raises several considerations. In the first place, the term itself could be objected to as foreign to the French social and political context. As I will discuss in detail in the chapters that follow, the 1958 Constitution reaffirms France as an "indivisible, secular, democratic, and social Republic ... without distinction of origin, race, or religion." This foundational language has served to delegitimize articulations of racial or ethnic differentiation within French identity, in contrast to the United States where one affirms Americanness through ethnic hyphenation. The French media and scholarly studies thus tend to deploy signifiers of national origin or immigrant generation to specify populations of nonwhite, non-European identity. However, this analytical move risks suturing those so designated to a non-French elsewhere, implying that they are not fully genealogically or territorially French, regardless of their actual citizenship status. Moreover, it does not recognize how people experience a commonality of racially or ethnically marked experience within France.

The PIR uses the term *indigènes* precisely to capture this common sense of otherness felt and experienced by those of postcolonial immigrant background, and inhabitants of lower-class neighborhoods (*les quartiers populaires*) more broadly, as well as to underline that they remain subjected to ongoing colonial state management and violence even in the putatively postcolonial metropole—*indigènes* being the term used by colonial administrators to refer to non-European subjects in North Africa and elsewhere. However, this translates poorly into English, where "indigenous" implies relative territorial autochthony and the fight for sovereignty in situations of settler colonialism—perhaps appropriate for describing regional ethnolinguistic minorities in Brittany or the Basque region, or the ongoing colonial situation in French overseas departments and territories, but less so for many of those racially stigmatized in the metropole. And the *indigènes* ethnonym is indelibly positioned within the very postcolonial politics that this book seeks to unpack.

In this sense, the fact that the term "French men and women of color" comes off as a foreign import has the benefit of giving it a relatively neutral status within the ongoing French polemic. Moreover, it actually does have a French genealogy in *gens de couleur* (literally, "people of color"), those emancipated people of mixed race background in the pre-abolition colonial French West Indies, ostensibly equal to white Frenchmen but in practice with limited social and political rights (see Dubois 2004a). In that regard, they were somewhat akin to today's French men and women of color who often experience their racialized social status as "second-class citizens" (*citoyens de seconde zone*). Many *gens de couleur* migrated to France after the Haitian Revolution (1791 to 1804), becoming among the first nonwhite communities in metropolitan France. In many ways, the Haitian Revolution and its violent politics of liberation set the stakes for future anticolonial movements and continues to provide the undertone to ongoing efforts to decolonize postcolonial France (see Dubois 2004b; Trouillot 1995).[12]

Secondly, hidden within the term "French men and women of color" are certainly nontrivial differences in the particular postcolonial trajectories of those with familial connections to North Africa, sub-Saharan Africa, the Caribbean, and Southeast Asia. Likewise, intersecting experiences of gender, sexuality, religion, and ethnicity fundamentally affect people's sense of everyday belonging and limit their enactments of solidarity. At various points in this book those specificities will be highlighted as they emerge as points of tension, stress, or even productive friction, as they serve as the bases for innovative collaborations across various terrains of difference.[13] In my other published ethnographic writings (see Silverstein 2002a 2004b, 2007b, 2008a), I have underlined the particularity of a Berber (Amazigh) perspective within the broader Muslim-French historical experience, and at various points in the chapters which follow I draw on this work. But in this book, I am particularly concerned with how these manifest differences come to be subsumed and lived within a generalized experience of racial otherness, as part of a common post-colonial condition, in the context of public moral panics about the future of France. Insofar as these moral panics have often centered around Islam as an index of radical, incompatible alterity, I will focus, particularly in the first half of the book, on the changing, stigmatized conditions of Muslim-French subjectivity. But, to a great extent, such a stigma is experienced by all French men and women of color. Frantz Fanon famously recounts how one of his Antillean philosophy teachers insisted, "When you hear someone insulting the Jews pay attention; he is talking about you" (Fanon 1967: 101). Much the same could be said about the ways contemporary Islamophobia in France encapsulates the racialized discrimination felt by all nonwhite French men and women.

As critical scholars and antiracist militants have long insisted, race and racism are not simply or primarily psychological attitudes, beliefs, or ideas premised on faulty reasoning, misconceptions, or an overwrought sense of superiority. They are rather social formations, forged in the violence of colonialism, embedded in the institutions of political governance, and reproduced for capitalist profit. As the structuring condition of the modern world, race and racism come to be internalized in bodily dispositions, affects, and perceptions, phenomenologically inscribed in lived social relations and everyday encounters. They produce durable inequalities that have the effect of social reality even if they fail the scientific tests of contemporary biology or the ethical aspirations of liberal sensibilities.[14] Such inertial, racialized structures cannot be overcome with words alone, and the popular cultural forms and modes of representation discussed in this book are but calls to arms for fundamental institutional change—if not a social and political revolution—yet to come. In chronicling these emergent representational forms, highlighting the postcolonial subjectivities they call forth, and situating them in a history of political and economic change, my hope is to give the reader a sense of the contexts and stakes of the present upheavals in France, all too often dismissed as "Islamic terrorism" on the one hand, or "white supremacy" on the other. As a historical anthropologist I am committed to taking seriously the complex ways in which the various stakeholders of the French postcolonial present seek to find meaning and future hope in uncertain times, whether or not one might agree with their analysis or vision.

THE COLONIZED AND THE DECOLONIZED

One such postcolonial stakeholder is the philosopher-novelist Albert Memmi. Born in 1920 in protectorate Tunisia to an Italian Jewish father and Tunisian Jewish mother, educated in Algeria and France, and expatriated to Paris after Tunisian independence, Memmi's life tracks the violence of colonialism and the shattered hopes of decolonization. His 1957 essay, *Portrait du colonisé*—later published in English as *The Colonizer and the Colonized* (1991)—stands with parallel manifestos by Césaire (2000) and Fanon (1963) as one of the most important and powerful indictments of colonial society written from within. Like

Césaire and Fanon, Memmi revealed the violent ways through which colonialism dehumanized indigenous peoples as much psychically as materially. While Césaire and Fanon wrote as black subjects who benefitted from the colonial educational system but remained the objects of everyday and institutional racial discrimination, Memmi's Jewishness brought a number of social and political privileges, and thus placed him somewhere betwixt and between colonizer and colonized.[15] Such a liminal position gave him a certain degree of purchase on what he, following Georges Balandier (1951) and later Pierre Bourdieu (1958), called "the colonial situation" as a total social phenomenon in which the worlds and subjectivities of colonizer and colonized were co-constituted and reciprocally determined. The colonial situation locked Europeans, whatever their politics or ideology, in a pathological dependency on indigenous populations, whose subjugation and durable impoverishment was the condition of possibility for the colonizers' wealth and status. "The colonial situation," he averred, "manufactures colonialists, just as it manufactures the colonized" (Memmi 1991: 56). And such manufacturing happened in and through a racial order: "Racism appears ... not as an incidental detail, but as a consubstantial part of colonialism. It is the highest expression of the colonial system" (ibid.: 74).

Yet, for all its indictment of the colonial situation as a "diseased society" (ibid.: 98) that can only be cured through radical surgery, *The Colonizer and the Colonized* is not a revolutionary call-to-arms. The dehumanization of the colonized does grant colonizers apparent superhuman status, but they do not actually act as super-agents. Their privilege is fragile and limited, subject to the whims of metropolitan policy and the disciplined compliance of the colonized whose recalcitrance necessitates continual policing. Equally, the colonized are not simply passive victims of racialized violence, and the "wretchedness" (ibid.: 117)—indeed, "mummification" (ibid.: 98)—of their world is as much the product of prior social configurations as colonial subjugation. Their eventual revolt, while in Memmi's analysis inevitable, does not predetermine an outcome. In the short term, decolonization takes the form of rejection, "defensive racism" (ibid.: 131), and the construction of a "countermythology" (ibid.: 139) that fetishizes the particularities of custom and tradition—for North Africa, particularly Islam and Arabic— to the detriment of universal human scientific, linguistic, and artistic accomplishments that, while remaining pragmatically necessary, became marked as European and thus rejected as imperialist. In the concluding pages of the essay, Memmi makes a humanist plea for those soon-to-be decolonized to transcend the strictures of cultural nationalism and territorial partition:

He can, of course, assert himself as a nationalist. But it is indispensable that he have a free choice and not that he exist only through his nation. He must conquer himself and be free in relation to the religion of his group, which he can retain or reject, but he must stop existing only through it. The same applies to the past, tradition, ethnic characteristics, etc. (ibid.: 152)

Only if he—and indeed, for Memmi the decolonizing subject is gendered masculine—succeeds in doing so will the colonized become "a man like any other" (ibid.: 153).

Given this guarded optimism, it should come as little surprise that Memmi's assessment of decolonization fifty years later in *Portrait du décolonisé*—published in English as *Decolonization and the Decolonized* (2006)—was acidly critical. As much as the 1957 essay was a thoroughgoing indictment of colonial society, the 2004 sequel condemned the postcolonial world as having failed to cure the underlying pathology of reciprocal dehumanization. Even more than in the first volume, Memmi draws on his intimate familiarity with the "Arab-Muslim" case in both the contemporary Middle East/North Africa and within postcolonial France. Testifying as a native informant to the postcolonial predicament, he accuses his fellow "Third World" intellectuals of having failed in their ethical responsibilities to denounce what he sees as the corrupt, totalitarian polities that have emerged in the wake of decolonization, and lambasts them for attributing such socioeconomic and political problems wholly to the colonial past or an enduring "neocolonialism." While he admits that "the actual face of the world's young nations bears the imprint of the colonial past," he nonetheless insists that, "Even in the past, colonization was not responsible for everything" (ibid.: 21). He is particularly critical of how successor regimes in the Maghreb have deployed Arabic and Islam to the exclusion of "an open and multicultural nation, one that includes the Algerian Kabyles, the Egyptian Copts, Jews and Christians" (ibid.: 32–33), instead condoning, even calling forth, "virulent anti-semitism" (ibid.: 33) and Islamic "fundamentalism," which he characterizes as retrograde and murderous (ibid.: 35). Building on his earlier psychological assessment of colonial mental life, Memmi diagnoses the decolonized Islamic subject as suffering from the interiorization of "submission" (ibid.: 50), a schizophrenic division of public piety from private ostentation (ibid.: 51), and a "general paralysis" of psychosocial development (ibid.: 58). He concludes that this produces, at least in the eyes of the "Third World," a veritable clash of civilizations: "the confrontation of two societies: one open, adventurous, dynamic and therefore filled with danger, wicked and depraved, the other static, turned inward, powerless to confront this challenge but virtuous and legitimate through its submission to God" (ibid.: 65–66).

In Memmi's assessment, however, these two mythical societies are in fact not separate entities, but conjoined in a single postcolonial situation that mirrors the prior colonial one. The putative "Third World" reproduces itself in the heart of the West through the aegis of immigrants and their children who carry with them the humiliation of their colonial past and the resentment of their racialized present. Muslim and black immigrants are, in Memmi's words, a "living reminder of the country's [France's] colonial enterprise" (ibid.: 78), of the failures of its self-aggrandizing "civilizing mission," and of an unpaid debt contracted in sweat and blood: "Immigration is the punishment for colonial sin" (ibid.: 82). Like Jews of an earlier period, Muslim Europeans confront the handicap of their unprivileged condition and subjection to racism with a Faustian dilemma of either assimilation or communalism, with many opting for the latter option and isolating themselves in what Memmi sees as "ghettoes" of "regressive" religious tradition. The second generation is likewise condemned to "digest the memory of colonial domination and the exploitation that followed within the former colonial power" (ibid.: 115) and responds with disaffected delinquency, if not overt rebellion against the racist structures of education, employment, and the police. While the "youth" feel solidarity with the plight of decolonized subjects elsewhere, mobilize for Palestinian rights, and come to adopt African-American popular culture as their own, they block themselves from becoming fully European. "The son of the immigrant is a kind of zombie, lacking any profound attachment to the land in which he was born. He is a French citizen but does not feel the least bit French ... And, in truth, he is from another planet: the ghetto" (ibid.: 119). To this predicament, Europe offers no hopeful vision but only either reactive policing or resigned complacency.

> In the face of Islam that is sure of its values because of its relative youth, Europe no longer has a system of ethics capable of providing new guidelines. Skeptical and blasé like the elderly, it promotes an easygoing leniency, but the lack of civic pride is not freedom, but anarchy. (ibid.: 133)

Most critics have unsympathetically read Memmi's analysis as a version of the controversial "culture of poverty" argument proposed by anthropologist Oscar Lewis (1966) and adopted by regressive blame-the-victim American social policy in the 1970s—through which the marginalized (whether American blacks and Puerto Ricans or European

Muslims) reproduce their own inequality by distrusting and ultimately giving up on the very institutions that provide for social mobility (read assimilation).[16] As in his earlier work, Memmi refuses to approach the postcolonial subject as a passive victim of discrimination and neo-colonialism, though in the process, he does treat them as dupes of fundamentalists preaching feudal violence. He views Islamic practices like veiling not as disciplined expressions of the cultivation of an agentive pious self as anthropologists of religion have proposed (Fadil 2009; Fernando 2014; Hirschkind 2006; Jouili 2015; Mahmood 2005), but rather as "coercive measures" and "constraints" (Memmi 2006: 15), as at best knee-jerk reactions to Western sexual decadence. He doubles down on his humanist philosophy, uncritically defending secularism (*laïcité*) as the "primary condition of true universalism" (ibid.: 142) and ignoring the ways it has exacerbated new hierarchies. He condemns capitalist greed but does not undertake a systemic analysis of the ongoing human and environmental ravages of global capitalism. For all his condemnations of racism, he seems to place the burdens of integration squarely on the decolonized subject. Ultimately, for Memmi, the disease of postcolonial Europe is not congenital, but rather the lingering symptoms of the original injury of colonialism.

Certainly Memmi's liberal philosophy and defense of *laïcité* put him in the company of Bernard Henri-Levy, Alain Finkielkraut, Pascal Bruckner, and other so-called "new philosophers" (*nouveaux philosophes*), many of whom are also of Jewish background, whose strident, existential defense of the French Republic, public support for bans on public veiling, and general alarmism over a feared Islamization have arguably bolstered an Islamophobic climate in France. However, unlike Finkielkraut and others, he does not suture his championing of French republican values to uncritical Zionism or colonial apologism. Indeed, Memmi has been a stalwart advocate for Palestinian rights, and even if he does not condemn Israel as a settler colonial society, he does nonetheless insist on the perduring effects of colonial discrimination in postcolonial Europe. In that sense, his approach is not wholly incompatible with that of the PIR who regard him as an elder statesman. Though his closest interlocutors are Arab intellectuals like Sadiq al-Azm, Aziz al-Azmeh, and even the late Edward Said, who long sought to ecumenically conjoin Islamic humanism with secular Marxian critique and a scathing condemnation of postcolonial authoritarianism. As he recounts in the Afterword to the English edition of *Decolonization and the Decolonized*, if the book was politely ignored by the French Left, it was embraced by much of the Franco-Maghrebi media and intellectual elite as a welcome contribution to their long struggle for rights and recognition as full French citizens despite their ethnic and religious differences.

Memmi is but one of a number of complex writers, activists, and artists I will profile in this book who have been differently engaging the Trotskyite question "whither postcolonial France?" These figures include Houria Bouteldja, Marwan Muhammad, and Abdelmalek Sayad, already briefly mentioned, but also the football stars Nicolas Anelka and Zinedine Zidane, rappers Abd Al Malik and Médine, French Jewish politician and scholar Esther Benbassa, parkour practitioners David Belle and Sébastien Foucan, secular feminist activist Fadela Amara, shock-comic Dieudonné Mbala Mbala, and several others. How they come to take voice and position themselves within public debates vary dramatically, but they are unanimous in their agreement that something has to give, that the liberal premises behind the French republican social compact have failed to live up to their universalist ideals, either because they have been incompletely applied or because they were conditioned on a racial, colonial order in the first place. All try to offer an alternative to the neo-nationalist slide on which they fear France to be. Such a formulation of France for the French would be both illiberal and racist; would exclude all French men and women of color, whether black or brown, Muslim or Jew; and would decidedly embrace the white privilege of neocolonialism. Such a postcolonial future would not only preserve coloniality as a durable entailment of present inequality but would make it definitive of France's identity. In response, Memmi, Bouteldja, Muhammad, and others have all reached out in unexpected ways across various terrains of ethno-racial and religious difference to forge new transnational solidarities and project untimely, alternative social configurations. However the details of their alternatives might differ, they call for us to think beyond France in order to rethink France. This book tries to remain attuned to their common call.

CHAPTER OUTLINES

The chapters that follow all bear distinct narrative arcs, but overlap and intertwine in their assessment of postcolonial France as a lived present and future orientation. Chapter 1 builds on the foundational work of Abdelmalek Sayad to explore mobility and transnationality as everyday, structuring dimensions of personal and familial lives in France. It argues that, while French men and women of color broadly identify and are embedded within the sociopolitical structures of the French nation-state, such belonging is largely mediated through ongoing processes of maintaining overseas connections. Finding a home in France, in other words, depends on the very capacity to physically and psychically transcend its borders.

In Chapter 2 I address Islamic veiling, conversion, and radicalization as a recurrent obsession of the state and media, and which generates legal efforts to regulate, delimit, and control religiosity, as well as new secular Muslim subjects like Fadela Amara. These concerns have come to a head with the growth and transnational violence of Islamic State, but the French state's surveillance of Islamic life long antedates the recent, tragic attacks. The chapter focuses on how postcolonial life in France is increasingly delimited by the militarization of urban space and the securitization of cultural and religious expression.

Chapter 3 examines the political obstacles to building a sense of home in postcolonial France that French men and women of color face in the form of racism and discrimination. It particularly focuses on twinned discourses and practices of Islamophobia and anti-Semitism, seen to divide postcolonial France from within and define the limits of tolerance. I explore how French men and women of color tend to be marginalized for their sensitivity to Islamophobia and seeming failure to adequately perform a proper critique of anti-Semitism—and the constraints such demands place on their own forms of self-expression. I also discuss the various efforts of creating dialogue across terrains of religious difference, particularly those of Esther Benbassa and Jean-Christophe Attias.

Chapter 4 continues with issues of anti-Semitism and Islamophobia in the context of the *Charlie Hebdo* attacks and the repeated prosecution of the shock-comic Dieudonné Mbala Mbala for hate speech. Rather than harping on the apparent hypocrisy evidenced by the differential treatment of *Charlie Hebdo* and Dieudonné, the chapter instead focuses on the inclusions and exclusions generated, and the different kinds of solidarity called forth, by public expressions like "Je suis Charlie" or a *quenelle* (a Nazi-like salute).

Chapter 5 centers on repeated controversies around the selection and performance of the French national football team. Taken as a bellwether of integration and multiculturalism, the national football team receives disproportionate scrutiny and its players of color are held to an impossible standard. The heroic figure of Zinedine Zidane—whose headbutt (*coup de boules*) during the 2006 World Cup championship match gave pause to but did not erase his legacy—is contrasted with Nicolas Anelka among a generation of Muslim-French players accused of self-absorption and uncertain loyalties, particularly in the wake of the spectacular failure of the French team at the 2010 World Cup.

In Chapter 6 I likewise focus on sports as a site of postcolonial culture-making. It explores the emergence of the athletic practice of parkour (or freerunning) among young French men and women of color grouped around David Belle and Sébastien Foucan as a means of reclaiming marginal spaces of suburban housing estates (*les cités*) and transforming their built structures of exclusion into a playground for self-making. Through such sporting engagements, young French citizens on the margins attempt to speak back to structures of power and enact a modicum of agency in local communities.

Chapter 7 likewise is centered in *les cités*. Focusing on the hip-hop innovations of Abd Al Malik, Médine, Kery James, and others, it contrasts different forms of hardcore and Sufi rap produced in the wake of the 2005 anti-police violence, the most mediatized of a series of confrontations that have occurred across three decades in France's suburban housing projects. These different hip-hop styles project opposed visions of "ghetto" or national patrimony and belonging, different articulations of visceral hatred against a racist "France" (and the police who seem to represent it) and spiritual love for it as a site of reason and culture.

The Conclusion takes seriously the demand to "love France or leave it" and how various Muslim-French subjects like Houria Bouteldja have responded to this demand through a reconfigured language of love. It explores the public debate that the interventions of the PIR have called forth, and how they have transcended France in moves of solidarity across Europe and the Atlantic.

1

Mobile Subjects

In the 2006 film, *Africa paradis*, the Béninois director Sylvestre Amoussou imagines a Europe of 2033, where economic recession and urban overcrowding have reached a point where Europeans are willing to risk their lives to cross the Mediterranean in search of a better life in a relatively prosperous and politically amalgamated "United States of Africa." There they face widespread racism and xenophobia, are relegated to menial jobs and underserviced urban peripheries and, as undocumented laborers, are under constant threat of deportation. Well-meaning politicians advocating multicultural policies of tolerance find themselves blocked by right-wing nationalist movements wielding a powerful populist rhetoric of "Africa for Africans." Antiracist protests are repressed by heavy-handed police, and a cycle of violence risks exploding. As undocumented immigrants from France, Pauline and Olivier are caught in the midst and are forced to make difficult choices and risk sacrificing their family's unity for long-term economic survival.

The film is a brilliant satire that works precisely because of how close it hits its mark, how recognizable the scenes are to the everyday lives of many in postcolonial France, albeit with the racial cast reversed. It reminds us of the arbitrariness of what we take for granted and denaturalizes the presumed inherent link between European culture and material wealth. Were it not for centuries of imperialist resource extraction and labor exploitation of the Global South, the film implies, our economic world order might look very different indeed. And, if theorists of disaster capitalism (see Davis 2006) prove to be correct, it might still look quite different in the not so distant future. Africa may be all of our future, and perhaps, as Jean and John Comaroff (2011), among others, have suggested, we might look to it for our theoretical models of sociopolitical life (see also De Boeck and Baloji 2016; Simone 2004).

I begin with this inversion fantasy in order to highlight contemporary political and economic anxieties over France's place in the postcolonial world, anxieties which broadly recapitulate past fin-de-siècle plaints about the decline of the West (see Spengler 1926). Such concerns undergird current alarmist depictions of the permeability of France's borders to migrants and refugees arriving from across the Mediterranean, and the negative effects such newcomers are feared to have on national unity and prosperity. As elsewhere across Europe, North America, Australia, and South Africa, these fears have strongly racialist and nationalist undertones, even in countries with official multicultural national policies or, in the case of France, putatively color-blind models of rights and access.

Of course, there is nothing inherently new about moral panics about the "flood" or "invasion" of needy newcomers carrying with them cultural-religious values or political ideologies seemingly at odds with national norms. Such panics seem to come to a head during moments of economic uncertainty, most notably in France during the 1930s and 1970s, moments marked by the concomitant rise of rightist nationalist movements. In the 1930s, French nationalist groups like Charles Maurras's Action Française transformed into fascist movements built around violent anti-Semitism. Even rival centrist and leftist parties feared that immigrants from southern, central, and eastern Europe would import foreign revolutionary (fascist, anarchist, or communist) ideologies and dilute or sully the national (biological or moral) character. Well before the German occupation, politically active foreigners were arrested, interned, and their associations banned. Meanwhile, the economic downturn of the early 1970s witnessed the foundation of Jean-Marie Le Pen's anti-immigrant National Front, as well as the publication of Jean Raspail's novel Le camp des saints (1973), a bestselling, apocalyptic nightmare of South Asian economic refugees invading Europe and setting off a global race war.[1] Nativist policies in both periods enjoined periodic attacks on (North) African immigrants by gangs generally composed of working-class white Europeans, themselves often of relatively recent immigrant ancestry and structurally vulnerable to economic downturns (see MacMaster 1997; Sternhell 1983; Taguieff 1991). The immigrant parents and grandparents of many of today's Muslim-French citizens survived such earlier scares, and the first wave of Muslim-French political activism in the late 1970s and early 1980s was a direct response to the violence and deportations that their parents and elder siblings faced (Aissaoui 2009; Derderian 2004). The 1983 March for Equality and Against Racism, colloquially known as the Marche des Beurs,[2] continues to be upheld by activists of color like the Party of the Indigènes of the Republic (PIR) today as the first political action of young French men and women from postcolonial immigrant backgrounds, as the preliminary step in the long, ongoing fight for civil rights (Hajjat 2013).

Contemporary concerns over "uncontrolled" immigration and asylum in France build on this older supremacist history, but in a context of an expanding wealth gap between an entrenched white bourgeoisie and a growing multiracial, postindustrial precariat pushed to the urban peripheries, in which the defense of privilege gets cast as a security issue and tied to a broader "global war on terror."[3] Indeed, the immigrant scapegoat for present fears of economic-*cum*-national decline has shifted from the European revolutionary to the Third World destitute to the Islamic jihadist, the abject figure par excellence of French secular republicanism. These Muslim men and women come from families who hail from across the Muslim-majority world (especially from North Africa, sub-Saharan Africa, Turkey, and South Asia), but—more frightening to some observers—many are also recent converts (or reverts) to Islam.[4] According to certain right-wing pundits, French born-and-raised Muslims are a fifth column of an Islamist reverse-imperialism that is in the process of transforming Europe into Eurabia and threatens to reduce non-Muslim populations to a marginal status of *dhimmitude*—akin to the ghettoized lives of Jewish and Christian minorities in the Ottoman Empire (see Ye'or 2005). In later chapters I will discuss the effects of this Islamophobia on the cultural and religious lives of Muslim-French citizens and denizens; in this chapter I will focus on their abjection as outsiders in relation to the French national project on the basis of their history of familial mobility and their ongoing transnational orientation toward and participation in trans-Mediterranean worlds—as well as their efforts to build robust communities in the face of such rejection.

In contemporary assessments of Europe's political economic crisis, Muslim immigrants and asylum seekers are triply to blame. First, media pundits and conservative politicians portray them as over-procreating, welfare-dependent abusers of increasingly limited public funds who naturally call forth native aversion. Since the 1970s, politicians and pundits have, drawing on 1920s Chicago School sociology, postulated a demographic "tipping point" (*seuil de tolérance*) of "outsiders" (*étrangers*) beyond which local communities will feel threatened and respond violently (MacMaster 1991). From this perspective, immigrants and their children are not only "matter out of place," to use the language of Mary Douglas's structuralist analysis of pollution (Douglas 1966: 36), but they are also what one might call "matter out of time." They are polluting insofar as their presence in postindustrial France is deemed no longer necessary; while Muslim immigrants may have played a key role in the wartime effort or the postwar reconstruction, for which France as a "host" nation should be grateful and respectful, they now only constitute surplus population, a problem to be managed, and a drain on state resources. They are guests who have overstayed their welcome, who should have left a long time ago, whose continued presence is a challenge to national decorum. As Abdelmalek Sayad (2004: 162–215) asked: What becomes of a migrant laborer who can no longer labor? And to the extent that French-born Muslims are still considered "second" or "third" generation immigrants, they have remained forever tied to that laboring past and still carry their parents' "original sin" of foreignness. Insofar as French women and men of color today demand equal rights and recognition *as* French citizens, they have violated both their parents' original explicit contract of paid mobility and their implicit agreement to quiescence and politesse. They not only stand out as reminders of France's past industrial glory, but also of the incapacity of the present state to live up to its social compact, which promised the opportunity for flourishing lives to all. From the perspective of the once providential Catholic-secular state, today's Muslim French—and those from postcolonial immigrant backgrounds more broadly—are a social embarrassment and an ethical challenge.

Secondly, their history of family mobility continues to haunt their performance of belonging within France, making them suspected of having never mentally or materially invested in what for many is their country of birth. Popular portrayals of Muslim and black French lives emphasize their alienation, their lack of homeliness, their failure to incorporate themselves into the French body politic. Their Africanness or Arabness tends to be treated not as a hyphenated modifier of their Frenchness, but an index of alternate patriotic ties, whether or not they hold dual citizenship elsewhere; it signals their theoretical or threatened deportability (see De Genova 2001). Indeed, French law allows for the revocation (*déchéance*) of French nationality for naturalized citizens in cases of terrorism or other crimes that "jeopardize (*porte atteinte*) the fundamental interests of the Nation,"[5] and French officials have considered extending such provisions to include polygamy and to apply to French-born dual nationals as well. Even for the latter, their consumption of non-French media, regular visits to family abroad, religious or cultural travel, and sending of remittances, making donations, or investing financially elsewhere mark them as only partially committed to French life.

Moreover, as with the equally marginalized Roma, the areas of residence associated with Muslim immigrants and asylum seekers come off as dilapidated, ramshackle, and unsettled, as lacking in community care and attention. State failures to provide and maintain adequate infrastructure not only discourage identification with French national geography but serve as stigmatizing signs of otherness for those without better residential options. This is true not only for temporary refugee camps like the now defunct "Jungle" outside of Calais, where undocumented migrants stuck en route to Britain have consistently defied French police efforts to disperse and deport them, but also for the long-term suburban housing projects (*les cités* or *quartiers populaires*) established in the 1950s and 1960s precisely to settle Algerian migrants and their families previously housed in worker hostels, "transit camps" (*camps de transit*), or shantytowns (*bidonvilles*). As has been well-documented, suburban housing-project residents often suffer from "postal code racism"—a mode of discrimination that supplements racial profiling based on perceived origin, physiognomy, or class status—when they apply for employment or merely traverse urban centers (Jobard & Lévy 2009; Silverstein 2008b). Their precarious living conditions—much like the economic poverty and reported criminality that characterize the *cités*—come to be taken as yet another defining characteristic of Muslim-French subjectivity: impoverished, criminal, and unstable.

Third, Muslim and black immigrants, asylum seekers, and their children are seen as not just mobile subjects but mobilizers of cultural and religious values fundamentally deemed incompatible with French secular, liberal norms. Islamophobic accounts warn over the expansion of enclaves of cultural difference within France, "lost territories of the Republic" (Brenner 2002) where otherness is deemed reproduced through Muslim-French endogamous marriage practices and the seeming refusal to secularize their religious practices. Recent international right-wing media reports about the existence of "no-go areas" in the *banlieues* run by criminal gangs and Islamist preachers, where police supposedly refuse to step foot, merely echo long-standing domestic fears of sectarianism (*communautarisme*) and the development of American-style ethno-racial "ghettos" as "areas outside the law" (*zones de non-droit*).[6] Of course, from the perspective of racialized residents of urban peripheries, the law is overly enforced and their lives overly policed, with various forms of everyday leisure (including merely hanging out in groups near building entrances) criminalized by the Anti-Criminal Brigade (BAC) in the name of a low-intensity war on drugs and delinquency (Fassin 2013; Mohammed & Mucchielli 2006).

As I will detail in later chapters, such enclaves are further characterized as particularly "Islamic suburbs" (see Kepel 1987), governed by rigid religious interpretations and norms that even former 1968 radicals and militant feminists fear will turn back the clock on postwar gains in gender equality, sexual freedom, and social justice more generally. The hyper-visible agent of this Islamization is, as Nacira Guénif-Souilamas has critically analyzed, the "Arab boy" (*le garçon arabe*), portrayed as a veritable Trojan horse of extremism, violence, and misogyny, and accused of forcing women to either submit to Islamic codes of modesty or be treated as sexually available "whores" (Guénif-Souilamas 2006; Guénif-Souilamas & Macé 2004). Revelations about *les tournantes* (gang rapes) of teenage girls by groups of mostly Muslim men in the early 2000s—as well as the tragic death of 17-year-old Sohane Benziane, burned alive by her boyfriend in Vitry-sur-Seine—ignited public furor and gave birth to the movement of Muslim-French women known as Ni Putes Ni Soumises (NPNS, Neither Whores nor Doormats), co-founded by Muslim-French feminist activists Fadela Amara and Samira Bellil (see F. Amara 2006; Bellil 2002).[7] Insofar as young immigrant women have long been constituted as a hope for the assimilative powers of the French secular Republic, the French state embraced NPNS, boosted Amara's political career, and championed NPNS's characterization of *banlieue* women living in terror in order to legitimate its subsequent bans on public veiling.

More recent public outcries over a perceived increase in public sexual harassment—as well as media coverage of sexual misconduct allegations against Swiss academic Tariq Ramadan whose long-standing critique of Islamophobia has made him popular among many young Muslim-French youth—have similarly pointed the finger at supposedly violent, sexually predatory, hyper-masculine men trafficking in foreign North African gender norms. In this analysis, misogyny is either an unreflexive cultural enactment or a product of the social dysfunction of postcolonial men frustrated in their own social and professional mobility, and in their failure to achieve full masculine autonomy through marriage and the establishment of their own households. Even those African and Middle Eastern male asylum seekers who have risked their lives in perilous trips across the Mediterranean come to stand in as expressions of pernicious patriarchy, their solo migration negatively interpreted as a selfish act at the expense of their female or child kinfolk left behind in lands ravaged by war or environmental degradation.

In many ways, then, the Muslim male, as a perpetual migrant, has come to encapsulate the threats and promises, the anxieties and hopes of post-colonial France. Once upheld as a laboring, fertile body promising social and economic renewal for a stagnant postwar France, he now emerges as a threatening vector of social disintegration and civilizational conflict. The past, present, and future mobility of Muslim-French residents—and those tracing their heritage across the Mediterranean more broadly—constitutes a racialized stigma, a sign of social alienation, and an alibi for proposed populist policies of "national preference" in state education and the civil service. As such, racialized immigrants and their children come to carry the burden and the blame for broader structural shifts, for the failure of the French welfare state to adjust to the postindustrial economic landscape and guarantee the same social mobility available to past generations or the same homely comfort to the white privileged few increasingly confronted with those disabled by global political and economic violence. Even supposedly balanced accounts, such as that of the American journalist Christopher Caldwell (2009), join in the blame-the-victim rhetoric, rehashing older Islamophobic and anti-immigrant scapegoating.[8] As Sayad has brilliantly put it:

> The immigrant is the perfect embodiment of otherness: he always belongs to a different "ethnic group" and a different "culture" (in the broadest, vaguest and ethnocentric sense of both words). He is also someone of poor social and economic condition, essentially because he originates from a country that is socially and economically poor. He is part of a different history, and the mode of his absorption into this society has nothing to do with its history. He belongs to or originates from a country, a nation, a continent that occupies a dominated position on the international chessboard, especially when compared with countries of immigration, and which is dominated in every respect. (Sayad 2004: 168)

As I argued in the Introduction, current anxieties around France's de facto multiracial trajectory reflect unresolved tensions within colonial racialized violence and the blowback of decolonization—all of which were predicated on mobility. The export of excess, undesirable, or criminal French and southern European populations to settle conquered lands was balanced by the import of colonized laborers to man the industrial, mining, and military machines during and after the world wars (Liauzu 1996; Noiriel 1988). The postwar reconstruction of France largely occurred through the backbreaking efforts of recruited immigrant workers, generally men with limited life choices after the agricultural infrastructure of their homelands had been destroyed by colonial land confiscations (Talha 1989).[9] These immigrant populations were joined by an educated colonized elite pursuing their advanced studies in the metropole before returning to the colonial periphery as teachers, doctors, and civil servants. Given this mix, France became a primary site for the development of anticolonial nationalist movements under the leadership of expatriate student or worker revolutionaries like Ho Chi Minh (Indochina), Frantz Fanon (Antilles), Habib Bourguiba (Tunisia) or Messali Hadj (Algeria), and for the organization and financing of independence movements. The 1960s witnessed the transnationalization of decolonization struggles, with nationalists assassinating or bombing targets in Paris, and with local immigrant communities subjected to curfews, arrests, and assassinations—the most egregious being the massacre of Algerian participants in a nationalist demonstration in Paris on October 17, 1961, already discussed (House & MacMaster 2009). In this sense, it should come of no surprise that France remains a base of support for and enactment of (organized or individualized) resistance to Western imperialism, or that contemporary Muslim-French communities—the children and grandchildren of anticolonial militants—are today subjected to similar modes of policing.

The policing and stigmatization of French men and women of color for their past or incipient mobility fails to recognize just how socially and culturally French they are. Most of those born or bred in France are neither fluent in their parents' or grandparents' native language nor feel any patriotic attachments elsewhere; occasional family trips to visit relatives abroad only serve to underline just how alienated they feel in their putative *bled* (homeland). As deterritorialized as some of the religious traditions and political ideologies upon which they draw may be, they are locally grounded and culturally indigenized in France.[10] As Marwan Muhammad (2017) and Edwy Plenel (2016) aver, their artistic endeavors, cultural crossings, verbal arts, linguistic innovations, and general entrepreneurial energy arguably provide dynamism to a French society and culture feared to lack innovation and a global competitive edge.[11]

In addition, postcolonial France is a decidedly heterogeneous social formation. While often caricatured as socioeconomically marginalized, many French men and women of color are squarely middle class or, like Muhammad, have successfully joined the professional ranks.[12] Some Muslim French come from Christian families and have converted to Islam for a variety of personal or social reasons; others come from mixed marriages, such as the Lévy sisters, children of a middle-class Muslim mother and a Communist Jewish father, who set off the 2003 French public debate over the *hijab* for refusing to remove their headscarves in class. The most precarious are indeed those undocumented asylum seekers who have crossed the Mediterranean fleeing political and economic instability, or simply in search of a better life. While it is the privileged few with the resources who make such a journey, in some cases these men and women have no home to which to return, and have discarded whatever identity papers once linked them to a particular country. Such a voyage of desperation is known in Morocco as *harrag*— literally "burning"—and has become not just a business for traffickers but a veritable rite of passage, especially for the younger generation (see Arab 2014; Pandolfo 2007). Laments of having to leave by any means— and the costs of emigration to families, communities, and human lives—are retold in newspapers reports, poetry, and popular song across the Global South. There is nothing particularly new about this, and indeed songs mourning migration go back at least to the 1940s in North Africa, but the scale of such movement has increased dramatically as the youth population of the southern Mediterranean has demographically exploded, as unemployment has rocketed to 30 percent and more, and as political uprisings, instability, and civil wars destabilize the once authoritarian control of populations in Tunisia, Libya, and Syria. Now, as my Moroccan friends recount to me with some amazement, one even hears mothers encouraging their own children to leave: "Go, son, go. There's nothing for you here." While France is now rarely the first port of entry, it remains the ultimate destination for many, given a prior history of family settlement and cultural and linguistic familiarity for many migrants from the former French Empire in North and West Africa.

As a number of scholars have documented, EU states have worked unsuccessfully to interdict such flows (see Ben-Yehoyada 2017; Feldman 2012). They have increased naval patrols in the Mediterranean and on the Atlantic coast to intercept smugglers' ships, and security services have infiltrated trafficker networks in order to gather intelligence and, minimally, filter out suspected terrorists. They have off-shored border patrols to migrant-sending countries and have offered development funds and free-trade agreements as incentives for North African states to fight domestic wars on terror and migration. This has led to regular abuses, and has sometimes served as an excuse for authoritarian governments to incarcerate and torture political dissidents or to evict undesirable populations. In Morocco, the fight against migration has been used as an alibi for police forces to round up and deport undocumented African migrants and transmigrants, in certain cases literally depositing them over Saharan borders without adequate food or water (Collyer 2007). In the wake of the 2015 attacks in France, attributed to men of North African heritage based in Belgium, some of whom may have entered Europe as asylum seekers, France reinstated passport checks along several of its European borders, essentially ignoring the rules of the Schengen security zone and calling into question the EU's practice of allowing unrestricted internal movement. Border security and terrorism once again have become a key issue in national elections, with Marine Le Pen's National Front making unprecedented gains in France's 2016 presidential race.

EVERYDAY AND STRATEGIC TRANSNATIONALISMS

Given the renewed focus on mobility as a security threat, it is of little surprise perhaps that the de facto transnational lives of French men and women of color should be a source of ongoing stigma. For all the historical recognition of the centrality of population movement in the form of labor migration, military conscription, and commerce to the slow transformation of "peasants into Frenchmen" over the long nineteenth century (Weber 1976)—from local attachments in discrete cultural-linguistic regions to some sense of a centralized national identity—and for all the genealogical acknowledgment of just how many white French citizens have parents or grandparents born abroad (Noiriel 1988), France has been remarkably slow to officially embrace immigration as central to its national narrative. In general, since at least the mid-nineteenth century, both nationalist ideologues and the folklorists, anthropologists, and historians who underwrote their efforts, have elaborated a culture concept based on rooted, territorial inhabitation, against which mobility and displacement come off as exceptional, if not problematic and threatening (Malkki 1992). It is only in the last few decades that social scientists have come to focus on the migrant and diasporic condition not as an issue of political stability or resource management, but as exemplary of the baseline conditions of cultural complexity (Hannerz 1991) and globalized modernity (Appadurai 1996). And such revisions—at least in their populist renderings—risk either celebrating transnationalism and cultural creolization as the next step of human evolution against which "Islamic fundamentalism" is a dangerous survival (see Barber 1996; Friedman 1999), or bemoaning cultural homogenization (sometimes equated with Americanization) and the loss of a sense of distinctive identity. Both triumphalist and apocalyptic visions of globalization coexist in contemporary French public discourse, and both converge to cast further suspicion on postcolonial migrants—and particularly Muslim-French citizens—as either out of step with France's global future or harbingers of France's national demise.

Of course a number of French men and women of color have achieved professional success. Others, meanwhile, are upheld as exemplary cases of positive assimilation, particularly women like Amara or Bellil who have become outspoken French patriots and public critics of Islam. But for the vast majority confronting institutional discrimination and popular Islamophobia, whose social integration and belonging is never fully acknowledged and always suspect, unqualified "loyalty" (to borrow Muhammad's use of Hirschman) to France's national-global future is simply not an option. Nonetheless, in spite of this racism and suspicion, they have worked to build flourishing lives in the circumstances presented to them. They have forged webs of sociality (material and virtual) both within and beyond the French nation. They have fashioned modes of interaction and alignment through which they can express themselves as French, but not just "French": as French *and* Muslim (and/or African or Asian or Caribbean). These webs of sociality, I want to argue, may be spatially located in a given city or even housing complex, but necessarily draw from wide and varied cultural arrays that transcend France's borders. I will call such an inescapable, lived, locally grounded experience of de facto community-making across diverse spatial fields "everyday transnationalism"—in contrast to the more conscious identity projects one might call "strategic transnationalism." In later chapters, I will focus on these latter forms of globally oriented identity politics, but for the rest of this chapter I am more interested in the mundane, banal postcolonial experience of living simultaneously within and beyond the nation-state.

Already in the 1950s, anthropologists of the Manchester School such as A.L. Epstein (1958), Max Gluckman (1961), and J. Clyde Mitchell (1956), who were studying rural–urban migration in Northern Rhodesian mining towns, insisted on the differentiation of social fields when studying identity formation. Rather than presuming that African villagers would naturally carry their tribal ties with them to the newly built cities, they argued that urban tribal affiliations took on new meanings as categorical markers of identification rather than social structures. If the racist colonial state sought to institute indirect rule in the mines through a system of tribal elders—much as postcolonial French governments have more recently tried through the French Council of the Muslim Faith (CFCM) (Davidson 2012; Fernando 2014; Laurence 2012)—the miners, for whom class interests often trumped tribal affiliation, quickly came to view the elders as mere toadies and rallied against them. Africans may be first and foremost tribesmen in rural settings, Gluckman (1961: 68–69) concluded, but in the town they were townsmen and had to be approached as such. Likewise today we should not presume an equivalence of being a Moroccan in Morocco and in France; French Moroccanness is an identity category that only takes on meaning within the French social field. Moroccan-French adjust their performances of Moroccanness and Frenchness as they move between different social fields, or even as they circulate from domestic settings to spaces of work, education, and leisure.

James Ferguson (1992), revisiting the Manchester School studies and the Copperbelt towns thirty years later, added some nuance to Gluckman's approach. In Ferguson's ethnography, there were two kinds of Zambian townsmen: "ruralists" and "cosmopolitans." Ruralists had maintained close ties with their tribal homelands and their kin, engaging in regular communication, monetary remittances, and family visits. While they had lived for decades in the Copperbelt, they had never stopped being tribesmen, and when employment became scarce they were able to return to their natal villages where they had invested in resources of kin and property. They could easily reintegrate because in a sense they had never left, socially speaking. Cosmopolitans, on the other hand, had not maintained equivalent ties. They had become townsmen par excellence, having invested primarily in their urban households, and had internalized the trans-tribal urbane culture and lingua franca of the city as their own. When circumstances occasionally forced them and their families to flee the city to rural areas, they became veritable strangers in their putative home, trying to rebuild their lives but finding their kinship networks frayed and their cultural practices outmoded. Ferguson offers no explanation for why one migrant became a ruralist and another a cosmopolitan. There was nothing predetermined in the act of migration; the distinction arose from unexpected circumstances and difficult-to-generalize personal situations.

Urban Villages

I would propose that the ruralist/cosmopolitan distinction might similarly prove to be a useful heuristic for thinking through the everyday transnationalisms lived by French men and women of color. In the first place, even if one burns one papers in the *harrag*, one need not necessarily burn one's ties to the country of one's birth. And even many of those born and bred in France remain strong participants in the lives of their parents' or grandparents' communities of birth, the equivalent of Ferguson's "ruralists." Many families take advantage of the services offered by consulate cultural centers, attending speeches by overseas politicians, voting in national elections, and enrolling their children in language classes and religious instruction. Following postcolonial independence, southern and eastern Mediterranean states engaged in explicit outreach projects toward their diasporic communities, in large part to head off the influence of opposition movements among their expatriate populations. In the case of North Africa, these efforts were coordinated by "friendship associations" (*amicales*), which provided education and social services for emigrant workers and their families in France and elsewhere, including organizing diasporic cultural and religious life through religious personnel and even financing mosque construction. Such "embassy Islam," as Jonathan Laurence (2012) has termed it, served in large part to surveil and re-suture the Franco-Maghrebis to North African nation-states.

More recently, a number of states have established fully fledged ministries for expatriate affairs. The Moroccan monarchy established a Ministry of the Moroccan Community Abroad in 2007 in an explicit effort to encourage "Moroccan residents abroad" (MREs) to channel them to send private remittances and homeland investment through national banks (Brand 2006: 74–80). The 2011 Moroccan Constitution—revised in the wake of massive countrywide protests against authoritarianism and economic stagnation—provided explicit measures to ensure emigrants' political rights in both Morocco and abroad, promising to "reinforce their contribution to the development of their homeland" (Articles 16–18). Some French-born Moroccans hold elected office in the resulting Council for the Moroccan Community Abroad.

If, in earlier decades, North African states regarded emigration as an "economic safety valve" (Brand 2006: 17), viewing emigrants as politically untrustworthy and good only for their hard-currency earning capacity, by the end of the twentieth century they had been reconfigured as co-partners in national development (Belguendouz 1999). This largely formalizes the intimate circulation of people, monies, and goods between the diaspora and the homeland that has long existed and compensated for the governments' inability to provide adequate services and infrastructure. In the case of rural Morocco, where I have done long-term field research, French-Moroccans broadly bypass the formal development and governance channels, but actively participate in village-based diasporic associations that mirror rural assemblies (jma'at), provide social welfare for members, organize festival celebrations, arrange for the repatriation of migrant corpses, and collect funds for rural development projects (see Khellil 1979). Their remittance monies finance the provision of electricity, running water, paved roads, and schools to villages bypassed by state infrastructure, as well as contribute to the purchase of land, the building of homes, and the capitalization of small enterprises (De Haas 2006). While some residents who have not left complain that the departure of able-bodied men and women has created veritable ghost villages and worry that emigrant remittances are leading to a brutal modernization of a once integrated rural way of life (see Hoffman 2002), in many ways remittances actually enable local socioeconomic vitality in the face of larger structural and ecological transformation, permitting a larger percentage of the population to partake in the evident signs and performances of distinction—including commodity consumption, domestic architecture, and conspicuous female modesty—normally reserved for a traditional elite (McMurray 2001: 64–97). In the case of the southeastern pre-Saharan Moroccan oases where I have carried out research, the emigration of "black" Haratin men—the former sharecroppers of "white" Berber tribesmen and Arab notables—to the mines and factories of northern Europe has enabled their families to purchase land, irrigation rights, and ultimately political power (Ilahiane 2004; Silverstein 2010).

For many migrants to France, as Sayad (2004: 36) has emphasized, a permanent return to the once-and-possibly-future homeland remains a "myth" perpetually deferred, and those who do return are forced to undergo "rituals of reintegration" and over-perform orthodox nativeness. Likewise, when those born and raised in France travel to visit family abroad, they are often negatively treated as "foreigners," or *Françaoui*. Yet most do travel when it is politically and economically feasible to do so, whether on holiday visits, as pilgrims, or simply as cultural tourists. Granted, these trips are now more planned around French school schedules than religious or agrarian calendars as they were for older generations, and they are increasingly being encouraged and channeled by overseas state agencies and corporate travel agencies. But the trips provide the infrastructure of an everyday transnationalism which continues to link many French men and women of color to elsewheres in often close-knit social structures.

Such transnational interactions are further facilitated through various forms of media, whether through older technologies of letters and mandates or newer modalities of telecommunication that provide not only for the sharing of news but also help establish a virtual sense of intimate co-presence, creating what Peggy Levitt (2001) has called "transnational villages." One family with whom I regularly stay in the southeastern Moroccan town of Goulmima has a daughter in Paris, the wife of an emigré engineer from the region. Between the oasis house and the Parisian apartment, they keep open a perpetual video Skype window, call out to each other when in earshot of their computers' microphones, and do daily domestic tasks such as peeling potatoes in front of the screen while chatting. The daughter may be physically far away, but she is still fully a member of the household, participating in every conversation or decision. The town also hosts several websites that those originating from the surrounding Ghéris valley have established to encompass a broader spatial dispersion. The splash page of Goulmima.com, maintained by the Association Arraw n'Ghriss (the Ghéris Congress) announces, "This site seeks to serve as a tie between Ghérissois from everywhere. It has the objective of keeping those Ghérissois who live away from their natal country informed of events occurring in the Ghéris and the cultural and organizational activities of the region." Such websites supplement village associations based in France. They recapitulate audiovisual media (song, poetry, fiction, film) that have long critically commented on North African emigrant experiences of exile (*lghorba*) in Europe (Goodman 2005; McMurray 2001: 98–109). I will discuss some of these media— particularly various genres of North African and hip-hop musical forms—in the chapters which follow (see also Silverstein 2002b). Today, state-produced broadcasting competes with more informal Islamist, ethnic, and multicultural media for those of postcolonial migrant heritage. Overall, they create an immersive audiovisual landscape in which identity and belonging within France is constructed, with both diffuse and actively negotiated dimensions.

Sacred Geographies

Such ambient connectivity to natal villages is clearly an important vector of everyday transnationalism. These overseas connections are present without reflection in the lives of many from rural-oriented families; for others, they are a strategic decision to explicitly seek out non-metropolitan genealogical rooting. But not all transnational intimacy depends on such a one-to-one link with a particular geographical locality. For many with postcolonial immigrant backgrounds born and raised in France, ethno-national identifications take on new meanings as cosmopolitan modes of classification. For instance, being called a "Berber" or *chleuh* in Morocco remains to this day an unforgivable insult, being tarred as a rural ignoramus or backward tribesman unfit for modern life, and the Amazigh cultural movement thus operates as a rear guard to gain official recognition for Berberness (Tamazight) as a living culture that is part and parcel of the modern nation (Maddy-Weitzman 2011). In France, by contrast, identifying as Berber or Amazigh amounts to a claim to urbane, secular modernity, to genealogical kinship with the Christian majority population as ur-Mediterraneans. Many Franco-Maghrebis of Berber descent are attracted to Amazigh politics as a means to separate themselves out from "bad" Arab Muslims too often amalgamated in French media and popular discourse with "fundamentalists" (*intégristes*) and terrorists (Silverstein 2002c, 2007b). Ethnicity becomes, in Herbert Gans's terms, "symbolic ethnicity" (Gans 1979), with European Amazigh associations hosting annual secular ritual celebrations of Ashura, the Berber New Year (Yennayer), or the commemoration of Tafsut—the 1980 "Berber Spring", when activists first rallied in Kabylia (Silverstein 2003). The celebrations center around ritual foods (particular preparations of couscous) and folk music with women wearing ceremonial Berber robes and jewelry. Store-front association locales are decorated with imagery and objects collected from Algerian Kabylia or villages in the Moroccan High Atlas. In so doing, a putative Berber homeland (Tamazgha) becomes less a node of transnational connectivity than a generalized object of what Michael Herzfeld has called "structural nostalgia" (Herzfeld 1997: 109), a diffuse desire among some Franco-Maghrebis for a time before migratory time. Pierre Bourdieu's famous "Kabyle house" (Bourdieu

1979), adapted to Parisian apartments, comes to function less as a structuring space of signification and sociality that defines a delimited cultural world than an index of distant belonging materially enacted in domestic architectural gestures (see Silverstein 2004b).

Other Muslim French similarly engage in everyday transnational practices that connect their lives in tangible as well as virtual ways to broader communities of faith. As I will discuss in more detail in subsequent chapters, pious men and women, through their daily prayers and dress, their speech and bodily habits, and their performance and consumption behavior, seek to construct ethical spaces within the built environments of France (see Fernando 2014)—spaces that now include *halal* fast-food chains, cola brands, and comedy clubs, as Jeanette Jouili (2015) shows. Theirs is a break from certain religious practices of their parents that, to certain Salafi reformers, are characterized by uncon-scious imitation (*taqlid*), if not heretical innovation (*bid'a*). In so doing, they connect themselves to a broader world of belief, reflection, and respect that transcends temporal borders and political divides. If the sacred geography of some pious Muslim-French believers centers around the Arabia of Muhammad and his righteous followers, that of an equally important neo-Sufi revival movement occurring across the Med-iterranean encompasses other sites and figures. As I will further detail in Chapter 7, in France, the 'Alawiyya and Boutshishiyya brotherhoods have grown significantly over the last decade, attracting both already practicing Muslims and new converts, as well as state recognition and support. Intellectualist and quietist in orientation, members seem at home wherever they can gather in collective study and meditation. Yet the orders definitely have particular spatiotemporal imaginaries that chart a differentiated sacred topography of love and communion with God, of fullness of grace and blessing (*baraka*). In the case of the French Boutsh-ishiyya studied by Deborah Kapchan (2009, 2013), the sacred center is in Madagh, Morocco, the home of the mother *zawiya* directed until 2017 by Sidi Hamza al-Qadiri al-Boutshishi (and now by his son Sidi Jamal), who trace their own spiritual lineage (or *silsila*) back to Abdelqadir al-Jilani and on to the Prophet. As such, Madagh, as a sacred place, comes to orient adepts' devotion and ritual pilgrimage, being the primary node through which Parisian worshipers connect to God. Regardless of one's particular ethnic descent, as a disciple one becomes spiritually and gene-alogically Moroccan without ceasing to be also French.

The Black Atlantic

Morocco becomes thus potentially meaningful for certain Muslim French as a vector of homeland connection, a locus of ethnic identification, and an ethical node within a sacred geography. However, for other young men and women growing up in France's impoverished working-class neighborhoods and public housing projects, being "Moroccan" might also be a more specific marker of local belonging, of living in a complex or area colloquially named for the original immigrant inhabitants. Such is precisely the case for a *cité* in Dreux, the Parisian suburb studied by the sociologist and former mayor Françoise Gaspard.[13] Or as Didier Lapeyronnie noted with regard to a 2002 survey, a young resident of a different Parisian housing project insisted that he too was "Arab" because he "lives with Arabs" (Lapeyronnie 2005: 215). Such identification points to a particular kind of everyday transnationalism I will explore in more detail later in the book, namely that which Robin D.G. Kelley (1996) calls "ghettocentricity": an orientation toward the proverbial "ghetto" as a site of multiethnic belonging and heritage that connects residents socioeconomically and politically to similar urban peripheries and marginalized zones across the world. Such transnational ghetto patrimony comes to be expressed via tropes of kinship, property, and blackness, tropes deployed by French men and women of color in everyday street-level interactions, as well as in artistic renditions by organic intellectuals, writers, filmmakers, and musicians. As I have tried to describe elsewhere (Silverstein 2006), such ghettocentric efforts have involved efforts to take back control of their neighborhoods as livable social worlds in the face of deindustrialization, corporate flight, and heavy-handed policing.

French *cités* and *quartiers populaires* have developed elaborate modes of social solidarity and reciprocity that are expressed through local norms of linguistic register (including the use of various argots and transidiomatic crossings), dress, and gender, generational, and kinship relations, as recently described by ethnographers like David Lepoutre (1997) and Chantal Tetreault (2015). As I discussed earlier, such forms racialize residents as a species apart for bourgeois inhabitants of city centers, but within the *cités* they are bases for a sense of home, solidarity, and even family. Importantly, this solidarity extends beyond the spatial boundaries of France. Not surprisingly, as Hisham Aidi (2014) has beautifully shown, the United States is a particularly rich source of inspiration for French men and women of color attempting to find an expressive style and political vocabulary, seeing in the history of African-American struggle an important precedent for their own politics of resistance.[14] Today's PIR, like generations of past activists, uphold black American civil rights leaders and Black Power activists as models for their own engagement. In the process, they connect themselves to the broader African diaspora constituting the Black Atlantic (Gilroy 1993) without detaching themselves from the Muslim Mediterranean, and all the while remaining resolutely French.

THE IMMIGRANT AND THE SCHOLAR

Everyday transnational attachments and strategic aspirations put immigrants and those from postcolonial migrant backgrounds in a decidedly ambivalent position. They provide a voice and body to France's ongoing, complex entanglements with its former empire and the broader racialized violence that begat current global inequality. And, in enacting those historical connections, they arouse the suspicion of nationalist ideologues, who see in those transnational gestures a lack of loyalty to France as a rooted culture and historical destiny. Perhaps no single figure has embodied or documented such dilemmas with more nuance, critical insight, and empathy than Abdelmalek Sayad (1933–1998).[15] Born in modest conditions in Kabylia, northern Algeria, Sayad's life tracked the ruptures of decolonization and the postcolonial and transnational worlds to which it gave birth. Taking advantage of colonial educational policies that privileged Berber-speaking regions, Sayad eventually pursued graduate studies at the University of Algiers, where he embarked on a prolonged research partnership with Pierre Bourdieu. Together, they recorded the economic dislocation and cultural "uprooting" (*déracinement*) Algerian peasants experienced under late colonialism and the French–Algerian war, both as labor migrants in the slums of Algiers and as displaced persons in military resettlement camps established in the countryside—including in Sayad's native region—built as part of a wartime counter-insurgency strategy to dismantle the rural support network of Algeria's National Liberation Front (FLN). Their study of the internment camps (Bourdieu & Sayad 1964)—publication of which was delayed until after the war, given its critical register—underscored the disabling effects of colonial violence on villagers' everyday practices and embodied habitus, on their spatial orientations and temporal rhythms, on their cultural values and aesthetic judgments, on their ability to conform to normative expectations of masculine honor and female modesty, and on their very sense of the social previously built through the organization of collective labor. Forced to live in the prefabricated world of military camps and pursue individualized occupations, all under the watchful eye of suspicious guards, they had become "de-peasanted peasants" (*paysans dépaysanisées*) without any clear model or possibility for regeneration.

> The peasant can only but live rooted in the land on which he was born and to which his habits and memories attach themselves. Uprooted,

there is a good chance he will die as a peasant, in that the passion which makes him a peasant dies within him. (ibid.: 115)

Sayad brought this colonial trauma with him to France, where he came to pursue graduate studies after the French–Algerian war ended and stayed on as a researcher and later as a professor of sociology. As an Algerian immigrant who wrote about Algerian immigrants, his work had an autobiographical quality to it, even if he never wrote specifically about his own life. As Bourdieu and Wacquant aver, "he was the phenomenon [of immigration] itself," living as an "organic ethnologist" (akin to Gramsci's "organic intellectual") and serving as the "public scribe" for others' parallel experiences (Bourdieu & Wacquant 2000: 177, 179). He was attuned to immigrants' psychic, physical, and cultural "suffering" in part because of his own life-long struggles with physical disability and employment, always living in the shadows of his French peers whose upbringing and family connections provided the social and cultural capital necessary for success in the rarefied and racialized world of French academia, as Bourdieu (1988) himself detailed. Indeed, Sayad wrote extensively about the embodied stigma that migrants carry and pass on to their children, whether as laborers or medical cases or suspect objects of the racializing gaze: "The immigrant is no more than his body" (Sayad 2004: 213).

However, Sayad refused to give into the temptation to relegate himself or his immigrant interlocutors to the status of victims or dupes. For all his emphasis on (post)colonial violence as the ground on which the figure of the immigrant was written (Boubeker 2010),[16] he insisted on the agentive role of immigrants in tracing their mobile trajectories and reflecting on their destinies. He took seriously their narratives not simply as empirical evidence but as self-conscious modes of analysis in their own right. Many of his classic articles consist largely of lengthy block quotes from his (often illiterate) interlocutors, certainly edited and ordered, which provide sophisticated insight into migration as a fraught social phenomenon with little commentary needed.

Moreover, Sayad underlined the heterogeneity of the immigrant experience and the hierarchies within it: that there were winners as well as losers, that the suffering and dilemmas immigrants and their children faced were as much the product of their home society as that of their French employers or lodgers or enforcers. Every immigration, he famously promulgated, is first and foremost an emigration, and to focus solely on their lives in France would be an act of ethnocentrism (Sayad 2004: 29). Words matter, he insisted in an interview with Jean Leca entitled "the evils of words," and terms like "immigration" and "integration" not only mislead but reproduce the French state's discourse on immigrants as an economic resource (Sayad 1990). Instead, he traced the forms of "collective mis-recognition and "lies" (Sayad 2004: 29) that permitted emigrants and their relatives to sustain the belief that relocation was temporary and for the benefit of home communities, allowing them to ignore both the unequal benefits to certain families and the general disruption emigrant cash brought upon rural lifeworlds. If the French state treated them as individualized bodies, from the perspective of Algeria they were social actors whose decisions (such as whether to take their families to France, or how to educate their children, or whether to naturalize as French citizens) reflected on and inflected broader communities—a broader social responsibility of which immigrants were painfully aware.

French men and women from postcolonial migrant backgrounds carry the weight of these past dilemmas and sufferings with them, incor-porated in their dispositions and worldviews, in their attitudes toward life in France and their imagining of future exit strategies. While many of their parents and grandparents—students, factory workers, and miners alike—did engage in the anticolonial struggle, their activities and their consequences have been rarely remembered, and many others were simply unable to take action given the precariousness of their position. Activists of color beginning in the 1980s, and continuing with the PIR today, give voice to their immigrant parents' history and call for reparations for their suffering, for the racist violence and labor exploitation to which they were subject, for the disabilities they now carry from work accidents or for the lack of opportunities open to them to pursue their education. For these activists, Sayad is their model and muse, his writings prescient in their critique but also in their recuperation of voices otherwise unheard, misunderstood, or deemed unimportant (see Boubeker 2010; Khiari 2006, 2009). Like French men and women of color today, Sayad's inter-locutors' lives were decidedly located in France, but not wholly delimited by it. Their mobility made them racially suspect, but their resulting double-consciousness, as W.E.B. Du Bois (1989) famously discussed for black Americans (see also Bourdieu & Wacquant 2000: 180), and the "veil" through which they had to see—their unavoidable perspective on themselves as an object and not only or wholly a subject—also gave them insight and the basis for critique.

But it is not only the PIR who have recuperated Sayad's legacy. His name also graces the media resource library of the National Center (*Cité*) for the History of Immigration (CNHI), a public institution charged with

> assembling, safeguarding, developing (*mettre en valeur*), and making accessible elements related to the history of immigration in France

particularly since the nineteenth century, and to contribute to the recognition of the trajectory of integration of immigrant populations into French society, and to expanding (*faire évoluer*) perspectives and mentalities toward immigration in France.[17]

Originally conceptualized in the late 1990s by a team of historians and scholars of immigration, including several with recent immigrant backgrounds themselves, by the time the CNHI opened its doors in 2007 under President Nicolas Sarkozy to little fanfare, most had become critical of the project and left its advisory committee. The CNHI is housed in the Palais de la Porte Dorée, a building originally constructed for the 1931 colonial exposition and covered in a bas-relief façade depicting racialized colonial subjects doing various forms of agrarian and industrial labor alongside natural resources and exotic fauna.[18] While one of the offices of the original colonial building is preserved intact, and one of the early temporary exhibitions did focus on the 1931 exposition, there are few other gestures to the site's colonial provenance. Indeed, most visitors come for the tropical aquarium housed in the building's basement. When the CNHI was finally officially inaugurated in 2012 by France's socialist president François Hollande, its name was formally changed to the Museum of the History of Immigration, and indeed even when I first visited it in 2010, staff already referred to it as a "museum." In addition to its resonance with the lived spaces of housing projects in which many immigrants and their children live, the earlier designation of *cité* implied a public space of encounter and debate; as a "museum" immigration comes to be relegated to a historical, monumental, dead past. Even those expositions which trace immigration to the contemporary period tend to principally whitewash present violence and wrap past suffering into a narrative of national development. Appropriately, when Sarkozy initially opened the museum, it operated under the auspices of the short-lived Ministry of Immigration, Integration, National Identity, and Co-Development. In the French state's logic, mobile past-presents that exceed the nation can only be understood as threatening.

CONCLUSION

Thinking beyond the nation-state has been a sustained project of both activist and scholarly concern for several decades. If states' efforts to maintain a monopoly on legitimate violence and fiscal control continue unabated, the nations they govern can no longer be contained—if they ever could be—by delimited ethnic and territorial borders. Under the rubric of transnationalism, scholars of migration have importantly highlighted these lines of potential fracture, particularly questioning the telos of assimilation that immigrants were presumed to undergo, calling into question the "melting pot" that supposedly magically transformed North African peasants into Frenchmen (see Glick Schiller et al. 1995). But to think of transnationalism as a unilineal vector that continues to unite migrants and their descendants with their geographical and cultural "homelands" is to presume that all migrants are like Ferguson's Copperbelt ruralists, and to risk substantiating neo-nationalist paranoia that Muslim French are but a fifth column of a future Eurabia. While new communication technologies have certainly allowed families living across borders to maintain themselves virtually, they have also facilitated a number of other everyday transnationalisms in which Muslim and other French men and women of color participate, and strategic transnationalisms to which they aspire. Their mobile pasts and present connections racially stigmatize but also allow for insight and critique. They call forth a postcolonial France that exceeds itself.

2

How Does It Feel to Be the Crisis?

This chapter addresses the various ways in which those French men and women from a postcolonial immigrant background discussed in the last chapter think of and feel themselves as Muslims, how they adapt their religious commitments (their prayer, dress, eating and drinking habits, ways of interacting with others, and so on) to the secular context of urban France, and how their religious commitments connect them intimately with other Muslims in North Africa, West Africa, and beyond, in spite of—and sometimes even through—the surrounding dominant paradigms of secularism—or what in France is called *laïcité*. In earlier work (Silverstein 2004a) I have called these kinds of connections "transpolitics" in order to emphasize, first, as discussed in the last chapter, that the lives and imaginations of the young Franco-Maghrebi men and women with whom I have previously worked are not limited by national boundaries. And, second, that there is something inevitably political about such expressed and embodied religious or cultural commitments in the context of the universalist claims of the French secular republic—so much so that some who speak in the name of the French state perceive them as a challenge or a problem that has to be dealt with either through institutional or legal or policing mechanisms. It is this "problem" or "challenge" that I will address in this chapter, one which since the late-2000s, with the rise of Islamic State and a spate of high-profile attacks in Paris, Nice, Toulouse, and elsewhere has developed to a crisis point—or at least to the perception of a "crisis" for French secularism and republicanism. Whereas in the last chapter I explored how Muslim-French mobility—their migrant past and transnational connections—underwrote a racialized stigma, here I want to unpack how Muslim French *qua* Muslims, in their beliefs and practices, have come to signal a crisis in secularism, and yet how they nonetheless work to build rich and flourishing religious lives for themselves in spite of the institutional constraints and Islamophobic exclusions they face. How is it indeed that a few schoolgirls dressing modestly or even fewer veiled women on public streets has come to be perceived as an existential threat to France? And how indeed, to gloss Du Bois (1989: 1), does it feel to be the crisis?

In the first place, it is necessary to interrogate the category of "crisis" as a category of political analysis and a lived experience.[1] Political philosophy, and social theory more broadly, has long vacillated between interpretive modes emphasizing *longue durée* continuity (see Braudel 1958) and those underlining discontinuity (Foucault 2002), rupture (Koselleck 2004), and revolution (Marx & Engels 1978) as randomly repetitive or predictably periodic. Both sets of interpretations have been mobilized for conservative and radical political agendas, with cultural continuity treated as either an index of the force of tradition or of its agentive inventiveness in encompassing and indigenizing new contingencies (see Sahlins 2004), with revolutionary crisis either bemoaned as a failure of social reproduction or celebrated as the condition of possibility of stagnant social formations finally rejoining History, with a capital H (see Marx 1978). Marxian, Foucauldian, and Bourdieuian approaches, in their emphasis on dialectical transcendence, discursive breaks, and moments of uprooting, have all too often overlooked just how internally labile and creative "traditions" (whether material, discursive, or structural) can be, and how much modes of production, cultures, and habitus are continually adjusting and adapting to new contingencies and frictions within lived environments (see Bourdieu 2000; Silverstein 2004b). On the other hand, more structuralist analyses fail to account for how contradictions dialectically accumulate within extant social systems and cultural logics, either discounting the resultant crises as prefigured within local *longue durée* historicity or attributing them to external, alien causes.[2] Furthermore, neither set of social theories—insofar as they focus their analysis on transcendental categories of culture, structure, discourse, mode of production, or habitus—does justice to the phenomenological experience of crises as they are actually lived by social persons, as world-shattering moments when all that seems solid proverbially melts into air (Berman 1982), when one is forced to reach into (or occasionally outside of) tradition to cobble together a stance from which to make sense of new circumstances (see Crawford 2013). Such new interpretive stances are not neutral or passive, but actually come to determine the shape the crisis and its aftermath end up taking. In what follows, I want to emphasize both the dialectical process through which contradictions within French secularism, as energized by changing postcolonial conditions, give birth to the present "crisis" (or at least the set of transformations experienced as crisis), but also how that crisis is lived as a moral panic, as a moralizing set of anxieties which call into question certain moral certainties, and how those French men and women of color caught within it respond by creatively building on certain cultural and aesthetic traditions within and beyond the French liberal tradition.

But before elaborating on the "crisis" and its aestheticized responses, let me first provide some very general background about Islam as a lived spiritual practice and basis for identification in France. My focus will be on Muslim-French lives and struggles and on social and political debates about Islam—not on Islam as a religious tradition as such, but on those who are hailed as or actively take on being Muslim. Just as a reminder, Islam is currently recognized as the second most practiced religion in France after Catholicism, surpassing Protestantism and Judaism. Muslims, broadly construed, currently make up as much as 7.5 percent of the population of France, numbering somewhere between 3 and 5 million, consisting primarily of those with family ties to North Africa and Sub-Saharan Africa, but also South Asia, the Levant, and, in light of recent events, Afghanistan, Iraq, and Syria, as well as at least 100,000 "native" converts.

Note, however, that the native versus immigrant distinction, as discussed in the last chapter, is deeply problematic. As Sayad (2004) powerfully argued, the taken-for-granted state discourse that labels certain Muslim French citizens as "second" or "third" generation immigrants, as if they carry foreignness in their genealogy, is ultimately a racializing gesture of exclusion. Much of the contemporary nationalist response to the perceived existential crisis consists in rallying white constituencies around the populist idea that they are the "real," main root French (*Français de souche*), and instructing racialized others that, as putative newcomers, they cannot ever truly belong.

Moreover, these population statistics presuppose a fundamental epistemological question of who to include as a "Muslim" in the first place. Is Muslimness traced through one's genealogy? Through one's ancestors' place/s of birth? Through one's actual religious practices such as praying five times a day, fasting during Ramadan, or more broadly living an ethical Muslim life? By regular mosque attendance? Or, perhaps more subjectively by how one self-identifies? But the latter raises the problem of how to account for the fact that some claiming to be Muslims are not recognized by others claiming to be Muslims. Who is the arbitrator of such quarrels?[3]

In France, as we have seen, censuses cannot officially ask such questions, as the republican social compact is constitutionally premised on a community of citizens beyond interceding diacritics of race, ethnicity, and religion. There is an incredible diversity of belief, practice, and self-understanding among Muslim French, though by and large they have adapted their religious lives to the social circumstances and contexts they inhabit, constituting what some have described or promoted as a

"French Islam" (see Ramadan 2004). Indeed, for the last few decades, the French state has explicitly sought to underwrite the formation of a specifically French Islam (*Islam de France*), adapted to French norms of secularism (*laïcité*) out of the diversity of varieties of Islam in France (*Islam en France*).

Moreover, these Islamic formations are not only a consubstantial part of France's contemporary demographic reality, but a constitutive element within its history. Muslims have been present in France since the eighth century, with Umayyad forces based out of Cordoba occupying parts of southern France repeatedly from the eighth to the tenth centuries, and Ottoman naval forces again in the sixteenth century. These histories have left behind their material and demographic traces. Arguably it was in opposition to Islamic forces that the idea of a singular France as a Christian realm—however later fractured by religious schisms and political rivalries—came to emerge in the first place. French history textbooks have long touted the victory of Frankish and Burgundian soldiers under Charles Martel over Umayyad armies at the Battle of Tours/Poitiers in 732 as a key unifying moment for a cultural-territorial France. Furthermore, as historian Ian Coller (2010) has shown, Napoleon Bonaparte's short-lived attempt to incorporate Egypt, the Levant, and their Muslim subjects into the French Empire between 1798 and 1801— which his nephew Napoleon III later attempted to revive as an "Arab kingdom" (*royaume arabe*) in Algeria—led to the constitution of a small community of Egyptians and Syrians in metropolitan France. Marseille would become an important entrepôt for travelers, traders, soldiers, and laborers coming from the eastern and southern Mediterranean (see Mandel 2014: 9–13; Temime 1990). During more than a century of colonial rule, France forcibly governed millions of North and West African Muslim subjects, whether as direct rulers (in the case of Algeria) or indirectly (in the case of Morocco, Tunisia, and elsewhere) through local Islamic forms of authority. After World War II, as James Le Sueur (2005), Todd Shepard (2006), and Gary Wilder (2005) have shown, Muslims in Algeria and elsewhere in French-ruled territories were further incorporated as citizens of the multi-national French Union, with some degree of representation in the French national parliament. And, as discussed in the last chapter, French colonial subjects played vital roles in the country's military efforts during both world wars, as well as the rebuilding that occurred in their wake. All of which is to say that Islam— as both a lived religion and imagined figure—has been central to, indeed constitutive of, France's past and present.

LAÏCITÉ AND ITS DISCONTENTS

The question then becomes less what is it about Islam as such that presents a challenge to France as a universalist ideal or cultural nation, but rather how it is that Islam has come to be understood not as a constituent part of but rather as a problem for France at the present moment. Why is it that over the last several decades, long-standing Muslim-French subjects and citizens have come to be seen not only as an issue of state management (read "integration"), but as a veritable crisis in social stability, economic viability, cultural unity, and national security—such that a veil or minaret or group of men praying on the street could come to be seen as requiring something to be done, as necessitating legal regulation? Common explanations tend to have recourse to presumptions of primordiality, to claims to some inherent qualities of a decontextualized Islam and its generic practitioners, thus side-stepping nuanced social-scientific analysis. Such ready-to-hand hypotheses effectively racialize Islam as a natural species of otherness, just as their practical effects legitimize the further exclusion of those French men and women committed to their Muslim faith.

The broadest claim, as mentioned in the last chapter, is about the cultural or institutional incompatibility of Islam with French ways of being, or its gender norms, or its secular organization of public life: *laïcité*'s putative exclusion of the religious from the political, or rather its supersession of religion by the liberal state. The presumption of course ignores the significant heterogeneity within both Islam and Frenchness, the sexism and patriarchal values still inherent within French gender performances, and the different (and often hypocritical) ways in which *laïcité* has been historically and presently applied.[4] People who identify as Muslims in France approach their faith in both relatively orthodox and relatively symbolic, flexible, or heterodox ways, much as French Jews and Catholics do. Mainstream French feminist anxieties about the spread of Islamic misogyny—as evidenced by often over-stated claims about veiling practices, seclusion, forced marriage, and genital cutting (or so-called "female genital mutilation")—index just how vulnerable critics feel France's belated and incomplete struggle for women's liberation to be. As recent revelations around the #balancetonporc (France's version of #metoo) movement attests, French gender equity is aspirational at best. Arguably, devout Muslim women do not hide their sexuality any more than devout Catholic, Orthodox, Protestant or Jewish women; the latter's dress is simply more normalized in the French public visual field than a *hijab* (headscarf) or a *niqab* (face veil). Without exclusionary legal barriers, such visual signs of modesty do not in and of themselves pose a barrier to active professional lives, or to devout women being serious feminists in their demands for equal pay, non-discriminatory access to public resources, or freedom from harassment. Indeed, the covered Muslim women I have met during past research in France tend to be among the most courageous and outspoken in these regards; they have learned to persevere in the face of regular experiences of Islamophobia, sometimes in the form of overt verbal or physical attacks, though more commonly in terms of covert acts of micro-aggression. Certainly many Muslim-French women build flourishing lives for themselves within the strictures of *laïcité* and even uphold its principles (see F. Amara 2006; Keaton 2006:188–89). Others struggle against secular constraints and legal prohibitions on dress and public religiosity. Ethnographies of pious women emphasize how much agency they do have in their religious lives, that their decision to cover or not emerges from a committed effort to live an ethical life following God's path, and that, in any case, they are not the submitted dupes the Ni Putes Ni Soumises (NPNS) movement and other pundits present them as being (see Fernando 2014; Jouili 2015).[5]

Moreover, the claim about Islam's incompatibility with French republican norms due to its failure to distinguish between public and private, and between religion and politics, likewise fails to capture the complexities within either France's institutional arrangements or the diverse ways in which Muslims in France or elsewhere conceptualize their relationship between their duties to God and to temporal powers. Christian and Islamic traditions each call forth spaces for public debate over guiding social and political principles. Each of these publics has its own genealogy and thus slightly divergent presuppositions about ethical norms of self-presentation and behavior. And each calls forth counter-publics (Warner 2002) that operate in parallel, and occasionally in opposition, to hegemonic governance structures. But for centuries these public spheres have been interconnected and accommodated alternate modalities of participation, most often in the name of coexistence and mutual respect. Christians and Jews living in Muslim-majority polities were historically not subject to *shariʿa* jurisprudence as such, but were delimited in their actions to the particular ways in which Christian or Jewish legal processes were locally recognized, instituted, and encompassed within a broader system of sovereignty (see Mahmood 2016). Likewise, Muslims have been expected and inclined to follow the laws of the lands in which they live, whether Muslim-majority or not, though of course some aspects of religious practice are obligatory and in theory non-negotiable. That said, devout Muslims, like all other people committed to a faith, do not always live up to their obligations, ask God's forgiveness when they fail to do so, and work to do better in the future. Versions of the same dilemmas can be illustrated for devout French Christians, Jews, and others, and in some cases very orthodox sects do isolate themselves so they can maximize a pious environment in order to facilitate fulfillment of their obligation. When Muslims groups are seen to organize like this, they are accused of sectarianism (*communautarisme*) or creating "ghettos"—of not wanting to "integrate" or "live together."[6]

As Talal Asad (2003), Saba Mahmood (2016), and others have shown, European secularism, particularly as it becomes ideologically ossified as a state religion premised on commensurable national citizens, fails where earlier, imperial forms of governmentality succeeded in ecumenically integrating a multitude of ethno-religious subjects (see Makdisi 2007). Whereas, late-Ottoman rule managed religious diversity through the unequal coexistence of Muslim and non-Muslim *ahl al-dhimma* collectivities, European imperialism in the Middle East and North Africa imported political secularism built around a Protestant notion of a privatized, individualized conception of religion that was ostensibly commensurate across all faiths. Yet, in order to maintain religion as a private mode of belief rather than a collective enactment, colonial and inheritor postcolonial states had to continually intervene, manage diversity, and regulate the legal borderlands that define the private sphere. Contemporary French public discourse around *laïcité* thus misrecognizes three key features: first, that secularism involves increased state engagement in, rather than retraction from, the religious sphere; second, that it emerges from a very particular Protestant understanding prioritizing private inner spirituality—as opposed to external collective embodied practices—as the true site of religiosity; and third, as Naomi Davidson (2012) has shown, that the imperative to secularize Islam merely extends a colonial logic of population management onto postcolonial France, a demand with which Muslim-French subjects have thus been long intimately familiar.

This historical forgetting of secularism's Protestant origins and colonial past allows contemporary spokespeople for *laïcité*—as well as the various governmental commissions that have been established over the years to defend and reinforce it—to treat Islam as differently different than the various other differences which have been historically accommodated or are otherwise seen as relatively unproblematic. Other ethno-religious subjects, including many French Jewish intellectuals and Amazigh activists, have found in their incorporation into the sociopolitical hegemony of secular republicanism a welcome protection from the stigma of otherness, and in some cases have become its ardent advocates. As Anya Topolski (2016) has detailed, the postwar elaboration of the civilizational category of "Judeo-Christian" as characterizing Europe's particularity—in broad opposition to Islam—emerges in part from this process of incorporation of formerly racialized others. It is this internal ambivalence between avowed religious neutrality and "Judeo-Christian" bias, this tension between theoretical universalism and practical particularism, that constitutes some of the key contradictions within French *laïcité* that, under present conditions of scaled-up super-diversity (Vertovec 2007), underwrite the present crisis.

In this regard, while France's 2004 *laïcité* law prohibiting "the wearing of signs or dress indicating (*manifestant*) religious belonging in public elementary, middle, and high school" ostensibly addresses all conspicuous religious paraphernalia (Jewish *kippas*, Sikh turbans, Orthodox large crosses, and so on), it was directly motivated by a set of cases of schoolgirls wearing *hijab* that had generated public controversy since 1989, and is commonly known as the "veil law" or the "headscarf ban."[7] The law emerged from the recommendations of a blue-ribbon commission established by President Jacques Chirac and headed by former minister Bernard Stasi. The Stasi Commission consisted of an erudite group of 23 scholars, government officials, and professionals working in the milieus of religion and migration, including ex-revolutionary philosopher Régis Debray, sociologist Alain Touraine, political scientist Gilles Kepel, immigration experts Jacqueline Costa-Lascoux and Patrick Weil, historian of *laïcité* Jean Bauberot, and noted Islamic scholar Mohamed Arkoun. In addition to Arkoun, the commission included two other members of Muslim background, attorney Nicole Guedj and school counselor Hanifa Cherifi, a self-defined "secular Muslim" who had in previous years mediated the return of covered girls who had been excluded from state schools. Over the course of four months, it held nearly 100 public and 40 private hearings with representatives of various religious communities, state agencies, NGOs, schools, and universities, as well as a public discussion with over 200 students from schools in metropolitan France and French territories abroad. While it interviewed a number of Muslim-French men and women, including representatives of NPNS, it only reluctantly and belatedly met with any women wearing the *hijab*.

The Stasi Commission's 77-page published report subtly traced the history of and present challenges to *laïcité*, and recommended a series of 26 measures to better enhance its mission of providing freedom of belief, the legal equality of religious groups, and the neutrality of the state vis-à-vis religion. These measures included not only proposed legislation to clarify the state's position on religious dress in schools, but also the incorporation of Yom Kippur and the Islamic feast of the sacrifice (Aïd el-Kebir) as public holidays; expanded classroom instruction on "religious facts" in addition to the history of slavery, colonization, decolonization and immigration; the teaching of non-state languages such as

Berber (Tamazight) and Kurdish as opposed to simply state languages like Arabic and Turkish in public schools; the rehabilitation of "urban ghettos" seen as the breeding grounds for Islamism; and the adoption of a *laïcité* charter to be invoked during various public rites including the naturalization of immigrants. Although several of these suggestions (including the teaching of Tamazight in schools) were subsequently considered and partially enacted, only the proposal for legislation against "ostensible" religious signs and dress in public schools promptly made its way into law. Several commission members later admitted to feeling forced to accept the ban in spite of their hesitations about its potential unequal application and exclusionary effects in order for their other recommendations to be taken seriously. As it turns out, they were right to be concerned. The law has disproportionately affected Muslim schoolgirls who, due to the relative paucity of accredited Islamic schools, find themselves forced to enter the fee-paying private school system (including, ironically, Catholic schools) or continue their education at home—leading to the criticism that it has resulted in their further social marginalization rather than foreseen integration.

Moreover, this refusal of French *laïcité* to accommodate Islamic practices, in spite of its ostensible religious neutrality, is often justified through the primordialist claim that Islam has a flat organizational structure and thus lacks representative institutions or ordered hierarchies that could speak and act on behalf of Muslims in France. While there is admittedly no equivalent of the Vatican for Islam as a whole (much as there is not for Judaism or Protestantism, to take two other minority religious groups in France), there is no lack of organizational hierarchies or authority figures within particular national, sectarian, or devotional Islamic structures, as the brief discussion of the Boutshishiyya brotherhood in the last chapter showed. The biggest difference is that Protestantism and Judaism have been officially organized in France for longer, and so they have been able to establish (sometimes rival) organizations that are recognized by the government and granted representational authority.

The French state's desire for an equivalent representative Islamic body dates back to the late 1980s. After several aborted earlier attempts, the then interior minister Nicolas Sarkozy established the French Council of the Muslim Faith (CFCM) in 2003, with 41 officers elected from the multiple federations, associations, and major mosques across the country. While election results have varied, the Ministry of the Interior has intervened in the organization's presidency, initially naming Dalil Boubakeur, rector of the Grand Mosquée de Paris—the oldest mosque in France, built by state authorities in 1926 to honor the sacrifice of

Muslim colonial forces during World War I (Davidson 2012)—given his seemingly moderate stance; he was subsequently reappointed on several occasions. The Ministry of the Interior has also progressively marginalized the influence of the popular Union of Islamic Organizations of France (UOIF), since re-named Muslims of France, which has been criticized as being too close to the Muslim Brotherhood and is currently excluded from the CFCM. The CFCM's authority and representativeness is frequently contested among many Muslim French, who bemoan the fact that it enthrones institutionalized mosque and religious association authorities, amounting to a "clericalization of Islam" (Bozzo 2005: 79), privileging men officially trained abroad and silencing Muslim-French women (see Fernando 2014). It has nonetheless become a site for officially-sanctioned negotiation around contested issues such as halal butchery, mosque construction, religious education, Islamic burial, and the provision of religious counselors in hospitals, prisons, and the military.[8] It has taken voice in solidarity with the victims of recent attacks associated with Islamic State, but also in response to egregious cases of Islamophobia. In 2016, the Vatican invited its president to participate in a Christian–Muslim dialogue. Meanwhile, its numerous regional councils have become an effective space for Muslim-French residents when they want to articulate and seek restitution for grievances concerning discrimination in housing, employment, and the provision of state services. Thus, at the local, national, and indeed international level, the CFCM does provide an official, de facto instance of Muslim-French collectivity that goes beyond the autonomous individual citizens that secular republicanism ostensibly recognizes de jure. In other words, in spite of the concern about "Islam" failing to provide a means for dialogue with the secular Republic, the French state—just like its counterparts in the Middle East and North Africa—has proven more than capable of creating institutional hierarchies and self-appointed interlocutors when it has deemed those to be missing and necessary for the management of ethno-religious diversity.

As with the exclusion of the UOIF, the political effect of recent moral panics, conspiracy theories, and media portrayals of the *banlieues* and *quartiers populaires* as hotbeds of Islamic State recruitment and jihadi extremism is to delegitimize the increasingly vocal demands for inclusion made by Muslim-French citizens outside of the aegis of the CFCM. As discussed in the last chapter, until at least the mid-1980s, the unspoken contract signed by French men and women of color exchanged begrudging legal tolerance for political quiescence and social politesse, requiring those from postcolonial immigrant backgrounds to relegate themselves to being laboring bodies and restrict their engagements to within their local communities. In contrast, Muslim-French citizens today actively use the streets and the courts to fight for their cultural and religious rights, for the right to wear what they feel obliged to wear, eat what they are doctrinally obliged to eat, and pray where and when they are obliged to pray.

This is an uphill battle twice over. First, as Mayanthi Fernando (2014) has insisted, Muslim-French petitioners are obligated to articulate their claims in the language of political liberalism, through a discourse of individual rights and freedoms: the right to practice their faith on an equal level as all others. To do so requires them to make commensurate that which is incommensurable, to effectively speak as if their Muslimness was defined and organized along the religious parameters of secularism, as an expression of private, inner belief rather than the social, embodied performance for which it is for them. Pious Muslim-French women have to claim their modest covering as a personal choice in order to defuse accusations of patriarchal coercion. But, liberalism treats individual choices as flexible, changeable, and adaptable—which is precisely not how they understand their nonnegotiable obligations to God. Their explanations—much like Tariq Ramadan's speeches (see Fourest 2010)—thus get read by unsympathetic commentators as double-talk rather than the unavoidable entailment of translating between the idioms of Islamic reasoning and liberal thought. The fact that Muslim French talk among themselves in the language of obligation, but to outsiders in the language of positive freedom, should not imply an incompatibility or untranslatability between "Islam" and "France," or, worse, a conscious effort to deceive, but simply the difficulties inherent in any situation where one is forced to present oneself (as an embodied, collective Muslim subject) in the terms of an (individual, secular) other.[9]

Second, Muslim-French claimants to equality in France are at a disadvantage because granting rights to perform their religious obligations is often averred by public officials and media pundits to deny the rights of the majority: the rights of schoolchildren to be free from the implicit proselytism of their classmates; the rights of young men and women to flirt in a sexualized public sphere; the rights of citizens to personal security; and the rights of animals to be humanely killed according to modern scientific (read non-halal) methods. Even prior to the 2004 ban, school administrators could legally dismiss covered students from class if they could reasonably claim their presence pressurized other students to cover and thus amounted to an act of proselytization (evidenced, perhaps, by other students' curiosity or subsequent covering). The original 1905 laïcité law specifically prohibited religious coercion, though to protect nonreligious schoolchildren from devout teachers, not from other students.

Likewise, the NPNS argued in favor of the ban as part of a broader effort of public sexual education for the *cités*, where young women, like Muslim women elsewhere, were ostensibly forced to hide their sexuality or risk sexual violence (see F. Amara 2006: 76–83; Djavann 2003). Other mainstream feminists more broadly defended the rights women had recently or aspirationally achieved regarding education, employment, and political parity *as women* without the need to hide their femininity (Scott 2006). In so doing, they refused to recognize the *hijab* or *niqab* as themselves expressions of femininity, as a form of modest fashion that could nonetheless be a beautiful and alluring individual gender expression (Jouili 2015; Tarlo & Moors 2013). Or, they saw such fashion trends as pernicious to women and, like liberal feminist philosopher Elisabeth Badinter, called for a boycott on brands that participated in Islamic marketing (Truong 2016). The 2011 ban on face veils in public spaces (sometimes referred to as the "*burqa* ban") carries a similar logic—particularly when it was over-applied by southern French police and mayors to ban full-body swimwear (so-called *burqinis*) on public beaches—insofar as the *niqab* was claimed to hinder sociosexual interactions taken to constitute the liberal public sphere.

The state moreover justified the ban on the face veil in terms of a broader public expectation of security premised on transparency, on the capacity of the police to surveil the public without intentional hindrance or deception.[10] The law explicitly prohibits "dissimulating one's face in public." Even prior to the 2011 ban, the French state required women to remove their hair and face coverings for photographs on mandatory state-issued identity cards, themselves required to be on an individual's person at all times outside of the home. Some civil servants, bank tellers, and other front-line receptionists found veiling to be threatening and in a number of cases had refused service to covered women, even before the ban provided the legal support for their Islamophobia. Other men and women interviewed by journalists felt visually subject to aggression by having to confront "walking coffins" (*cercueils ambulants*) on the street. NPNS spokeswomen explicitly articulated the rights of Muslim women to be protected from the coercion of their husbands.

At the extreme, some Islamo-skeptics have wrapped their anxieties in the language of animal rights, criticizing halal butchery—whether in industrial slaughterhouses or in private settings during the Aïd sacrifice—of causing undue harm to animals as they are not stunned before being killed.[11] All of which has made it more difficult for Muslim-French consumers to ensure adequate halal provisioning for state schools, hospitals, administrative offices, prisons, the military, and private corporations.[12] The 2012 revelations that many non-Islamic abattoirs had switched to Islamic methods in order to take advantage of the burgeoning halal market created a minor moral panic, both fanning Islamophobic theories of a Eurabian conspiracy and more generally calling forth a broader critique that the public had a right *not* to eat halal, or at least to know under what tradition its meat had been produced. In each case, freedom is pitted against obligation, public rights against private rules, tolerance against intolerance, modernity against tradition—with hegemonic secularism consistently failing to recognize its own traditions, impositions, and intolerances. The point is not to jettison liberalism altogether or give up its persistent critique of structural inequality enabled by a discourse of rights and freedoms, but to note its blind spots and hypocrisies, its cultural assumptions and privileging of certain kinds of subjects over others, its colonial genealogy and postcolonial entailments. As I discuss at the end of this chapter, some Muslim-French men and women have found in secular liberalism a powerful ally in their fight against postcolonial injustice. Others, however, have been disabled by the laws and political discourse that the panicked defense of secular liberalism has called forth. These pious men and women experience its crisis as their own racialization and exclusion.

GLOBALIZATION AND THE ETHNIC FIX

Thus the crisis surrounding "Islam in France" is ultimately a crisis not of an inherent cultural or religious incompatibility, but of postcolonial France sorting through its own liberal secular premises and promises within an undeniably multiracial, multiethnic, and multireligious environment where French men and women of color have increasingly taken voice to demand full and equal citizenship, the terms of which they seek to participate in the making. While Muslim-French men and women are living the effects of the current "crisis," the challenge they seem to present to a French way of life has more to do with historical changes and social transformations that have happened in France itself—a France which, again, we need to understand as always already including Muslims and Islamic practices, even before decolonization. What is at stake, as I emphasize throughout this book, are the changing contours and conditions of social, political, and economic life in France in which the contradictions and tensions immanent within secularism and liberal modernity create friction and spark crises. Efforts to exclude and treat France's Muslim constituent as abject others therefore amount to an attempted ethnic fix—akin to what David Harvey (2001) has termed a "spatial fix"—to a broader socio-material problem of late capitalist French modernity.

The fundamental transformation underwriting France's current existential crisis over the fate of liberal secularism is the end of the Cold War, which shifted geopolitical attention from a West–East axis back to a North–South one of imperial times. It was in this context that Bernard Lewis (1990) and Samuel Huntington (1996) proposed their "clash of civilizations" thesis as the new world paradigm—a paradigm that has, in spite of its many problems and critiques, become the dominant lens for mainstream publics on both sides of the putative divide. The end of the Cold War likewise animated political contestation and democratization processes in the former French Empire, in which Marxist and Islamist opposition movements called into question authoritarian states that had been alternately propped up by NATO or the Soviet Union since decolonization. The subsequent heavy-handed but incomplete suppression or exporting of this opposition would ultimately give birth to radical transnational movements like the Islamic State. Arguably, the 2011 uprisings in Syria, Tunisia, Libya, and beyond mark the end game of these post-Cold War transformations (Silverstein 2018), with no clear new model of state–society relations taking hold in the region. In the meantime, the uncertainty and precariousness emerging within the region as it struggles against reassertions of state authoritarianism and global neo-imperialism gets coded in France and elsewhere across Europe as a security threat easily attributable to Islam.

The second related transformation in terms of how a now externalized internal Islam comes to constitute a "challenge" and become a scapegoat for the current crisis is related to France's ambivalent place within the process of European integration. Europe, as a unified sociopolitical entity, certainly has its historical roots in the 1957 Treaty of Rome, if not to earlier experiments in industrial cartelization, but really comes to be more than merely a delimited customs union only in the wake of the Cold War with the 1992 Maastricht Treaty. The process of political integration has had profound socioeconomic and cultural ramifications directly related to France's broadly Catholic socialist underpinnings. On the one hand, it has entailed France harmonizing its migration policy and social welfare program with its eastern neighbors, balanced by demands for fiscal austerity in the context of economic contraction. All of which has translated into increasing numbers of Muslim-French and other communities of color with full citizenship rights making demands on a postindustrial French state that no longer has the resources to assure the productive futures of the younger generations. This has underwritten a situation of precarity—including high unemployment, housing shortage, crumbling infrastructure—in parts of outer-city and small-town France not profoundly different from other global sites ravaged by neoliberal shifts in production and expanding wealth inequalities. On the other hand, EU regulations since the 1990s have required member states to protect the cultural, language, and religious rights of their inhabitants, calling into question the privileged relationship Christian churches had to the state, as well as the ostensibly universalist model of secular republicanism itself. The French state has actively resisted and violated some of these regulations. For instance, in 1992 France signed the European Charter for Regional and Minority Languages, designed to recognize, protect, and promote regional languages such as Basque, Breton, and Catalan, but has failed to officially ratify it on the basis that it violates the constitutional definition of France as "indivisible," with all citizens equal before the law "without distinction of origin, race or religion," with the second article of the Constitution specifying that, "The language of the Republic shall be French." These same constitutional provisions have made it difficult for France to officially and specifically track anti-Muslim discrimination and attacks, a point I address in the next chapter.

As discussed in the last chapter, such continental challenges to national narratives and practices—in the wake of deindustrialization, transformations of the agricultural core, and repeated economic crises—have animated the populist appeal of far-right nationalist parties like the National Front running on Euro-skeptic, anti-immigration and often Islamophobic platforms. As anthropologists like Terence Turner (1995) have long insisted, support for anti-immigrant and Islamophobic groups should be understood as much an act of racist exclusion as an aspiration for national inclusion by those white working-class residents who feel increasingly left behind by the postindustrial shifts of late capitalism, who take past state efforts to embrace multiculturalism as calling forth a new France in which they do not seem to have a place (see Sveinsson 2009). While mainstream French political parties have explicitly distanced themselves from the racist undertones of the National Front's platforms, they have nonetheless adopted many of the more stringent migration and asylum policies, antiterrorism security measures, states of emergency, and limitations on Islamic public religiosity called for by the radical right—what is generally referred to as a "LePenization of the [French] soul" (*lépenisation des esprits*) (see Le Goaziou & Mucchielli 2006: 155). In recent years, mosque constructions have been repeatedly blocked and, as of 2011, street prayer in Paris has been banned in the name of public security, in spite of a lack of mosques to accommodate worshippers for Friday prayers, especially during the holy month of Ramadan. Islamo-skepticism, if not even outright Islamophobia, pays politically, and socialist governments such as that of François Hollande (2012 to 2017) are as likely to adopt such measures as their rightist counterparts. Indeed, Marwan Muhammad writes of "a veritable Islamophobia bonus [*prime*]: a media bonus, a political bonus, even an electoral bonus" (Muhammad 2017: 188).

The third transformation has to do with the changing nature of protest and opposition in Europe, from one based on class solidarity and international revolution to one based on identity and culture, as already alluded to with the radical-right nationalist movement. Faced with policing and deportation measures, bans on Islamic dress and public gathering, regulations over halal butchery, and a wider set of surveillance practices legalized under post-2015 state of emergency conditions, many of which are now integrated into standard law, all of which repeatedly single out Muslim populations for special attention, it should perhaps come as no surprise that a number of young, marginalized Muslim French have adopted an increasingly stigmatized Islam as a banner of local and national protest and have been attracted to visions of a global Islamic future.[13] Muslim populations in France, as in surrounding countries, have been expanding as much because of new waves of immigrants fleeing violence in the Middle East and North Africa— balanced in part by the out-migration of French-born Muslims to places like North America or the Gulf—as because of the conversion of young men and women growing up in poorer, mixed-ethnic urban areas like the Parisian *banlieues*. Such conversions should be taken seriously as forthright expressions of spiritual convictions and moral strivings, and not merely as reactions to social marginality or politically felicitous modes of identification (Allievi 1999; Oujibou 2009; see also Özyürek 2015; Rogozen-Soltar 2017).

At the same time, however, they do contain political valences, and such political engagement itself can derive from an Islamic ethico-moral sense of responsibility. Whereas previous generations, including those who animated the 1983 Marche des Beurs (or March for Equality and Against Racism) (Hajjat 2013), spoke in the language of international revolution or a cultural revolt of global youth or a liberal discourse of civil rights, new protest movements by French men and women of color draw on Islamic ethical discourse, sometimes via a rhetoric of jihad, more often in terms of a broader anti-imperialism in which young Muslim-French protesters in particular liken their social situation to the repression of Palestinians or the plight of Muslim Brothers in General Sisi's Egypt. Their orientation is thus decidedly transnational, though, as we saw in the last chapter, not inherently delimited to the spaces marked out by their particular family history of migration. So, if "Islam" does seem to present a challenge to the French secular republic and has become indexical of its contemporary crisis, then it is not because of any inherent incompatibility with secular modernity as such—particularly insofar as Islam has always been immanent to and constitutive of France—but because Islam has become increasingly the language through which social injustice, economic marginalization, political stagnation, and cultural racism is being explicitly challenged by men and women of color within France.

BREAKING THE SILENCE

The central question is then: How do Muslim French come to take voice within the hegemonic secular republic? How do they make spaces of social, cultural, religious, and political exclusion, like the housing projects of the Parisian *banlieues*, their own? How do they construct rich, meaningful, and flourishing lives for themselves *qua* Muslims in such places? How do they make sense of these spaces through various forms of artistic, textual, and political representation, and, in so doing, animate them in new ways and even project possible, hopeful futures? Such efforts take many forms, and in the chapters which follow I will be particularly attuned to the forms of writing, music-making, embodied practice, and political organization through which young French men and women of color refuse the silence of exclusion and enact membership within and beyond France.

A key interlocutor with French secularism and an important figure in public articulations of agentive belonging for Muslim-French women has been Fadela Amara. As mentioned in the last chapter, she co-founded the feminist movement Ni Putes Ni Soumises (NPNS) in the *banlieues*, and rose to become secretary of state of urban policy during the presidency of Nicolas Sarkozy from 2007 to 2010. Born and raised in Clermont-Ferrand (central France) to Algerian Kabyle immigrant parents, she writes of being "shocked" into antiracist activism when as a teenager she witnessed police mistreatment of her parents after her baby brother had been killed by a drunk driver (F. Amara 2006: 53). She subsequently joined SOS-Racisme, the national antiracist organization with close ties to the Socialist Party formed in the wake of the 1983 Marche des Beurs. Her primary interventions have centered around organizing women from the *banlieue* housing projects, which she presents as being "abandoned by the state" (ibid.: 84) to "Mafia-like organizations" run by local young men, and thus degrading into American-style "ghettos" (ibid.: 92).

In Amara's analysis, the true victims of this process have been young Muslim-French women like herself and her younger sisters. Echoing Nicolas Sarkozy's 2003 distinction between official Islam and the "Islam of cellars and garages" (*Islam des caves et garages*), Amara contrasts the spiritual beauty and serenity of the Mosquée de Paris with the implacable "religious obscurantism" of contemporary "basement Islam" (ibid.: 93). She outlines the "harmful influence" of the latter, particularly its misogyny. "Through its religious propagation of intolerance basement Islam offered young men a theoretical framework and tools with which to oppress young women" (ibid.: 97). The veil (*voile*), she continues, "is the most visible and telling evidence of this lapse into obscurantism" (ibid.: 98). Self-describing as a "practicing Muslim" and absolutely condemning Islamophobia that wrongly amalgamates Islam, fundamentalism, and terrorism, she finds in *laïcité* a "common framework" to guarantee women's freedom and provide for "peaceful coexistence of different religions" (ibid.: 100–1).

The NPNS was similarly constituted within this secular republican frame. In 2001 she organized a national Estates General of Neighborhood Women (*femmes des quartiers*) drawing on the legacy of the 1789 Revolution, from which emerged the 2002 NPNS manifesto, a direct appeal for women to take voice against their oppression:

> No more silence during public debates over the violence, the precariousness, and the discrimination ... For us the struggle against racism and exclusion, and the battle for our freedom and emancipation, are one and the same struggle. We alone can free ourselves from this double oppression. We are speaking out in this appeal in order that our sisters and our mothers in each housing project in France may hear this call to freedom and join our struggle for a better life in our neighborhoods. (ibid.: 163–64)

In 2003, the NPNS spread this message across France in a self-conscious commemoration of the twentieth anniversary of the 1983 march, thus placing the NPNS directly in the civil rights genealogy. Whatever gains had been garnered in the 1980s in terms of equality had not been extended, Amara argues, to Muslim-French women, who continued to suffer from social exclusion and sexual violence within their communities. The movement's goal remains to provide sexual education and encourage women to engage and rebel against forces of continued oppression, to break free from the local, religious chains of the "ghetto" and engage as "active citizens" (ibid.: 143) within the French Republic. Such a fight entails breaking with the dominant "cultural relativism" (ibid.: 159) of the Left, which, she argues, in the name of respect of "culture and tradition" and its championing of anti-imperialism, has bolstered global Islamism and its deleterious effects on Muslim women. Rather, in the conclusion of her autobiographical text, she vows to "carry on our unrelenting combat [*sic*] to preserve secularism, equality, and a plurality of social identities in a multicultural republic" (ibid.: 162).

Amara's activism has generated considerable critique for being self-serving and politically conservative, and for playing into the broader Islamophobic stereotype of the "Arab boy" (*le garçon arabe*), whose disabling politics Nacira Guénif-Souilamas (2006) and other critical scholar-activists have systematically analyzed. While Amara's book certainly relies on a caricature of "ghetto" living conditions, her plea certainly comes off as heartfelt and sincere, an existential cry for women to stand up to social and cultural-religious conditions under which they continue to suffer, and moreover to the men who impose them. The liberal-secular political framework offers her precisely the platform from which to make her case, and she sees and lives no contradiction between her rights and duties as a liberal citizen and her obligations as a practicing Muslim. She does not connect that framework to its colonial history or to the violence accomplished in its name. She broadly ignores the fact that others may not find the secular and Islamic logics so obviously commensurate, or may not find it so easy to adopt a rhetoric of rights and freedom to articulate their continued sense of abjection—and indeed at times active exclusion—from the French republican project. Her solution seems to be the political equivalent of Sheryl Sandberg's neoliberal feminist model of "leaning in" (Sandberg 2013). It is the perspective of those who have already achieved some measure of success and who view their own past suffering as only yet another challenge they have overcome through the force of individual courage and will. For all of her discussion of social exclusion, she does not engage in a structural critique of power or of the effects of enduring anti-Muslim racism on the possibilities of postcolonial agency.

Amara's is clearly but one of a number of ways in which Muslim-French citizens and other French men and women of color have taken voice to express and respond to what is posed as an existential crisis. Some have elaborated a Sufi vein of inner spirituality likewise consonant with dominant ideologies of liberty, equality, and fraternity, but via a more quietist embrace of pan-religious humanism. Others have found themselves in the so-called "Islamic revival" in which communal piety and solidarity is critically opposed to state-sponsored forms of socio-political life (see Jouili 2015). Others, as we have seen in the last chapter, construct transnational ethno-racial movements, sometimes via Berber/

Amazigh or African culturalist projects, sometimes via an identity politics centered on global blackness and the hip-hop nation. In some cases, Islam provides a rich semiotic code through which to interpret the trials and tribulations of so-called "ghetto" life; it provides a framework of belief that allows artists, writers, singers, and audiences to contextualize their current struggles within a longer collective history and situate their wanderings along a more consequential personal path toward God. It provides poetry and musical forms that enrich their artistic endeavors and appreciation. In other cases, as we will see in later chapters, other cultural or spiritual traditions become the basis for such claims, though in many cases they too at times mix with Islamic themes. While it is unclear whether France will prove to be a place of efflorescence for new generations of Muslims, such engaged artists, activists, and intellectuals—including Amara as well as many of her outspoken critics—have nonetheless pushed back against widespread Islamophobic suspicion, opposition, and violence, and insisted that Islam is immanently part of France, and part of what makes the country so great.

For Muslim French and other French men and women of color, then, the contemporary "crisis" as bemoaned by state officials, polemicized in the media, and experienced in popular moral panics is not an external challenge coming from the Islamic world to an already constituted France, but something internal to the postcolonial tensions and contradictions within secularism and political liberalism—modes of governmentality that claim to accommodate and represent all citizens but only to the extent that they remake themselves into autonomous self-regulating and self-alienating individual subjects of the Protestant ethic and the spirit of capitalism. The freedoms implied in such a subjectivity ultimately prove to be illusory—subject to a variety of nonnegotiable obligations and restrictions that are inequitably distributed across class, ethnicity, racial, and religious terrains—increasingly precluded by contemporary conditions of socioeconomic precarity where fulfilling labor is no longer an existential condition or a social right but increasingly an exclusive ethno-racial privilege. The crisis then is not about Muslim French violating the implicit contract of secular citizenship, but about secular citizenship failing to live up to its own promise to recognize and pay forward all the work done by generations of Muslim French and other French men and women of color to make France what it is today and what it might become in the future.

3

The Muslim and the Jew

In a particularly poignant moment in Matthieu Kassovitz's celebrated 1995 film, *La haine*—a bleak, neo-realist portrayal of marginalization and violence in the Parisian *banlieue* housing projects—the white Jewish protagonist Vinz attempts to justify to his close Franco-Algerian Muslim buddy Saïd his fantasy of killing a police officer if their mutual friend Abdel, a victim of police violence, dies.

> VINZ: You want to be the next Arab (*rebeu*) killed in a police station?
>
> SAÏD: No.
>
> VINZ: Well, me neither.
>
> SAÏD: *You* neither? *You* don't want to be the next Arab killed in a police station?
>
> VINZ: Exactly …

Ten years later, Karin Albou's *La petite Jérusalem* explored the fractures of this cross-ethnic and cross-religious imagination. Set in another Parisian peripheral *cité*, the film relates a very different coming-of-age story—not of young men trying to survive in the shadow of police violence, but of a young Orthodox Jewish woman, Laura, trying to navigate the "religious law" of her community, her studies in Kantian philosophy, and her growing sexual desire for a Muslim man, Djamel, a refugee from Algeria's protracted conflict. If Kassovitz's film self-consciously presents a fable of class and spatial solidarity emblematized by Vinz's self-presentation as an "Arab," Albou's film—set in the midst of and portraying a series of attacks on Jewish synagogues and persons that marked France during the early 2000s—presents the ultimate impossibility of cross-ethnic and cross-religious imaginings, culminating in the failure of Laura and Djamel's relationship and the emigration of Laura's family to Israel.

These two films, in their overlaps and their divergences, underline the dilemmas of ethno-religious identification in postcolonial France, a country with both the largest Muslim and largest Jewish populations of Europe. Much as has occurred for African-American men in the United States, in contemporary French media and political discourse, young Muslim-French men from the *cités* are demonized as culturally violent, sexist, homophobic, and anti-Semitic (Guénif-Souilamas 2006 Guénif-Souilamas & Macé 2004), at the very same moment as their modes of dress, musical forms, and speech patterns are appropriated as styles of resistance by non-Muslim youth across the *banlieues* and even within bourgeois city centers. If the recently expanded rates of conversion to Islam, particularly but not only on the peripheries of French cities, index the tentative growth of an Islamic chic and the local characterization of Islam as a religion of social protest (Daynes 1999; Lakhdar et al. 2007)—much as Hisham Aidi (2014) has discussed in the United States and Latin America—this putative "Islamization" of the *banlieues* has, as we saw in the last chapter, called forth Islamophobic concerns about "lost territories of the Republic" (Brenner 2002), viewed as the forward outposts of an Islamic imperial "Eurabia" (Ye'or 2005).

In particular, anxious observers have characterized these areas as rife with a "new anti-Semitism." Contrasting the reported rise of anti-Semitic attacks in France since the early 2000s with the "classical anti-Semitism" whose ties to rightist expressions of French nationalism have been carefully detailed by Zeev Sternhell (1983), many commentators— including Emmanuel Brenner (2002), Raphaël Draï (2001), Alain Finkielkraut (2003), Pierre-André Taguieff (2004), and Shmuel Trigano (2003)—have linked the "new anti-Semitism" to the progressive turn to Islamic identity politics by those from postcolonial immigrant backgrounds. While careful to distinguish Islamism from Islam, these authors posit Muslim-French anti-Semitism as a continuation of an older Muslim anti-Zionism and anti-Semitism imported from North Africa by immigrants, transmitted from parent to child, and left to fester by a state fearful of offending its minority populations and Arab diplomatic partners (Brenner 2002: 14; Taguieff 2004: 14–15).[1] For Trigano (2003: 91), this assessment leads to a wholesale condemnation of "Arabo-Muslim" society as in need of complete reform if it is to fit into a secular modern world (see Draï 2001: 191). These authors follow Bat Ye'or (2002) in projecting an apocalyptic future in which French Jews—like other non-Muslims—risk being treated as *dhimmi* subjects, vulnerable to the whims of a new Islamic caliph—what Trigano (2003: 106–118) calls "the Ottomanization of Europe." Indeed, they see this renewed Ottoman form of governance as already in effect in the *banlieues*, which Finkielkraut (2003: 10) has characterized as "savage lands" (*lieux féroces*) where political norms of democracy and *laïcité* simply do not exist.[2] More recent acts of violence—including the 2006 abduction and murder of the French Jewish cell-phone salesman Ilan Halimi, the 2012 attack on a Jewish school in Toulouse, and the 2015 hostage-taking at the Hyper

Cacher Jewish supermarket in Paris in the wake of the *Charlie Hebdo* attack—have only reinforced this perception of an encroaching Islamic menace.

If Islam comes off as a danger to the future of France, French Jewishness (*judaïté*)—in spite of its many fractures along lines of devotion, class, and ethnicity (Ashkenazi versus Sephardi, among others)—is projected in parallel as the primary object and victim of this threat, in need of protection by the secular republican state. As Wendy Brown (2006) has argued, tolerance has become a central modality of secular liberal governmentality, regulating the behavior of citizens, bracketing the tolerant "civilized" from the intolerant "barbarians," and constituting an alibi for state violence against the latter. In the wake of World War II, Jews have emerged as "the ultimate champions and foot-soldiers of tolerance by virtue of their need for it" (ibid.: 135). In France, as elsewhere in the Global North, Muslim citizenship is considered suspect insofar as Muslims are accused of being genealogically and/or politically intolerant of women, homosexuals, and Jews. To overcome such suspicion and be recognized as tolerant, individual citizens, Muslims must performatively denounce not only terrorism, but also misogyny, homophobia, and anti-Semitism. In so doing, they are called upon to declare their "fealty to the nation-state over transnational Islam" (ibid.: 94).

The French state makes no equivalent demand of French Jews, but as a protected class whose narrative of belonging in France is intimately connected to a history of victimhood and betrayal, of the past failure of the French state to protect, their own citizenship can feel tenuous and vulnerable.[3] As historian Esther Benbassa (2004) has underlined, Jewish citizenship in France came at the price of disavowing their community institutions and embarking on a fraught path of cultural and social assimilation. The Dreyfus affair and the Vichy government's complicity in the Holocaust only underlined the uncertainty of this incorporation and the tenuousness of French Jewish citizenship more generally. Jews, as a group, make a double ethical claim on France, both as moral censors to whom an unpayable debt is owed, and as potential victims of ongoing global hatred deserving of special protections. Given this history, many French Jews have aspirationally tethered their cultural belonging to a post-revolutionary republican ideology of civility, solidarity, and *laïcité*, while at the same time articulating their past suffering as unique, incommensurable, and repeatable. This dynamic helps explain the self-righteous efforts of certain French Jewish intellectuals—like the "new philosophers" Alain Finkielkraut, André Glucksmann, and Bernard-Henri Lévy—to position themselves as ardent defenders, even spokesmen, for the secular republic on whose protection they depend.

Unfortunately, as discussed in the last chapter, practical applications of *laïcité* can have Islamophobic dimensions and exclusionary effects on Muslim-French citizens.

In this chapter, I focus on the categories and subjectivities of "Muslim" and "Jew" as they have come to be projected and implicated opposition-ally in recent moral panics around the future of postcolonial France as a social, cultural, and political project, and the seemingly sectarian politics which appear to be driving the country apart. As Matti Bunzl (2005) outlined, if Jews were abject figures of modern European nationalisms (as much as they were its intellectual architects), it is now Muslims who are excluded from the global neoliberal order (even as Gulf petrodollars have broadly financed this order's establishment). By the late-twentieth century, the previously derided "cosmopolitanism" of Jews—their lack of rooted belonging within a given European territorial ethnos, their seeming physical and cultural mobility, their "mercurial" (Slezkine 2006) role as borderless go-betweens—all of which had animated past anti-Semitic ideologies, became emblematic of a projected borderless Europe. Their seeming capacity to seamlessly integrate (indeed assimilate) into urbane social and professional life was no longer understood as insidious but positively contrasted to Muslims' apparent sectarianism and ghettoiza-tion. Their ostensible accommodation to (and indeed advocacy for) the strictures of an increasingly hegemonic state secularism—in spite of its Protestant genealogy, dividing private from public religiosity, inner faith from external expressions, individual belief from group practice—is likewise now contrasted with Muslims' seeming inability to domesti-cate their religious expression and obligations and separate their faith from public life. Jews' seeming political quiescence as French subjects stands in stark contrast with contemporary Muslim-French demands for rights and recognition that defy the limits of liberal politics, with their outspoken and embodied activism and engagement in struggles beyond France's borders. Muslims *qua* migrants are, as I argued in previous chapters, stark public reminders of the demise of Europe's imperial and industrial past and of its inability to fully or successfully turn the page to a postimperial or postindustrial future built around the very service sector in which Jews historically prospered. Their culture of (Islamic) poverty is blamed for the durable inequality (Tilly 1999) from which Jews and other exemplary or model minority subjects have supposedly escaped through sheer effort and an encultured work ethic.

Within this public accounting of minority difference, and within this "hierarchical, unequal multiculturalism" (Rogozen-Soltar 2017: 4), European Jews and Muslims are not only contrasted but actively pitted against each other. Whether the conflict is taken to be the continuation of age-old hatreds or the recent product of the Israeli–Palestinian struggle, it is projected as a surrogate for a broader "clash of civilizations," opposing Occident and Orient, the Global North and the Global South. The centrality of Auschwitz to the making of the European modern, instead of underlining the common Jewish and Muslim (Oriental/ Semitic) experience of dehumanization by the Occident (Anidjar 2003), has served only to accentuate their ideological separateness. If the Holocaust has legitimated the exceptional status of Israel as an illiberal, racial project, Palestinian resistance and Muslim anti-Semitism more broadly seem to threaten to repeat its horrors. For many Muslim-French citizens, however, Israel can only but be a settler colonial state, a living reminder of the incompleteness of decolonization not only in the Middle East but also in the lived, everyday experience of themselves as post-colonial subjects. The "solidarity of 'condition'" (Benlabbas 2015: 23) Muslims in France feel for Palestinians is mirrored by the common threat of expulsion many French Jews feel with Israeli Jews, particularly for those Jews "expelled" from North Africa after decolonization (Benbassa 2006: 69; see also Benbassa 2004).

   This chapter explores how such postcolonial interpellations translate into contemporary political imaginations and social engagements for European Jews and Muslims. Drawing on recent historical scholarship of Muslim–Jewish relations in France (Arkin 2014: 15–55; Katz 2015; Mandel 2014), I will try to show how current dilemmas over identification and action connect to the unresolved contradictions of an imperial project and the violence of decolonization, the present-day effects of which are still felt by many, albeit in altered and renovated ways. In contrast to scholars and pundits who would characterize present Jewish–Muslim tensions as but a contemporary instance of an age-old conflict, I will underline its particular situatedness within the French postcolonial context, itself transected by emergent invocations of diasporic and transnational belonging that connect French Jews and Muslims to groups beyond France's borders. Departing from those who would treat the French Jewish experience as exceptional to the broader immigrant and postcolonial experience, I conceptualize Muslims and Jews in France within the same analytic field, and approach the violence of anti-Semitism and Islamophobia together as interlaced and co-constitutive, as part of a set of structural tensions within postcolonial France in which a low-intensity "war on terror" has been pursued since the early 2000s.[4] As I discussed in previous chapters, whereas the previous generation of Franco-Maghrebi social and political actors—that of the Beur movement of the 1980s—primarily limited their activism toward improving their daily lives as citizens of France and residents of dilapidated suburban localities, and looked to the struggles of black Americans and South Africans for their political inspiration (see Derderian 2004; Hargreaves 1995; Silverstein 2004a), many French men and women of color today—projected and acting as "Muslims" and largely disavowing the ethnonym "Beur"—rather orient their political consciousness to the violence in Israel/Palestine and elsewhere in the Middle East. They find in these contexts of neocolonialism salient analogies for the conditions of political alienation, social discrimination, economic precarity, and cultural embattlement they experience in France.

It is in this context of marginalization and Islamophobia that the Muslim-French reaction to the French state as an ongoing colonizing force can take on the form of a generalized anti-Zionism and an occasional anti-Semitism. From the perspective of many Muslim French, Jews seem to incarnate French bourgeois success, to have benefited from an upward mobility that seems to be foreclosed for them. Moreover, they seem to have done so, in defiance of French republican norms, as an integrated, organized "community" and not as a set of atomized, alienated individuals. The Muslim-French politician Mehdy Benlabbas has recently spoken of the admiration and even "jealousy" this produces for Muslim-French citizens aspiring for some heightened degree of sociopolitical belonging:

> In its solidarity, its structuring, its organization, its institutions, [the Jewish community] incarnates everything lacking among today's French Muslim [*Français musulmans*]: a tightly-knit community, united around collectively defended fundamentals ... Muslims of France aspire for this solidarity, this organization which would permit them to exist beyond being an object of critique, of suspicion, of stigmatization, indeed of hate. (Benlabbas 2015: 23–24)

This French Jewish success seems to occur among even those of a North African/Sephardi background, distancing them from their colonial past and their fellow Maghrebi immigrants. If the 1970s and 1980s witnessed at least tentative efforts to coordinate Jewish and Muslim-French antiracist and civil rights efforts—whether through community organizations or via umbrella groups like SOS-Racisme, the Movement Against Racism, Anti-Semitism, and for Peace (MRAP), and the International League against Racism and Anti-Semitism (LICRA), affiliated with the mainstream political parties—by the late-1980s French Jewish organizations increasingly separated themselves from Franco-Maghrebi activists' support for Palestinian rights and the apparent "religious revival" that seemed to be occurring among Muslim French (Arkin 2014: 80–96;

Mandel 2014: 125–52). Such refusals of common cause at times took on alarmist, Islamophobic dimensions,[5] were paralleled by a similar religious revival among French-born North African Jews, and became entangled with the increasingly Zionist, pro-Israel ideological positions taken by representative associations like the Representative Council of Jewish Institutions (CRIF) or the Union of Jewish Students of France (UEJF) within the French Jewish "community." By the 2000s, the French Jewish teenage girls interviewed by ethnographer Kimberly Arkin were avowing their own racism and Islamophobia, declaring "I hate Arabs" (Arkin 2014: 2).

It is in the context of these divergences and reaffiliations that some Muslim French have expressed deep suspicion and even antipathy to French Jews as stand-ins for the French and Israeli states. As Michel Wieviorka has argued:

the Jews in Israel behave towards the Palestinians as the "French" in France do towards the "North Africans" … In the atmosphere of racism and disaffiliation which characterises them, the "Arabs" are therefore thought to be doubly mistreated by the French Jews who repress them as Jews, reproducing the model of the Israeli Jew towards the Palestinian Arab, and as French, racist and disrespectful towards them. (Wieviorka 2007: 142–43)

In its extreme, the violent racialization of French men and women of color as "Muslims," and the postcolonial violence they confront from the French state, is responded to in violence directed back at the state and those (including Jews) who seem to represent it. Of course, not all such violence necessarily follows a logic of religious interpellation and invocation, in spite of presumptions by certain Islamophobic critics (see Mishani & Smotriez 2005). During the urban uprising in the *banlieues* of France of October and November 2005, young men on the street were primarily organized according to ties of residence and socioeconomic marginalization that transcended ethnic and religious differences. Calls for calm by local Islamic associations and even a fatwa against the violence by the supposedly fundamentalist Union of Islamic Organizations of France (UOIF) fell on deaf ears (see Silverstein & Tetreault 2006), and no Jewish persons or institutions as such were targeted by protesters. In still other cases, French men and women of color—including Berber/Amazigh activists with whom I have worked—engage in contrasting practices of cultural imagination, identify with persecuted Jews, and adopt philo-Semitic, pro-Israel, and even Islamophobic platforms.

All of which is to say that postcolonial Islamophobia and anti-Semitism are far from "homogeneous or coherent" phenomena (Wieviorka 2007: 13) While I reject the explanation of reciprocal violence as but a continuation of long-standing, Jewish–Muslim sectarian conflict, I nonetheless insist that the violence of colonial governance and decolonization continues to provide the framework through which various groups have made distinct claims to French subjecthood in increasingly oppositional ways (Arkin 2014: 15–55; Bahloul 1996; Benbassa 1999: 185–89; Hyman 1998: 193–214; Katz 2015). If Franco-Maghrebi Jews and Muslims, particularly of the first generation, have been similarly racialized as "immigrants," and found themselves inhabiting similar urban French neighborhoods and housing projects where they shared urban services and resources (such as halal/kosher butcher shops), their differential memories of colonial and wartime Algeria underwrote their affective distance (Mandel 2014: 59–79). The exacerbation of these relations in the wake of the increasingly violent events in Israel/Palestine (Benbassa 2004; Hyman 1998: 202–5) has made family recollections of closer Jewish–Muslim relations in North Africa the object of palpable nostalgia (Benbassa & Attias 2006: 88). Like all nostalgia (see Boym 2001; Herzfeld 1997), the pain of loss can enable or disable, merely underline just how separate today's French Jews and Muslims have become, or spur actions toward dialogue and reconciliation. I will discuss both conciliatory and conflictual trajectories in the pages which follow.

However, for most younger Muslim and Jewish citizens of France, coming to terms with the past matters less than confronting present inequality and future threats. The past tends to be engaged, if at all, primarily through the lens of trauma, as one of colonialism and slavery on the one hand versus the Holocaust on the other. The resulting competition of memory and victimhood (Benbassa 2006: 75; 2015: 12) further drives a wedge between young French men and women of color who are instructed in state schools to internalize the collective loss and guilt of the Holocaust, while simultaneously finding little mention of the colonial violence or enslavement their own ancestors suffered. Hence the occasional acts of rebellion against Holocaust lessons that some observers have taken as a sure sign of the propagation of a "new anti-Semitism" among the younger generation (see Brenner 2002).[6] Hence also the prov-ocations of French shock-comic Dieudonné Mbala Mbala, discussed in the next chapter, or the shrill commentary of activists from the Party of the Indigènes of the Republic (PIR), who call into direct question the sacrosanct quality of Holocaust memories in contemporary France and the ways in which certain Zionist ideologues and organizations have instrumentalized them for Islamophobic purposes. In these cases, it is not that contemporary activists are continuing the anticolonial struggles of their parents, but they are objecting to their exclusion from the official narrative of contemporary France. None of which forecloses the kinds of "multidirectional memory" Rothberg (2009) explores, where colonialism and the Holocaust can be understood together as constitutive of the racialized, postcolonial present. The rest of this chapter explores precisely the conditions of possibility for such an articulation.

COLONIAL CONTEXTS OF ISLAMOPHOBIA AND ANTI-SEMITISM

As I have discussed elsewhere (Silverstein 2002c, 2004a; see also Lorcin 1995), the French colonization of North Africa operated as what Jean-Loup Amselle, referencing Michel Foucault (1997), has termed a "war between the two races" (Amselle 2003: x). The French colonial administration formally distinguished "European" (*européen*) citizens from native subjects (*indigènes*), sometimes termed "nationals," legally inscribing this division in a *code de l'indigénat* (Native Code) that, until 1870 for Jews and 1944 for Muslims in Algeria, denied natives French citizenship and made them subject to different court systems and legal codes as standardized and officialized by the French administration (Shepard 2006).[7] In general, access to French citizenship required the renouncing of one's religious "personal" or "local civil" status, which was understood as tantamount to apostasy and thus almost universally avoided. Yet, within this larger, racialized citizen/"national," *européen/ indigène* divide, French colonial ethnologists further classified indigenous populations according to cultural, linguistic, and religious traits, treating them as differentially assimilable in relation to French "civilization" (Lorcin 1995; Silverstein 2004a: 35–75). These divide-and-rule strategies broadly belied fears of Islam as a unifying political force during nineteenth-century anticolonial revolts, a fear that was re-energized during the twentieth century by Arab nationalist movements in Tunisia and Egypt that would eventually give birth to the fight for North African independence.

In brief, French administrators perceived the essentially Islamic fatalism and fanaticism of Arab indigenous populations as an inherent stumbling block to their administrative or legal assimilation into the French nation. In contrast, they treated certain minority populations— particularly Jews, blacks, and Berbers—as somehow more proximate to French civilization, even if still culturally separate, sectarian, and potentially xenophobic. While Berbers and blacks were not enfranchised like Algerian Jews, they were repeatedly singled out for French paternalism. Berbers in particular were incorporated into educational experiments, were subject to customary/tribal codes ('urf, in Arabic; izerf in Berber) rather than Islamic law for civil matters, and were preferred recruits as migrant laborers, working on colonial farms, mines, and abroad in France, due to their perceived hardy work effort. Claims of Berber consonance with and contribution to French modernity have been reiterated in the contemporary period, as many of today's Berber/Amazigh activists present French Imazighen as the exemplary avatars of indigenous laïcité and the models for an Islamic practice compatible with and supportive of French republican values.

The divisions between Muslims and Jews, and among Muslims between Berbers, blacks and Arabs, played themselves out during the late-colonial period and struggles over decolonization. The rise of virulent anti-Semitism among French settlers in Algeria, coupled with the perception that Jews were exploiting Muslim populations, led to inter-communal violence in Constantine in 1930 (Cole 2010). Similar "riots" broke out in Oujda and Jerada in northeastern Morocco in the wake of the 1948 Palestinian Nakba/Israeli war of independence, and again across the country during the 1967 Arab–Israeli war, encouraging further emigration. Although a number of Algerian Jews were sympathetic to the Algerian nationalist cause, many sought to maintain some form of French Algeria, and were almost universally "repatriated" (to use the French state's rhetoric) to France at the end of the French–Algerian war (1954 to 1962). While Arabs and Berbers fought side by side against the French in the war and during the 1950s nationalist movement in Morocco, the two anticolonial movements drew directly on pan-Arab ideology that excluded explicit articulations of Berberness or blackness. Those who did call for multiethnic, multiracial, or multi-confessional independent states were broadly marginalized from the movements and subsequently exiled (or in some cases assassinated) after independence (Chaker 1990; Stora 1995a).

The intimacy of state violence against both Muslims and Jews is embodied in Maurice Papon, the Paris police chief responsible for the massacre of over 100 Muslim Algerian demonstrators at a rally in Paris on October 17, 1961 in support of the National Liberation Front (FLN). Not only was he also a former high official under the Vichy regime (and later found responsible for the deportation of thousands of French Jews to concentration and death camps in Nazi Germany), but he subsequently earned his mettle for instituting a regime of state-condoned torture against members of the nascent Algerian nationalist movement when he was governor of Constantine in eastern Algeria. Not only was the Holocaust broadly an extension of colonial violence within Europe, with Jews dehumanized as "Muslims" in the death camps (see Agamben 1999), but decolonization also victimized Muslims and Jews as both excess to the reformulation of French nationality as defined by the secular republican metropole.

POSTCOLONIAL VIOLENCE

In the wake of decolonization, there were over 400,000 North African Muslims and Jews living in France. By the early 1980s, this number had increased to approximately 1.5 million, as labor migration continued apace until 1974, and family reunification policies and the continued (albeit limited) availability of student, professional, and asylum visas afterward facilitated the arrival of more men and women.[8] Postcolonial migrants and their children faced consistent racist, anti-Semitic and Islamophobic rhetoric, which repeatedly resulted in physical attacks. Earlier, during the Vichy government, Muslims, and particularly Muslim nationalists, were subjected alongside Jews to internment and deportation, both in the metropole and in the North African territories. In occupied Paris, the Nazi administration sought to co-opt Muslims into their practice of anti-Semitism, though many Muslims ended up joining the Free French partisans. The rector of the Mosquée de Paris, Si Kaddour Bengharbit, while maintaining formal relations with the German administration, hid Jews and partisans in the mosque and arranged for their transportation out of the occupied zone—efforts for which he has been recognized as one of the "Righteous among the Nations" by the Yad Vashem Holocaust memorial.[9]

The French–Algerian war witnessed an upsurge of popular and police violence against immigrants, principally directed at breaking down the nationalist movement, but often indiscriminately affecting North African men and women in general. Attacks against North African immigrants and their children persisted in the 1970s and 1980s, as I have described elsewhere (Silverstein 2008b), with mostly working-class white males (*beaufs*, short for *beau-frères*)—threatened by deindustrialization and unemployment—performatively reasserting themselves as the defenders of the French nation through the violent exclusion of immigrants and their capacity for social and biological reproduction (see Turner 1995). Largely in response to such anti-Semitic and Islamophobic violence, as enacted by both individual men and the security forces, young French men and women of color began in the early 1980s to mobilize collectively in opposition to racism, police violence, and deportations in what subsequently became known as the "Beur movement." Their activism further drew broad support from Catholic social-service organizations, as well as from local Jewish groups, and thus became a space for productive interfaith dialogue. It also was a springboard for initial articulations of Berber/Amazigh identity politics. While such inter-religious and cross-ethnic solidarity would subsequently break down, particularly following the Israeli invasion of Lebanon in 1982 and the growing Muslim-French support for specifically "Arab" causes, its legacy remains important for those activists today who seek to forge new multidirectional futures. Indeed, activists involved in the PIR continue to point to the large number of people involved in the 1983 March for Equality and Against Racism ("Marche des Beurs")—a direct response to racist and police murders of young French men and women of color (Bouamama et al. 1994; Hajjat 2013; Jazouli 1992)—as the first battle of an ongoing postcolonial revolution (Khiari 2009). Other groups of young men of color sought retribution directly against the police, state institutions, and the cars of their middle-class neighbors in a series of uprisings (termed "riots" or *émeutes* by the media) that have become a periodic, ritualized episode of life in certain over-policed *quartiers populaires* from the early 1980s through the present. Through their embodied, violent engagement with the police, the subjectivity of Muslim-French men became premised not only on their status as objects of violence, but also on their role as agents of violence, avengers of their "brothers," and defenders of their "parents."

From the point of view of former Beur activists, as well as a number of other state and media observers, such violence came off as dystopian, as the failure of the state's multicultural policies and of 1980s liberal narratives of the "right to difference" within a "plural France" (Derderian 2004). Younger French men and women of color in the *cités* appeared to retreat from politics, suffer from historical amnesia, and embrace a culture of riot and "hate" (*haine*). Police and media representations of the *banlieues* as "lawless zones" (*zones de non-droit*) emerged from these fears, resulting in the further securitization of the *cités* and the calling forth of further cycles of periodic violence.[10] This violence was moreover strongly local in its rubric, oriented to the specific conditions of marginalization experienced by young men and women of color at the hands of the state and its socioeconomic agents and icons. The youth of the *banlieues* in question were by and large *not* motivated by global ideologies of Marxism or Islamism, even if such political movements were, and continue to be, present in the housing projects in question. In this sense, it is of little wonder that anti-police "riots" should target not only police stations, but also gymnasiums, shopping centers, schools, and other such institutions associated with state economic, political, and cultural dominance. As well as acts of destruction, these attacks entail occupation and appropriation, as local residents inscribe the sites, through graffiti and tags, as their own. I will return to these violent acts of appropriation in Chapter 6.

Nonetheless, as we have seen, this local violence became increasingly portrayed in the French media in Islamophobic terms, as part of a global jihad or transnational Intifada (Deltombe 2005; Geisser 2003; Liogier 2012). This portrayal tracked what some scholars have termed an "Islamic revival" among Muslim-French citizens in France, in which the monopoly maintained by the state agencies of North African countries over the organization and transmission of Islamic knowledge and worship has largely broken down. In its wake, a great diversity of Islamic associations, mosque structures, and activist organizations have prospered in France, tracing their lineage to various Sufi and Salafi movements originating from the Middle East, South Asia, and West Africa (see Bowen 2010; Cesari 1994; Kepel 1987; Roy 2004). While religious beliefs and practices remain quite diverse, many younger Muslim-French men and women have joined evangelical Islamic groups, and have rejected the "traditionalism" of their parents for modernist, streamlined interpretations of the Qur'an and the science of hadith.

Since the mid-1990s, state attempts to control these grassroots religious developments have taken two forms: first, as we saw in the last chapter, the building of a "French Islam" through state-affiliated agencies like the French Council of the Muslim Faith (CFCM); and second, through an expanded "war on terror." In response to the summer 1995 bombings of Parisian and Lyonnais transport lines by attackers associated with the Islamist insurgency in Algeria, the French government activated the Vigipirate anti-terrorist plan.[11] The plan was kept in effect until the September 11 attacks in New York in 2001, at which point it was elevated to a "reinforced" level of "high surveillance" of public institutions, a level at which it stayed through the 2015 Paris attacks and the enactment of a formal "state of emergency." These policing measures have lowered the bar of probable cause and authorized extensive identity checks, property searches, electronic surveillance, and preemptive detentions. Young French men and women of color have been particularly targeted by resulting "random" police stops (contrôles au faciès), resulting in countless judicial detentions, arrests, and, in the case of undocumented migrants, deportations (Fassin 2013; Jobard 2009). During such identity checks, security agents literally hail (in the Althusserian sense) young Muslim-French citizens as potential Islamist terrorists.

Through these processes of state interpellation, French men and women of color find themselves increasingly racialized as "Muslims" whose belonging to the French nation and loyalty to the French state is, as we have seen in past chapters, subsequently questioned. Whereas earlier forms of youth identification and organization during the 1980s and early 1990s had been based on shared diacritics of class and locality—being poor inhabitants of marginalized housing projects—that superseded divisions of race and religion and thus underwrote Vinz's racial conversion into an "Arab" as depicted in the film *La haine*, private practices and state policies have fostered a new racialization and deployment of religious categories. This is not to say that local ethno-racial categories of *rabeu* (Arab), *feuj* (Jew), or *renoi* (black) had not been part of the *banlieue* vocabulary prior to the mid-1990s, but rather that these were relatively flexible terms of address and reference that marked personal idiosyncrasies as much as ethno-religious roots. Moreover, youth solidarity crossed these racialized boundaries, with local *bandes* (gangs) forming largely on the basis of residence. New modes of religious identification, however, outline increasingly bounded modes of sociality that, while not excluding crossings of racial or religious frontiers, mark local social struggle as expressions of a larger, transnational religious conflict that threatens to become a self-fulfilling prophecy.

In other words, when Franco-Maghrebis *qua* Muslims witness the events of September 11, the American occupation of Afghanistan and Iraq, the civil war in Syria, or the ongoing violence in Israel/Palestine, they increasingly witness a reflection of the struggles they are undergoing in their daily lives. In spite of obvious diplomatic and policy distinctions between France, the United States, and Israel, some Muslim French understandably make the implicit analogy between the American army, the Israeli IDF, and the French riot police. They reinterpret, in other words, their battles with French forces of law and order as akin to (though not precisely) an Intifada of their own, as a resistance to forces of imperialism.[12] If their older brothers and sisters saw their struggles as inimically local and based in a larger fight for civic rights in France, many of today's young men and women of color see themselves additionally (if not primarily) as transnational Muslim subjects in solidarity with oppressed Palestinians, Afghanis, Iraqis, and Syrians. As Wieviorka observed in what he calls "ghetto anti-Semitism" with global reach: "The experience of Muslims [in France] becomes an illustration of what Muslims are said to experience at [an] international level and is constantly associated with images of the Israeli domination of Palestinians and the violence inflicted on the Iraqi people by the Americans" (Wieviorka 2007: 112). And this association of Islam with anti-imperial resistance has contributed to increased rates of conversion to Islam in the *banlieues* as a mode of "social protest" (Daynes 1999: 316).

Moreover, this set of alliances—which racializes religion over class—implies a different orientation toward other racialized groups. If previous struggles had unified all *cité* residents in opposition to white racists (*beaufs*) or bourgeois Parisians—even as the latter adopted *cité* styles as a mode of their own symbolic protest—the recent generation of *cité* youth tends to approach their Jewish coresidents as representatives of international imperialism and, ironically, of an anti-Muslim French state whose own history of anti-Semitic violence is ignored. "The Jews are resented quite simply because they are said to elude injustice and, not assimilated but fully integrated, they seem to be particularly well treated by France" (Wieviorka 2007: 109). As Wieviorka poignantly concludes: "This ghetto anti-Semitism constitutes a historical paradox: those who, in the past, lived in ghettos... and have endured racist hatred have today become, in an impressive turnaround, the imagined root of the evils from which they themselves have suffered" (ibid.: 140).

THE "NEW ANTI-SEMITISM" REVISITED

It is this shift in identification that helps explain reported spikes in anti-Semitic violence since the early 2000s and its attribution in part to Muslim-French *banlieue* residents. Granted, the statistical rise must be, to a certain extent, questioned given new, state-wide reporting guidelines that—particularly for schools, where the vast majority of reported incidents occurred—streamlined the collection of data on race-related crimes and arguably over-reported minor schoolyard incidents as hate crimes. Further, spikes in reported anti-Semitic violence have been accompanied by even greater spikes in racist and xenophobic violence particularly against Muslims over the same periods. While anti-Semitic attacks seem to go up and down in ways that broadly track events in Israel/Palestine, anti-immigrant and anti-Muslim violence has broadly increased (see Geisser 2003; Muhammad 2017).

It is worthwhile examining in some detail the high-profile attacks that have been at the source of recent Islamophobic moral panics and French soul-searching around the "new anti-Semitism," and that have been instrumentalized by right-wing Israeli leaders Ariel Sharon and Benjamin Netanyahu to encourage French Jewish emigration to Israel.[13] I will discuss the 2015 Hyper Cacher attack in the following chapter, but here will focus on the abduction and murder of the French Jewish cell-phone salesman Ilan Halimi by a multiethnic group of young French men and women from the *banlieues*, but spearheaded by Youssouf Fofana, a young Muslim-French man of Ivoirian background.

As Brian Klug (2003) has convincingly argued, "anti-Semitism" should be defined as the targeting of Jews *qua* Jews for violence, repression, or derision. In this sense, not every attack on Jews is necessarily an anti-Semitic attack, as any given attack may follow a very different economic or racial or political logic; this distinction is crucial in differentiating anti-Zionism (a political platform against a colonizing Israeli state) from anti-Semitism (racism directed against a people). In the case of Halimi, Fofana claimed that the kidnapping was purely motivated by financial goals, and that Halimi was chosen not because he was a Jew per se, but because he was presumed to be rich. Or, as another of the abductors claimed, "Ilan was Jewish, and Jews are rich" (Lévy-Willard 2006). In this sense, the attack cannot be assimilated into the narrative of a "new anti-Semitism" perpetrated by Muslims and tied to events in Israel/Palestine. Rather, it seems to be connected to an older anti-Semitic stereotype of the Jew-as-financier, one which has endured in the historical rhetoric of the French far right and has been further appropriated into contemporary Islamist ideology in France and abroad, some of which has clearly been assimilated into *banlieue* common sense. Moreover, whatever the exact motivation of the attackers or their personal (old or new) anti-Semitic beliefs, the killing did raise for both French Jews and the French state the specter of a renewed anti-Semitism, encouraged several thousand Jews to emigrate to Israel (as Laura's family do at the end of *La petite Jérusalem*), and led to increased social mobilization against this form of racism. All of which points to the fact that there may exist a social reality of anti-Semitism in France, regardless of the nature of any given attack.[14]

Moreover, attacks such as that on Halimi point to how some young Muslim-French citizens share ideological space with an anti-Semitic far right that, ironically again, has made its political bed on xenophobic and Islamophobic rhetoric. Rather than seeing acts of violence by Muslim youths on Jewish people and property as a failure of republican integration, as observers like Brenner (2002) and Trigano (2003) would have it, one could make a strong case that it is a sure sign of their very integration into a French nation premised simultaneously on a disavowal of cultural difference and on an avowal of a "true France" of the countryside (*pays réel*) historically connected to Catholic anti-Semitism. Indeed, it is an old sociological truism (and not an inherently false one) to take an immigrant group's racism against those who have more recently arrived as an index of their assimilation. In this light, it is interesting to note the timing of the clarion calls from academics like Brenner (2002), Trigano (2003), Taguieff (2004), and Finkielkraut (2003). Not only do their works correspond closely to the post-September 11 war on terror, and to a call for greater policing of Islamism in France (Deltombe 2005:

267–92), but they also can be read as reactions to the formal political incorporation of Muslim French via the state-run CFCM, an organization that seeks explicitly, in the words of former interior minister Nicolas Sarkozy, to "bring Islam to the table of the Republic" on the same terms as Jewish agencies like the CRIF with long-term official status. Indeed, Trigano (2003: 15–17) explicitly rejects comparisons of the Muslim-French and Jewish "communities" as commensurate groups who can be interpreted as being in conflict. Works like his constitute a hostile (if not Islamophobic) reaction to the incorporation of Muslims as fully fledged citizens of France.

BEYOND VIOLENCE

Yet the mutual resentment of Muslims and Jews in France as differently integrated and differently politically positioned French subjects need by no means be the norm. Just as Islam has become an idiom of social protest and source of identity conversion for a number of men and women on the French urban peripheries, and even (especially via Sufi interpretations) in bourgeois centers, so too can Jewishness become an object of desire. Philia, as well as phobia, can also serve as bases for inter-communal relations in France. In other work, I have underlined how many Amazigh activists in France have a very different relationship to Islam, secularism, and anti-Semitism than those Muslim French represented in the media (Silverstein 2007b, 2011). As mentioned earlier, colonial ethnologists treated Berbers as exceptionally suitable for French civilization due to their supposedly minimal and superficial Islamization.[15] Some Amazigh activists today echo the colonial stereotype with an explicit embrace of the heteropraxy and pre-Islamic origins of popular modes of Berber religious practice. A number of these activists have rejected Islam as their primary mode of identification, emphasizing instead the historical (if ambivalent) separation of religious and political spheres in Berber customary law and decision-making.

Moreover, some have rejected the generalized anti-Zionist (and occasionally anti-Semitic) politics of the Islamic world, adopting instead an avowedly philo-Semitic (if not pro-Zionist) discourse. In this discourse, Jews function totemically for Amazigh militants as a people similarly marginalized under the historic mantle of Arabo-Islamic hegemony in the Middle East and North Africa. More generally, a number of activists see in the Zionist movement a model for the Amazigh struggle: the successful codification and preservation of a threatened language, and the obtaining of political and territorial autonomy that some hope for within extant North African states or in a trans-nation of

Tamazgha. While by no means the agents of the Israeli state that Islamists occasionally accuse them of being, these Amazigh militants have actively sought to reconcile Jewish and Berber populations, and have publicly advocated a normalization of relations with Israel. Beginning in the early-1990s, delegations of French-Kabyle artists and intellectuals visited Israel and published reports of their voyages in Amazigh newsletters and blogs that circulated across France and North Africa. Ongoing efforts of solidarity and cooperation have transpired over the years since. In Wendy Brown's model of tolerance as a governmental mode discussed earlier, it is precisely through their claims to solidarity, if not identification, with Jews that Amazigh activists project Berbers as modern cosmopolitans, as true (civilized) French citizens. Such philo-Semitism (if not pro-Zionism) helps these activists distinguish themselves from the apparent intolerance of other Muslim French, stigmatized for their primordial anti-Semitism. Through their wholehearted support for laïcité, such Amazigh activists thus present themselves as the exemplary, "good Muslim" (Mamdani 2004) immigrants and ultimate defenders of the French Republic. In this respect, Amazigh philo-Semitism represents a racial project of national and transnational inclusion, of anti-anti-Semitism and cosmopolitan secularism, of imagined cross-communal identification that remaps postcolonial France in contradistinction to a "clash of civilizations" rhetoric that would racially divide the country between the "Muslim" and the "Jew."

But Amazigh politics of inclusion is not the only way out of the racialized violence called forth locally by the current politics of neo-imperialism justified by the "global war on terror." If Amazigh activists seek broader inclusion within a post-Auschwitz secular, cosmopolitan world, others imagine different kinds of cosmopolitanism where the mode of interaction and terms of inclusion remain open for negotiation. Less inspired by the utopian imagination of an Andalusian convivencia, of peaceful coexistence and interfaith harmony that supposedly existed under Islamic rule in Iberia, these proposals call forth a more mundane form of accommodation of difference, of "living together" (vivre ensemble).[16] From 2003 to 2005, Palestinian anthropologist and ambassador Leila Shahid, Israeli human rights advocate Michel Warschawski, and French journalist Dominique Vidal toured quartiers populaires of French cities to share their experience of working in solidarity with Palestinian struggles, with a message of ta'ayush (literally "living together") they saw as missing in France. Inspired by previous moments in French antiracist history where articulations of Palestinian rights did not imply anti-Semitism, they sought to help create new grounds for dialogue across communities of experience, underlining the shared human values within social justice movements beyond the racializing discourse of identity politics (Shahid et al. 2006).

Similar efforts have been undertaken by the French Jewish historian and politician Esther Benbassa. Born and raised in a Sephardic family in Istanbul, she migrated to France as a teenager, and completed her studies in France and Israel. In addition to her work as a scholar and university professor of modern Jewish history in France and the Sephardic diaspora, she has also engaged in national politics as an elected parliamentary senator for the Green Party (Europe Ecologie Les Verts), where she has sponsored legislation against discrimination and for social justice. In that role, she has also been an outspoken supporter of Palestinian rights. Charged with overseeing "de-radicalization" efforts in the wake of the 2015 attacks, she expressed deep reservations about such programs and those who were profiting from them (Muhammad 2017: 200–1). Deeply concerned by the simultaneous rise of anti-Semitism and Islamophobia in the early 2000s, which she saw as but "two sides of the same coin" (Benbassa & Attias 2006: 87), she and her husband, Jewish theological scholar Jean-Christophe Attias, founded the association Pari(s) du Vivre-Ensemble (Paris/Betting on Living Together), and sponsored a series of interfaith dialogues bringing together Muslim and Jewish scholars, activists, and religious leaders.

The dialogues were broadly motivated by a sense of urgency over the future of France and its republican model, but also a sense of hope. As they wrote in 2006:

> France is undoubtedly experiencing the last spurts of its centralizing Jacobinism, scorning anything that disagrees with its one and indivisible republican model. These are serious, anxious moments of direct resistance, but which perhaps call forth a multicolor France, a France of affirmative action, not negative discrimination, a France where all histories are shared in order to rebuild our shared history and memory in mutual respect. (ibid.: 10)

In 2015, in the wake of the *Charlie Hebdo* and Hyper Cacher supermarket attacks, they organized a similar dialogue and returned to similar themes:

> It is today urgent for Jews, for Muslims, and for the country itself to re-suture our ties, to restart the dialogue, without pretense, empty words, mere gestures, or hidden agendas. To say things—to admit them to each other—clearly, frankly, and in mutual respect. (Benbassa & Attias 2015: 6)

Concerned that interfaith dialogues are often but state-directed symbolic gestures in which Muslim leaders are publicly pressured to performatively distance themselves and their constituents from terrorism and offer their condolences to the victims, Benbassa and Attias seek to promote grassroots conversations, a "citizen dialogue" that promotes a sense of belonging "beyond the borders of their 'communities', for laying the foundations of a *Cité* not only of coexistence and mutual recognition, but of sharing" (ibid.: 54). For these efforts and her public critique of Israeli state policy, Benbassa has faced criticism for being a self-hating Jew and naively ignoring the reality (*angélisme*) of, if not apologizing for, terrorism. But she persists in her effort to combat the "disenchantment" (*désamour*) and inter-communal violence emerging from identities taken as races rather than the bases of mutual understanding and cooperation (ibid.: 13). Her vision of postcolonial France is one of hope, not of despair or submission.

CONCLUSION

Any analysis of contemporary Islamophobia and anti-Semitism needs to recognize moments when categories of identity and analysis fragment. The social positions of the "Muslim" and "Jew" in postcolonial France emerge from a long history of violence, but also hope, in which various actors who are today identified (and self-identify) along these taken-for-granted religious axes have been differentially placed vis-à-vis various state practices of exclusion and assimilation. The legal separation of Jews from Muslims, and later Arabs from Berbers, by the colonial administrations of North Africa—a distinction that better reflected metropolitan social castes than the state of communal interactions in precolonial North African societies—gained social facticity as it was reproduced in new postcolonial settings of the progressively securitized French *cités*. In France, the self-presentation and subsequent interpellation of Franco-Maghrebis as "Muslims" underwrites contemporary avowals of solidarity among French men and women of color with occupied Palestine and civil war Syria, and thus the resulting anti-Zionist (and occasionally anti-Semitic) orientation of some French street politics. Yet, as I have tried to insist, even this trajectory has been contested throughout, with, for instance, a strong Amazigh activism continuing to challenge the unquestioned pro-Palestinian orientation of Muslim-French advocacy, countering anti-Semitism with their own philo-Semitic and occasionally Islamophobic rhetoric.

Postcolonial France thus remains marked by an ambivalence of identification and dis-identification, of solidarity and exclusion, as marginalized Muslim populations become at various moments embraced as fantasy objects of national regeneration or anti-imperialist protest, and at others demonized as perpetrators of violence and barbarity—as Jews vacillate between objects of racial and religious revulsion and icons of cosmopolitan modernity. If the contemporary rhetoric of the "war on terror" has fragmented French Jews around their political support for Israel and alarmism over the rise of the "new anti-Semitism," so too has it served to divide Berbers, blacks, and Arabs into "good" and "bad" Muslims—to follow Mahmood Mamdani (2004)—as measured by their relative avowal of the rights of women, homosexuals, and Jews. It is the contemporary challenge of multiply hybrid postcolonial subjects in contemporary France to find new spaces of solidarity and new modes of identification that avoid the extremist rhetorics of Islamophobia and anti-Semitism, that reimagine social interaction and belonging beyond the poles of love and hate.

4

Dangerous Signs
Charlie Hebdo and Dieudonné

Racism, Islamophobia, and anti-Semitism, as I noted in the Introduction, are structural relations of inequality and exclusion, historically produced and embedded in institutional arrangements, and tied to larger processes of material exploitation. As such, they are not simply attitudes, perceptions, or feelings which can be remedied through education and enlightenment. But they nonetheless do directly affect how people see, feel, and inhabit the world, insinuating themselves into individuals' embodied dispositions and habits, their modes of interaction, discussion, and representation. Racism, Islamophobia, and anti-Semitism are expressed in words as well as deeds, through spoken and written signs, in gesture and fashion, in anger as well as solidarity. And signs, like words, do things. They tear people apart and bring them together. They exclude and include. They promote violence, demand retribution, and call forth security states. They destroy people's lives, provide solace to others, and occasionally heal.

Determining which words and signs are which is one of the fundamental ways in which states enact power and sovereignty. In France, freedom of expression is constitutionally guaranteed, but anti-defamation laws and restrictions on hate speech place distinct limits on public speech and writing. In addition to stringent laws on libel and those aimed to shield minors from pornographic or pro-drug images, a suite of relatively recent legislation aims to protect minorities and the relatively disempowered. A 1972 law prohibits incitements to hatred, discrimination, or racism. The 1990 Gayssot Law further prohibits "racist, anti-Semitic or xenophobic" speech, including Holocaust denial or revisionism. It specifies that "All discrimination based on belonging or non-belonging to an ethnicity, nation, race, or religion is forbidden" (Article 1). A 2004 law extends those protections to those subject to prejudice because of their "gender, sexual orientation, or disability."

This regime of legal censorship was gradually extended to protect the broader French public, and the Republic itself. As we saw in previous chapters, efforts to promote and protect *laïcité* involved the prohibition of religious signs in public schools. This was part of a suite of security measures enacted in the early 2000s through which it became illegal to "offend the dignity of the republic," including insulting the national anthem, flag, or any state functionary such as the police. A 2014 anti-terror law specifically made "apology for terrorism" a crime punishable by up to seven years in prison for statements made online. As the Collective against Islamophobia in France (CCIF) has tracked, these last laws have been used disproportionately to prosecute Muslim French and other French men and women of color (PEN America 2015). In the process, French censorship went from protecting legally vulnerable classes to projecting the Republic itself as in need of protection. It both responded and added to the larger sense that the French nation was in crisis, endangered by its postcolonial diversity.

In this chapter, I examine the racialized political processes through which certain words become sacred and others dangerous. To get at this, I focus on the *Charlie Hebdo* attacks and their aftermath, as well as the repeated prosecution of shock-comic Dieudonné Mbala Mbala for hate speech. Rather than harping on the apparent hypocrisy evidenced by the differential treatment of *Charlie Hebdo* and Dieudonné, the chapter instead focuses on the inclusions and exclusions generated, and the different kinds of solidarity called forth by a public declaration like "Je suis Charlie" or a *quenelle* (a Nazi-like salute). Powerful signs, I want to argue, certainly debar and disempower, but they can also open up new possibilities for identification and alliance. When thinking about the future of postcolonial France, becomings are as important as the crises they appear to generate.

JE SUIS CHARLIE, JE SUIS AHMED

Charlie Hebdo stands as a potent symbol of France's postcolonial predicament. With its origins in the 1960s and regularly published since the early 1990s, the weekly magazine has regularly courted controversy by graphically mocking public figures, religious symbols, and national rituals.[1] In 2006, it republished twelve cartoon caricatures of the Prophet Muhammad from the Danish newspaper *Jyllands-Posten* that had sparked violent international protests, leading to the French Council of the Muslim Faith bringing a suit of incitement to racial hatred against the magazine. In 2011, in the wake of revolts in North Africa against authoritarian regimes and the victory of the Islamist Ennahda party in the Tunisian elections, it published a special issue, "Charia Hebdo," with another depiction of the Prophet on the cover. In apparent response to the publication, unknown assailants firebombed its Paris offices, forcing the magazine to relocate to an unmarked building. In 2013 the magazine followed with another cover depicting Muhammad, which appeared in the wake of further international protests over the release of the American-produced Islamophobic film, *The Innocence of Muslims*. In the same year the magazine's cartoonist and editor-in-chief Stéphane Charbonnier (Charb) drew a two-part special edition, "The life of Mohammed," for which Al-Qaeda in the Arabian Peninsula (AQAP) publically called for his death in their English-language magazine. On January 7, 2015, the brothers Chérif and Saïd Kouachi, claiming to act on behalf of the AQAP, stormed into the *Charlie Hebdo* office and murdered Charb as well as ten other cartoonists, journalists, and support staff, severely injuring three others.

The January attack produced an incredible outpouring of public mourning in France and beyond, and Charb and his colleagues quickly became national martyrs. Over 100,000 people gathered that evening across France, and millions more over the next few days, culminating in a massive set of "republican marches" on January 11 led by political leaders and international heads of state. The Marianne statue in the Place de la République in Paris—the locus of the largest rallies—overnight became a memorial to the victims, with thousands leaving flowers, candles, and remembrances; the memorial has stood in the years since and incorporated further victims of the November 2015 Islamic State attacks in Paris as well (Hollis-Touré 2016). All ostensibly rallied around the ever-present slogan, "Je suis Charlie" (I am Charlie), originally tweeted as a hashtag by artist Joachim Roncin hours after the attack. At its most basic level, the meme expressed solidarity and empathy with the victims, mirroring a series of earlier slogans including particularly the "Nous sommes tous Américains" (We are all Americans), expressed widely in France (and notably in a *Le Monde* editorial) in the immediate aftermath of the September 11, 2001, attacks (Welch & Perivolaris 2016: 288). At a broader level, it signaled identification with a courageous act of standing up for one's secular liberal principles in the face of threats, in this case for the freedom of expression and the right to offend, even blaspheme (Klug 2016b).[2]

As Nadia Kiwan (2016) has argued, the freedom/right/duty to offend quickly became enshrined as definitive of French identity and the basis for republican national unity, which brooked no dissent. In a critical book about the "totalitarian rush (*flash*)" following the attacks, French social scientist Emmanuel Todd provocatively wrote, "'Je suis Charlie' became a synonym for 'Je suis français' [I am French] ... being French was not only having the *right* but the *duty* to blaspheme" (Todd 2015: 12–13). Within a few days of the attack, police arrested over 50 people on charges of "apology for terrorism" on the basis of verbal or written statements that they had made. School officials reported students who refused to participate in the minute of silence held the day after the attack, accompanied by outraged national media reporting that such refusals were majoritarian in some schools in the *banlieues*. The Ministry of Education, under Moroccan-born Najat Vallaud-Belkacem, directed school officials to not tolerate "any comportment contrary to the values of the Republic" (cited in Kiwan 2016: 235), and Vallaud-Belkacem followed up with further measures designed to prevent "radicalization" and reinforce *laïcité*. In the meantime, Guénif-Souilamas and other Francophone scholars of color (Guénif-Souilamas et al. 2015) quickly decried—in an open letter that drew its title, "How does it feel to be a problem," from W.E.B. Du Bois (1989)—how the national media maintained an exclusive narrative of a nation courageously standing up to Islamic "fanaticism," "extremism," and "intolerance," thus marginalizing or condemning analysts like Emmanuel Todd or other critical scholars who did not toe the mainstream editorial line or focused on broader issues of Islamophobia, racism, and social exclusion (Kiwan 2016: 236–37).

Much has been written about the irony and hypocrisy of banning, in the name of freedom of expression, those who expressed opinions contrary to the national script. Or of making national icons of people who made mocking public figures and national pretenses the very raison d'être and origin story of their publication. Or of enshrining a magazine which the state itself had repeatedly censored and prosecuted under hate speech laws. As Brian Klug (2016b) has brilliantly showed, there is a significant ethical difference between satirizing those sanctimonious individuals and institutions in power, and deriding those who find themselves politically voiceless and socially excluded, even if the latter also happen to be believers and take their beliefs seriously. And *Charlie Hebdo* was itself often guilty of the latter—and without much self-irony about the liberal, secular principles which animated its cartoon critiques. Yes, all could surely identify with—or, perhaps, "follow," to use an alternative connotation of *suis*—"Charlie" as a collection of fellow human beings victimized by violence, but many found it very difficult to identify or follow their repeated public belittling of the faith of those who already felt deeply vulnerable within French society.

Indeed, in parallel and response to the "Je suis Charlie" meme arose an alternative formulation: "Je suis Ahmed." The reference was to Ahmed Merabet, a Muslim-French police officer killed by the Kouachi brothers while confronting them on their exit from the *Charlie Hebdo* offices. Merabet was one of three police officers killed during the set of apparently coordinated attacks that occurred over several days, in addition to four Jewish patrons of the Hyper Cacher supermarket killed by Malian-French Amedy Coulibaly, who claimed to be working in concert with the Kouachi brothers. At its most basic level, "Je suis Ahmed" recalled that the staff of *Charlie Hebdo* were not the only victims, or the only ones whose lives should be remembered, mourned, or considered worthy of identification. If the French nation was indeed under attack, it was minimally a much more heterogeneous body than could be easily encapsulated by abstract principles like "freedom of expression" or the "right to offend."

At a deeper level, "Je suis Ahmed" encapsulated the dilemmas of belonging for Muslim-French citizens, particularly during moments of moral panic and heightened patriotism. As Marwan Muhammad explained, even as Muslim-French citizens felt

> strong emotions and unanimously condemned the abject violence, [they] could never resolve "to be Charlie" quite simply because *Charlie* never tried to be them, was incapable of stepping back from itself and trying, even for a moment, to feel how its articles and cartoons affected other people. (Muhammad 2017: 117)

'We (too) are the nation," as Muhammad titles his book from a 2012 CCIF public relations campaign that attempted to speak back to formulations that spoke of Islam as exterior to France or surveyed Muslim-French citizens to determine whether they felt "more French or more Muslim" (ibid.: 101).

To a great extent, "Je suis Ahmed" might simply be translated as Muslim Lives Matter. The slogan underlined that Ahmed Merabet was not merely collateral damage, a footnote to the "*Charlie Hebdo* attack," but a human being, a social person, and a full subject of the French nation, whether recognized or not. Like black Americans, Muslims in France and elsewhere seem to be repeatedly excluded from the set of rights and protections granted to those whose lives are deemed sacred and deaths mourned. Given a history of police brutality, state pronouncements, legal bans, and media portrayals, they perceive themselves to be but killable objects, liable to be killed in a police stop, bombable at a distance, assumed to be terrorist *hostis humani generis* (common enemies of all), or at least apologists for them, unless they speak up otherwise. "Je suis Ahmed" was a plea for human recognition and an act of identification, or at least solidarity, across the de facto color line (see Du Bois 1989; Fanon 1967).

But in other ways, "Je suis Ahmed" could also be translated as Blue Lives Matter. For Ahmed Merabet was more than just another man whose life matters, another national subject to be publicly recognized, represented, and memorialized. He was a police officer, an official representative of the French state, and he died in the line of duty. He was not only a member of the nation but a constituent of the state; not only deserving of protection, but an empowered protector. The "Je" of "Je suis Ahmed" is not only the particular speaking subject, whether Muslim or otherwise, but in some ways France as a whole. The declaration recalls the sacrifices of countless Muslim-French subjects and other men and women of color who gave their lives and livelihoods fighting France's wars, building its economy, and defending its values. It reminds us of the daily efforts of thousands of Muslim French and other French men and women of color in public service, working as police officers, civil servants, schoolteachers, judges, and even government ministers like Vallaud-Belkacem (under-represented as they may be)—people of whom the French state is also made, even if it does not always obviously operate in their name. It speaks to the fact that, if the French state is indeed a juridical apparatus and coercive instrument, as many French men and women of color largely experience it to be, a good number of those engaging in such authorized violence are themselves from a post-colonial migrant background.[3]

Thinking of the state in terms of its policing function and in terms of its aspirational monopoly of violence underlines a related aspect of the postcolonial dilemma made manifest by the attacks. As we have seen, the attacks predictably called forth yet another public reckoning of the proverbial "Muslim question," of the compatibility of an exteriorized Islam with French secular, republican values. While certain commentators repeated undeniably Islamophobic amalgamations of Islam and extremism (see Fourest 2015; Zemmour 2014), most were at pains to distinguish Muslim French as individuals from the intransigent beliefs which supposedly called forth the violence—all the while demanding that Muslim-French individuals positively affirm their commitment to *laïcité* through identification with "Charlie." For many, the explanation for the violence had to be found in some breakdown of the French Republic's motor of social integration and cultural education.

Journalists quickly tracked the Kouachi brothers back to their *banlieue* upbringing in search of the social vectors of their radicalization. They emphasized their upbringing as orphans in foster care and their petty delinquency. They discovered that Chérif met Coulibaly in prison, where they came under the spell of Djamel Belghal, a young militant with ties to London's Finsbury Park mosque, who was serving a prison sentence on terrorism charges for membership in the Algerian Armed Islamic Group (GIA) and training with Al-Qaeda in Afghanistan. The story thus became once again one of jihadist networks connecting Islamic warzones abroad to disenfranchised European working-class neighborhoods and housing projects—just as it had been in previous moral panics over young *banlieue* residents migrating to Syria as Islamic State fighters or wives. This narrative underlined the failures of French intelligence to properly track and dismantle such networks, leading to a renewed call—and appropriate exceptional powers under "state of emergency" (*état d'urgence*) legislation—for the heightened surveillance and detention of suspects, regardless of the effects on broader civil liberties.

Critics immediately and understandably pushed back against this state of exception (Agamben 2005), against this racial profiling of French men and women of color as suspect citizens on the basis of their background, residence, or religion (Guénif-Souilamas et al. 2015). They emphasized the material conditions, social exclusion, and racist discrimination that gave lie to republican myths of equality and integration. They historicized the present bloodshed within a longer history of colonial racialized violence, much as I have done in previous chapters. They placed at least part of the responsibility, in other words, on the French postcolonial republic and the Islamophobic discourse, such as the *Charlie Hebdo* cartoons, it sanctioned. In this way, they presented Coulibaly and the Kouachi brothers as the products of the secular republic, not as exceptions to it.

While clearly sociologically justified and politically well intentioned, such an approach risks overemphasizing the attackers as victims of national exclusion rather than as historical agents and global political actors in their own right. It does not sufficiently take seriously their own claim to being soldiers fighting a transnational battle on behalf of the AQAP and Islamic State. Certainly there may be reasons to doubt such claims, given the purported desire among some disenfranchised individuals to affiliate with a global Islamist brand as a mode of identity formation (see Roy 2004), and given the seeming random nature of Coulibaly's violence.[4] But the particular background, circumstances, and level of organization of the attack on the *Charlie Hebdo* offices—like the ones orchestrated later in November of that year—signal it as a veritable military operation, which is indeed how French police and intelligence officials would describe it (see Penketh 2015). Even though President François Hollande did not effectively declare war until after the November attacks, the *Charlie Hebdo* and Hyper Cacher attacks cannot be disconnected from the broader "global war on terror" in Syria and Yemen, and from the multiple commando raids, targeted assassinations, and drone strikes in which the French military and intelligence had participated. Much as the American government authorized the assassination of AQAP leader and US citizen Anwar al-Awlaki for his online and print publications allegedly inspiring terrorism—for his dangerous speeches, writings, and videos—so too did the AQAP condemn Charb for his dangerous and demeaning images. While Western states may refuse to recognize AQAP or Islamic State as equivalent actors or interlocutors, or their actions as legitimate means of war, the Kouachi brothers certainly acted as if they were. Their actions were essentially a low-tech drone strike on what they took to be a military target, not a random act of desperate, self-annihilating "terrorism."

By not recognizing these broader geopolitics of war and the attackers as actors within them, the French state and critical social scientists alike engaged—for vastly different reasons—in the "re-territorialization" of the attackers and their victims within a bounded French nation-state (Welch & Perivolaris 2016: 285). But, if nothing else, the January 2015 attacks underlined the fact that postcolonial France remains indelibly connected to elsewheres well beyond its territorial borders, to ongoing conflicts over territory and resources between various neo-imperial formations in which thousands have been killed and displaced. While the editors and cartoonists may have presented themselves as heroically defending French *laïcité*, the reach of *Charlie Hebdo*'s offense was significantly greater. Few may have risked prosecution by declaring "Je suis Chérif" or "Je suis Saïd," but "Je suis Ahmed" does signal postcolonial France as a global France, and that the globe as a complex place of dangerous politics in which we are all, in one way or another, responsible actors and potential victims.

THE DIEUDONNÉ EFFECT

One French public figure who did come close to identifying with the attackers was the shock-comic Dieudonné Mbala Mbala, a black French citizen of mixed Cameroonian-French ancestry who calls himself an "Islamo-Christian." On January 10, 2015, three days after the *Charlie Hebdo* attack and the day after the Hyper Cacher siege, Dieudonné wrote on Facebook that "I feel like Charlie Coulibaly" (*Je me sens Charlie Coulibaly*). The statement followed the basic form of earlier slogans, though notably shifted from "to be/to follow" to the verb "to feel". It was arguably less a form of identification or solidarity as such than a sense of being viscerally caught in the middle, half-French and half-African, half-Christian and half-Muslim, stuck existentially between those like "Charlie" who have the racial privilege to stand in for the French Republic and its liberal secular values, and those like Amedy Coulibaly who feel excluded from it and occasionally take up arms (military or otherwise) against it. In a later letter posted on the internet, he went on to liken his irreverent humor to that of *Charlie Hebdo*.[5] Such nuances were broadly lost on most observers. The minister of the interior, Bernard Cazeneuve, immediately condemned Dieudonné's statement and called for an investigation. The comic was subsequently arrested, tried, and found guilty of charges of "apology for terrorism," for which he was given a two-month suspended sentence and fined €10,000.

Dieudonné is no stranger to public controversy or legal proceedings. In 2014 he caused a similar stir by calling for the liberation of Youssouf Fofana, the head of the gang which kidnapped and murdered Ilan Halimi. Consequently, the Union of Jewish Students of France brought a civil suit against Dieudonné, but the court found him not guilty. More generally, he has been repeatedly accused—and on a number of occasions found guilty—of propagating racial hatred, particularly against Jews. He is an outspoken critic of Israel as a settler colonial state, running for election to the European Parliament on the Euro-Palestine list in 2004, and more recently affiliating with Yahia Gouasmi's Anti-Zionist Party. While he began his theatrical career working in close partnership with the French Jewish comedian Élie Semoun, in more recent years he has provocatively blurred the lines between anti-Zionism and anti-Semitism, and has even shared the stage with Holocaust denier Robert Faurisson and right-wing polemicist Alain Soral. He has visited Iran on several occasions and regularly evokes his friendship with Mahmoud Ahmadinejad; he has similarly praised Muammar Gaddafi and Bashar al-Assad. More recently, he toured North Korea and scheduled himself to perform there. Jean-Marie Le Pen is the godfather of one of his children.

Given such unrepentant provocation, Dieudonné has emerged as the black militant artist the French secular republic loves to hate. Perhaps more than any other contemporary figure, he has come to encapsulate mainstream fears of a new anti-Semitism, Islamic radicalism, and reverse racism propagating in the *banlieue* periphery from which he and many of his fans hail. Running political campaigns on first an antiracist, then an anti-globalization, and most recently an anti-Zionist platform, his staged comedy and public persona have had a polarizing effect on an already tense French public debate over free speech and the limits of toleration. His linked comedic and political engagements play precisely on the ambivalences of belonging, traumas of toleration, and the narcissism of privilege that mark the lives of French Jews, turn fears of anti-Semitism into the reality of attacks like Coulibaly's, and raise the specter of a new "exodus." As with *Charlie Hebdo*, Dieudonné turns offense into a right, indeed a duty, and like the magazine he directs this offense at those who already feel socially vulnerable.

Indeed, Dieudonné lays bare what he takes to be the hypocrisy in the French state's vigilance against anti-Semitism while allowing other forms of institutionalized racism to propagate, as well as the double standard of the recognition and indemnification of past suffering. Much of his artistic and political work has centered on raising public awareness about France's past participation in the African slave trade and its contribution to contemporary white privilege. He has been part of a broader effort by activists of color to force the French state to recognize and apologize for its role in colonialism and slavery, and to grant these forms of genocide equivalent moral and memorial status as the Holocaust. In the early 2000s he attempted to make a film on the history of the Code Noir— the French royal edict that authorized slavery in the colonies—but was refused state funding for the project.

Moreover, he directly links Jewish privilege to black suffering, both in terms of his claims about the historical role of Jewish financiers in the slave and colonial economies, and with regards to what he decries as the contemporary racism of the "Jewish lobby." In a 2003 television show, he played a Jewish settler who pronounces Israel as "Isra-heil!" accompanied by a Nazi-like salute.[6] His *quenelle* (suppository) arm gesture, which caused international controversy in the late-2000s when a number of football players and other personalities of color publically replicated it, while ostensibly a scatological commentary on how one takes it "up the arse" by the "system"—has been similarly condemned as an inverted or repressed Nazi salute.

In the absence of state protections for French citizens of color similar to those that benefit French Jews, Dieudonné presents himself as what Wieviorka terms a "moral entrepreneur" (Wieviorka 2007: 15). He calls forth popular resistance to the "bankers and the *békés*"—the class of white colonial settlers in the Antilles who are still socioeconomically dominant in the Caribbean, but who for Dieudonné stand in for white privilege more generally—elites, he claims, who still control today's political and economic system. After being attacked by militants of the Jewish Defense League during a visit to Martinique in 2005, a 92-year-old Aimé Césaire welcomed Dieudonné, whom he saw as a "brother," as part of a younger generation who spoke harsh truth to harsh power and gave hope for the future.[7]

Not all, of course, have been so generous with Dieudonné. Most fellow artists and activists, like Moroccan-French actor and comic Jamel Debouzze, have distanced themselves from him, especially given his recent associations with Soral and Le Pen. Tariq Ramadan bemoans his polarization of the French public, which has left little room for nuanced analysis or critique.[8] The Party of the Indigènes of the Republic (PIR) have been outspoken in their critique of his alliances with figures of the radical right, accusing him of "erasing without scruples more than forty years of immigrant struggle against the far right ... insulting the memory of all those who have fought against colonialism." They go on to note that, "consciously or not, he is doing the work of the Zionism he pretends to combat" (Boutledja & Khiari 2012: 418), The PIR spokeswoman, Houria Bouteldja, later added nuance to this critique in an interview, expressing more "ambivalent feelings":

> I love Dieudonné; I love him as the *indigènes* love him; I understand why the *indigènes* love him. I love him because he has done important things for dignity, *indigène* pride, black pride: he refuses to be a house negro (*nègre domestique*). Even if he isn't running a good political program, he has an attitude of resistance towards the white world ... What whites don't understand is that the *indigènes* essentially see that in him and that's why they love him, because he hasn't bowed down and, as *indigènes*, one can't but respect that. (ibid.: 389)

Of course, in some nontrivial ways Dieudonné is simply following in a very French tradition. In his comedy sketches, Dieudonné draws on the comic legacy of Pierre Desproges and Coluche (and indeed the Americans Lenny Bruce and Richard Pryor) who all sparked controversy through their rejection of respectable discourse to call out ethnic and racial prejudice. Dieudonné arguably takes this strategy a step further, courting controversy with his statements, gestures, and performances, and then incorporating the resulting accusations of anti-Semitism and apology for terrorism directly into his sketches as a meta-critique of French hypocrisies of tolerance, freedom, equality, and rights. By presenting the accusations as a selective regulation of freedom of expression, he implicitly questions the privilege of those who determine the bounds of liberal toleration.

Journalist Sylvain Cepel (2014) has likened the *quenelle* to the repressed Nazi salute performed by Peter Sellers in Stanley Kubrick's satirical film *Dr. Strangelove* (1964), and one might indeed interpret Dieudonné's gesture as a commentary on repression and mandatory self-regulation. Dieudonné and most of his fans vehemently deny that the *quenelle* has anything whatsoever to do with a Nazi salute, but like his comedic performances, the *quenelle* precisely plays on the slipperiness of meaning, the polysemy of signs, and the ambiguous relations between verbal, facial, and gestural expression. Therein arguably lies the brilliance of Dieudonné's comedy, where lines between performer and character are multilayered and blurred, and where the racialized irreverence dares the spectator to take seriously that which is presented in the frame of satire. Who are the real racists, it seems to ask us: those who play with popular stereotypes or those who can only see race and racism in the play?

The uncomfortable frisson of having one's liberal moral commitments laid bare clearly drives part of the mass appeal of Dieudonné's performance art, as does the blatant populism of the comedian speaking directly to those who feel screwed by the political and economic establishment—a sentiment that the *quenelle* graphically illustrates. For all of their condemnations and controversies, Dieudonné's shows and online performances gather together an incredibly heterogeneous audience from across the French racial, ethnic, class, and ideological spectrum, a veritable counterpublic (Warner 2002) that better represents postcolonial France than the public intellectuals who participate in the official public sphere of television talk shows and parliamentary debates (see Cassely 2013). While the Muslim-French *cité* residents, neo-Nazi punks, and even French soldiers who have all posted *quenelle* performances online may not agree on much, they share a general belief in the existence of a hopelessly sclerotic "system" in which they see little personal future, and thus find in Dieudonné's politically incorrect comedy and semi-serious activism a welcome attempt to figuratively upend it. That such postcolonial populism, as anthropologist Jean-Loup Amselle (2013) and other commentators (see Wieviorka 2013) have noted, builds on extant anti-Semitic prejudice as a rallying point is surely deplorable, and it is highly doubtful that the counterpublic called forth by Dieudonné's multimedia act universally upholds his broader ethical critique of a seemingly untouchable Jewish monopoly of suffering. Dieudonné and his fans may repeatedly insist that they are not "anti-Semites," that they do not harbor any particular hatred for Jews,[9] but in doing so they misrecognize anti-Semitism as an individual mental state rather than as a set of social effects, historical practices, and institutional forms that give it an undeniable reality even for those who in other regards benefit from relative political and economic privilege. Satire may provide plausible deniability for those within its arena, but it does not eliminate the sting for those who understandably feel targeted by it.

Lamentable as well is the instrumentalization of Dieudonné by the French political establishment, who have once again sought to displace the burden of public civility on French men and women of color. In the wake of the 2013 *quenelle* controversy, and responding to a public outcry particularly from French Jewish advocacy groups, French interior minister and presidential hopeful Manuel Valls moved to legally block Dieudonné from staging his show *Le Mur* ["The Wall"], claiming that it was a risk to "public order"; the representation of Jewish characters was also adjudged by the French High Court to challenge "human dignity."[10] The appeal to humanitarian principles struck many as particularly ironic coming from a public figure who had gained notoriety and bipartisan political capital for his support for immigration quotas, calling for the deportation of Roma, and being caught on tape deploring the lack of white residents in suburban Evry.

Ultimately, provocations like the *quenelle* or Dieudonné's ambiguous identification with Coulibaly arguably risk amplifying rather than bringing nuance to the sense of contemporary crisis, namely the moral panic surrounding the idea that the French Republic is under threat from internal incivility from an increasingly fragmented postcolonial population that refuses to sign an already-written contract of liberal toleration. And that is probably the last lesson one might hope would be drawn from the comedian's insistence, problematic as the forms it takes may be, on a necessary reckoning with the colonial past, on the long-term of effects of colonial violence and slavery, and on the inclusion of a broader population in national narratives of suffering, belonging, and protection. As the PIR worried, Dieudonné's words and gestures might dangerously play into the hands of ongoing exclusion.

CONCLUSION

What is it, then, that distinguishes *Charlie Hebdo* as an expression of French liberal values from the comedy of Dieudonné, prosecuted as their anathema? Both mock the privileged and powerful. Both poke fun at social pretenses and moral certitudes. Both transform provocation into an art form, a principled political position, and ultimately a lucrative commodity. Both seem to disproportionately target vulnerable minority populations, and both have repeatedly had to defend their words, images, and gestures from accusations of racism, Islamophobia, and anti-Semitism. Both seem eminently part of a vibrant French tradition of irreverent satire.

The easy answer would be that Islamophobia is simply more acceptable in contemporary French society than anti-Semitism, given memories of the Dreyfus affair and the shameful history of France's role in the Holocaust, as well as the relatively greater access French Jews have to the halls of cultural, economic, and political power. As detailed in the last chapter, French Jews are simply no longer asked, as Muslims are frequently, whether they feel more Jewish or more French. Perhaps it is indeed simply a matter of time, that in another generation or two Muslim-French subjects will simply be French citizens, no more different than any other differences in a postcolonial France that capaciously embraces diversity as simply part of what it is. In that future France perhaps all offense will be taken equally seriously, or equally mocked and dismissed. Racializing signs will be equally dangerous, or equally impotent.

But there is something unsatisfying about such an answer, about an approach that demands that those presently excluded simply be patient and wait for more enlightened times. As sociologists have long remarked, racist inequality has a durable quality, reproduced through political institutions, economic structures, educational policies, and the law (see Omi & Winant 1994; Tilly 1999; Winant 2004). Institutional change requires human political agency in the form of civil rights movements, localized rebellions, or broad sociopolitical revolutions. For all of its irreverence, *Charlie Hebdo* operates in the idiom of the secular republic and the logic of liberal politics. It may produce a frisson for its broadly middle-class, educated readership, but they can rest assured that its critique will be contained within the end pages of the magazine. Dieudonné, in contrast, has no truck with the civic discourse of *laïcité* and political liberalism. He wears his identity politics on his proverbial sleeve, and calls forth an eminently diverse counterpublic that is containable only with difficultly within the *banlieue* peripheries. The memes and gestures he introduces, like the *quenelle*, rapidly disseminate, ramify, and become the basis for new, unexpected alliances. There is something unpredictable and uncontrollable about Dieudonné's performance and audience that frighten those who carry the mantle of defending the French Republic. They bespeak a postcolonial France in the making, one which will not bend to the pre-existing liberal secular parameters, but which seeks to set its own terms for belonging, inclusion, and social remaking—a postcolonial France that explodes the territorial borders of France while still remaining culturally its own, if different. And for some ardent defenders of the secular Republic, those are dangerous signs indeed.

5

Anxious Football

On December 28, 2013, upon scoring his first goal for his new football club, the English team West Bromwich Albion, the veteran French striker Nicolas Anelka ran across the field holding his right arm in a *quenelle* gesture. Completely unremarkable by the flamboyant standards of goal celebrations in professional soccer, the gesture touched a raw nerve in France, where the match was being televised live and where, on the same day, the French interior minister Manuel Valls had publicly stated his intention to ban Dieudonné's shows because of their alleged anti-Semitism. Anelka tweeted that the gesture simply meant that he was dedicating the goal to his "friend Dieudonné," and that there was nothing inherently anti-Semitic about it.[1] "Of course I'm neither an anti-Semite nor a racist, and I totally stand up for (*assume*) my gesture." The French minister of sport, Valérie Fourneyron, responded on Twitter, calling it a "shocking, nauseating provocation. No place for anti-Semitism or incitement to hatred on the football field." The Union of Jewish Students of France denounced Anelka's "cowardice," and the Paris-based European Jewish Congress called upon the English Football Association (FA) to suspend Anelka for his "inverted Nazi salute".[2] The FA ultimately determined that the gesture was not intentionally anti-Semitic, but nonetheless suspended Anelka for five matches, after which West Brom terminated his contract (James 2014).

Anelka, long considered the enfant terrible of French football, had in many ways encapsulated the racialized anxieties and disappointed hopes of French football over the past decade. A convert to Islam, he was born and raised in the western *banlieues* of Paris to parents from Martinique. He showed prodigious talent as a young player and entered the Clairefontaine national training academy aged 13, where he trained alongside a generational cohort of other young French footballers of color. After getting his start as a striker for powerhouse Paris-Saint Germain (PSG) in 1996 when only 16, he transferred to the London club Arsenal, where he had success under iconic French manager Arsène Wenger, before moving on for a massive transfer fee in 1999 to play for the Spanish giant Real Madrid. In spite of scoring some important goals, he fell out with the Real Madrid manager Vicente del Bosque, returning to PSG within a year, the transfer fee being 40 times that paid to PSG when they had earlier sold him to Arsenal—a fee so high that it required supplemental aid from corporate sponsors Nike and Canal+. In this sense, as Geoff Hare (2003: 12) has averred, Anelka came to stand for both France as an exporter of footballing talent and for its broader sporting commercialization.

The rest of Anelka's professional career followed a similar peripatetic path. He played for seven different clubs in England, Italy, Turkey, and China from 2002 to 2012, interspersed with periodic clashes with his coaches, including PSG's Luis Fernandez, the Spanish immigrant who led France to victory in the 1984 European Championships alongside the legendary Malian-born Jean Tigana and Michel Platini, himself from an Italian immigrant background. Throughout, Anelka was a semi-regular player for *les Bleus*, the French national side, featuring in 69 matches and scoring 14 goals, though he frequently ran afoul of the coaching staff and was excluded from a number of major tournaments. During the half-time break of the 2–0 defeat by Mexico in the 2010 World Cup in South Africa, he got into a verbal altercation with French head coach Raymond Domenech, who was unhappy with Anelka's positional play. The French Football Federation sent him home from the tournament and later suspended him for 18 matches. In an act of solidarity, his teammates staged a walkout during the subsequent day's training, producing a public reckoning in France, with the national media accusing the players of unprofessional behavior, if not treason. For right-wing pundits, it merely underlined the fact that the multicultural dreams of the French *black–blanc–beur* (black–white–Beur) side that won the 1998 World Cup and the 2000 European championship was but an illusion, and that a "black–black–black" side (as some referred to it) could never truly represent France.[3] Anelka's *quenelle* merely confirmed the obvious.

The demonization of Anelka, as well as fellow Muslim-French foot-ballers Samir Nasri and Mahmadou Sakho, who have posed with Dieudonné performing *quenelles*, reiterates a long-standing demand that sporting figures and other celebrities of color serve as representatives of multicultural quiescence: that they express themselves exclusively in the audible language, visible signs, and palpable emotions of the nation, "one and indivisible." Whereas earlier chapters have largely addressed national anxieties raised by embodied expressions of piety by (veiled) Muslim-French women, in this chapter and the ones that follow I focus primarily on masculine bodily performances. Here I contrast Anelka to Zinedine Zidane, the hero of the 1998 and 2000 international tour-naments as alternative figurations of the supposed threat and promise of France's postcolonial future. I explore how football—particularly on global platforms like the World Cup—has become an anxious national spectacle, in which rituals of social and cultural renewal are subject to commercialization, racialization, and politicization to the profit of some and the exclusion of others. It is a preeminent stage on which national loyalty and adhesion are performed and scrutinized, and in which passions of identification are felt, expressed, and evaluated.[4] In many ways recapitulating early-twentieth-century colonial exhibitions, such moments condense existential hopes and fears over the capacity of the postcolonial French nation to parlay its past glory into future planetary prominence. The stakes in football are high, and while all footballers from Anelka to Zidane ultimately just want to play their game, the game they end up playing extends well beyond the football pitch.

NATIONAL SPECTACLES

There is something deeply ironic about French football becoming a locus of postcolonial hopes and anxieties, as a (perhaps fun-house) "mirror" which reflects back national aspirations and fears (see Boli et al. 2010: 11). While today the most practiced sport in the country, football has been largely disdained by the country's cultural and political elite, with the older aristocracy and professional classes still broadly preferring individual sports like tennis, swimming, fencing, cycling, and equestrian events, and rugby today competing for dominance in the southwestern part of the country. As we will see in the next chapter, beginning in the mid-nineteenth century, the French state primarily invested in gymnastics and other forms of physical education over team sports as a means of promoting national strength at home and in the colonies. If there are many French observers today who laud team sports like football for their promotion of democratic values of equality and responsible citizenship, others dismiss it as encouraging selfish, antisocial violent passions and for being a vector for corporate greed (Dubois 2010: 17; see also Redeker 2002).

Football was a relatively late arrival in France, and was originally mostly associated with English expatriates. It only really gained social traction in the interwar period, mostly in medium-sized manufacturing, industrial, or mining towns like Sochaux, Saint-Etienne, Sedan, Lille, Roubaix, and Lens, where employers sponsored teams as a means to promote work discipline and defuse labor politics, as well as to promote their brands. These were also centers of labor migration from within Europe (Italy, Poland, Portugal, Spain), but also from the colonial periphery; indeed, as

Stéphane Beaud and Gérard Noiriel (1990) remarked, the maps of immigration and football in France are effectively one and the same.

The legendary playmaker on the French national team in the 1950s, Raymond Kopa (Kopaszewski), was born to Polish immigrant miners outside of Lens, and famously recounted that he saw football as a means to escape work in the depths of the mines (where he had lost a finger) to a better job as an electrician. The footballing lives of other iconic players from Michel Platini through Anelka and Zidane similarly recount family histories of immigrant struggle. Moreover, as Laurent Dubois recounts, French football "also has its roots planted firmly in the history of empire" (Dubois 2010: 8–9), with the annals of French footballing glory since the 1920s marked by players of color like Larbi Benbarek, Raoul Diagne, Marius Trésor, and Jean Tigana hailing from colonial North Africa, sub-Saharan Africa, and the Caribbean. Colonial historian Pascal Blanchard (2010: 122) notes that fully 35 percent of those who have played for the French national team since its beginnings are of diverse backgrounds, and that since at least the 1930s, newspaper and political commentators have publicly questioned how "French" the national team was, usually in deeply racist ways. In this respect there is nothing at all new about Le Pen and other right-wing pundits' racism and Islamophobia; what is arguably new is that others have come to take such remarks—and football more broadly—so seriously as a gauge of national unity and strength.

In part, this is related to how France has come to recognize and experience itself in the postwar and postcolonial era. Despite the French Republic's secular liberalism, citizenship has never been merely a juridical category involving a calculus of dispassionate individual rights and responsibilities, but is also a racialized performance of patriotic belonging that is highly policed and publicly surveilled. A nation is neither simply shared homogeneous, empty space–time nor a delimited arena of rational debate, but also a sentimental community, a coalescence of fellow feeling, an "intimate public sphere" (see Berlant 1997). Benedict Anderson (1991) famously framed this affective aspect of nationhood in terms of patriotic sacrifice, the willingness to die for one's country. Certainly tragedies have been particularly salient occasions for heartfelt articulations of national unity and the transformation of their victims into martyrs to a higher cause. The *marche républicaine* and other rituals of collective mourning in the wake of the *Charlie Hebdo* and subsequent November 2015 attacks constituted performative avowals of steadfast recalcitrance and a refusal of blind terror and equally blind revenge. Whether or not one identified with *Charlie Hebdo*'s politics or supported the government's Middle East policy or its lukewarm embrace of domestic diversity, one might nonetheless find oneself, at least for a brief moment, in a motto like "Je suis Charlie" or the later "Je suis Paris" as an articulation of a basic feeling of togetherness and solidarity as fellow French men and women, or simply as fellow human beings, who could have also been victims.

Triumph as well as tragedy can also provide such a heightened sense of national affect. The early-twentieth-century Jewish-French sociologist Emile Durkheim (1995) spoke of the "collective effervescence" that took place in large ritual gatherings, whose primary function he saw as making the values and obligations of the social group viscerally palpable for individuals who otherwise live a more profane, workaday existence. Indeed, Durkheim was a key advocate and minor architect of the Third Republic's efforts to sacralize laïcité and transform public education into a new church of liberal political and moral values. In the wake of what he took to be the dying of old religions, he called forth a "new faith" (ibid.: 430) to express itself with new ceremonies. Fellow countrymen Pierre de Coubertin, the founder of the Olympics, and Jules Rimet, the first president of the French Football Federation (FFF) and founder of the World Cup competition, thought in similar (if more Catholic) terms, and likewise saw the events that they created as forms of moral pedagogy through which the nationalist frenzies that underwrote World War I—from which they, like Durkheim, were deeply scarred—could be channeled in less violent and more socially productive forms (Dubois 2010: 23–29; MacAloon 1981, 1984: 251–52; see also Rimet 1954).[5] Both events focalize participants and spectators on patriotic symbols of their respective countries, as equal rivals and commensurable loci of affiliation.

Since the Third Republic, the French state has invested heavily in sporting infrastructure, building training facilities and stadia, developing physical educational curricula, and sponsoring competitions. To this day, France dedicates a significantly larger amount of public money to football than other European countries do (Hare 2003: 31). These efforts are centralized through the Ministry of Youth and Sports and the National Institute of Sport, Expertise, and Performance (INSEP),[6] in coordination with the FFF, which operates as a nongovernmental association but which receives several million euros in state subventions.[7] The Clairefontaine academy where Anelka and others trained emerges from these explicit state efforts to build the French nation through sports training.

Sports stadia become spaces for people to viscerally feel local or national attachment as an overwhelming, multisensory experience (see Bromberger et al. 1995). Packed in with thousands of cheering others, they literally can feel the nation on their skin.[8] Particularly for many French citizens of color, French nationalist symbols are largely suspect, instrumentalized by the radical right to promote white supremacist agendas, or at best mandatory ceremonial dressings during school assemblies or the national Bastille Day holiday. In the absence of European wars and in the wake of the termination of national military service, "the nation exists as a widely shared and performed symbolic form only thanks to international football games" where, for supporters, "the national football team really *is* the nation, at least for a time" (Dubois 2010: 8, 5).

The state profits from these international sporting occasions to orchestrate a ritual composition of nationhood through player processions, award ceremonies, and the performance of national anthems; through the athletes' uniforms and the omnipresence of flags; and through attendance and speeches by heads of state. As I have discussed elsewhere (Silverstein 2000b, 2004a), France's hosting of the 1998 World Cup presented a unique occasion to celebrate the diversity of *les Bleus* as emblematic of a modern, multicultural France, a connection that was reinforced through advertising slogans and enthusiastic media coverage. Defying critiques from the radical right that racialized the nonwhite players as foreigners, mainstream politicians jumped on the team's early victories to lionize a hybrid (*métisse*) France re-presented as an "alternative, antiracist nationalism" (Dubois 2010: 105–6). Such an orchestrated performance of national diversity in many ways recapitulated older colonial exhibitions, where colonized subjects and their products were put on display as a means to advertise France's imperial economic venture and civilizing mission (see Bancel et al. 2002). In the 1998 World Cup, postcolonial immigration was similarly celebrated as a resource that not only built France's infrastructure during the postwar period known as the *Trente Glorieuses* (1945 to 1975) but continues to bring glory to the nation today. Indeed, *les Bleus* midfielder Christian Karembeu's great-grandfather Willy had been forcibly transported from New Caledonia for the 1931 Colonial Exposition (Dubois 2010: 111). The 1998 team was later immortalized in an exhibition, "Allez la France! Football and Immigration" at the National Museum of the History of Immigration (CNHI), housed in the Palais de Porte Dorée built for the 1931 exhibition. Celebrating the contributions of immigrants and those from a postcolonial immigrant background to France's footballing glory, portraits of the 1998 players were hagiographically displayed alongside past legends from immigrant backgrounds, and an edited video of the final championship match won by Zidane's two headers was played on a loop in a dedicated video installation.[9]

But national sensibilities can transcend the official enactments in the stadium and the museum. Immediately after the 1998 victory, an estimated 1.2 million Parisians descended on the Champs-Elysées, draped in French flags and dancing under the Arc de Triomphe, on which the faces of Zidane and his teammates were projected. Rivaling the famous scenes of the return of de Gaulle along the same avenue and the liberation of Paris from Nazi occupation, they historically condensed layers of military and sporting victories into a single projection of a triumphant France, not as an object of textbook study or mere ritual acknowledgment, but as a fully felt aspect of who they were. Those who came experienced an unbridled joy of mutual self-recognition—what Victor Turner (1974) called "communitas"—in which the diversity of everyday social differences were momentarily subsumed into, without necessarily being erased from, a common feeling of national belonging. Indeed, Algerian flags and those of other nationalities represented by players with families from Argentina, Armenia, Ghana, Senegal, as well as the overseas French territories of the Antilles and New Caledonia, mixed freely in the crowd, leading numerous observers to celebrate the festivity as a triumph of diversity over xenophobia, a victory for a plural postcolonial France. Dubois commented that the celebrations, although short-lived and no doubt over-exaggerated,

> did provide a space for people to cross and even trample on the borders and suspicions that shaped their daily lives, to enact, at least for a few days, a concrete utopia of harmony and to experience, if in a fleeting way, what it might mean to live in a very different world—one in which France was at ease with itself in all its diversity, accepting of its global past and multicolored frame. (Dubois 2010: 157)

Yet, as John MacAloon (1984) has compellingly argued, official, sacred rituals of national allegiance and joyous (or mournful) popular festivals of communion are always at risk of being undone by overly orchestrated, politicized, or commercialized spectacle. Examples of such subversions abound for mega-events like the World Cup and the Olympics, when the grandiosity of their ideological narratives or visual productions overwhelm the human feelings they are ostensibly meant to invoke, perhaps most famously during the 1936 Berlin and 2008 Beijing Olympics. While the original Parisian *marche républicaine* maintained its communal sense in spite of the presence of world leaders, its one-year commemoration came off to would-be participants as utterly staged and overly policed. Rather than the bonds of sadness and outrage providing a sensation of common identity, the "stiff choreography" of remembrance seemed to dictate how and in what patriotic form one was supposed to feel the nation, fragmenting for good any capacity to unite in multi-directional memory under "Je suis Charlie" (Hollis-Touré 2016: 297).

Given their massive size and global media transmission, major sporting events likewise can serve as compelling platforms for ideological messages that may run contrary to the peaceful national or urban rivalries officially enshrined. The kidnapping of Israeli athletes by the Palestinian Black September group at the 1972 Munich Olympics is certainly the most iconic such event, but the targeting by Islamic State militants of the France–Germany friendly being played at the Stade de France during the November 2015 Paris attacks follows the same spectacular logic. On a less violent but equally political scale, Anelka's *quenelle* broadly recapitulated the Black Power salute by American sprinters Tommie Smith and John Carlos at the 1968 Mexico City Olympics. Like Smith and Carlos, Anelka was ultimately sanctioned not for the content of his gesture as such, but for its violation of the ban on any political or religious signs beyond those directly associated with the teams at play. That football, like all sport, is deeply tied to politics at local, national, and transnational scales has been well-documented (see Boniface 2002; Dorsey 2016; Farred 2008; Fatès 1994; Foer 2004; Kuper 2006). What is at issue here is when politics itself breaks down; when the national spectacle of unity-in-diversity reveals itself to be little more than superficial, commercialized theater; and when rival, racialized expressions of postcolonial difference emerge in forms that cannot be easily contained in a stadium ritual or a museum display.

SINGING AND HISSING

For many observers, the multicultural promises embodied in the 1998 World Cup victory came crashing down during an October 2001 France–Algeria friendly played at the Stade de France in the northern Parisian *banlieue* of Saint-Denis. Organizers billed the first ever meeting of senior national sides as a moment of "reconciliation" (Dubois 2010: 198–213).[10] As discussed in earlier chapters, the French–Algerian war remained a raw nerve in France, broadly effaced from official memory and rarely publicly discussed or taught. Indeed, it was only two years earlier that the French government finally officially recognized the anti-colonial conflict as a "war" rather than simply "events" or an internal policing operation. The following year, General Paul Aussaresses publicly admitted to running a campaign of torture and murder of captured fighters of the National Liberation Front (FLN), but no apology followed either from him or French officials.[11] The match occurred shortly after the September 11 attacks in New York, in an atmosphere of reinforced Vigipirate security measures that had originally been introduced in the mid-1990s in the wake of bombing attacks associated with the ongoing Islamist insurgency in Algeria, itself presented as a "second Algerian war" with new mujahideen fighting against the authoritarian FLN and military power (see Stora 1995b).

And football itself had been part of this long process of decolonization. Most famously, shortly before the 1958 World Cup, in the midst of the anticolonial conflict, ten Algerian Muslim players based in France, including several like Rachid Mekhloufi and Mustapha Zitouni, who had played for the French national side, clandestinely left France to join the FLN's team based out of Tunis. While never recognized by FIFA, the international football body, the team would eventually include 35 players, all but one of whom had been playing professionally in France, and would play 80 matches across the world in the explicit goal of promoting Algerian independence (Abderrahim 2008; Nait-Challal 2008; Yahi 2010). While several would return to France after the French–Algerian war, the FLN heavily regulated the emigration of footballers, refusing to authorize transfers and, in the case of Ali Bencheikh, forcibly returning them to Algeria (Frenkiel 2010: 113). But regulations were gradually loosened, and by the 1990s the Algerian state was explicitly recruiting players from the French-Algerian diaspora. Six of Algeria's starting eleven in the 2001 match were born in France but were dual nationals and opted for the Algerian national side, and all but three of the eleven were currently playing their professional football in France.[12] While the choice of whether to play for Algeria or France was a complex one, based on personal circumstances, mixed emotions, and rational calculations of one's sporting chances, it was often read through the lens of rival patriotisms (Andrès 2010: 135). Ultimately, there was no doubt that the match would be experienced through a living history of (post) colonial antagonism.

For the organizers, the timing of the match nonetheless seemed propitious given France's recent victories in the World Cup and European Championships under the dominant performance of the French-Algerian Zidane. The son of a Kabyle immigrant raised in the La Castellane *quartier populaire* of Marseille, Zidane seemed to present the perfect figure of postcolonial reconciliation. Journalists for the widely circulated sports newspaper *L'Equipe* fantasized about the normally reticent Zidane picking up the microphone and addressing the multicultural "*black–blanc–beur*" crowd in the stadium and those watching at home:

Just a few words to say that, nearly forty years after Algerian independence, this match that we thought for so long would be impossible carries with it immense hope, and he is one of the sons who will make it possible to heal the wounds. (cited in Gastaut 2008b: 133)

Zidane himself had never been to Algeria, and while he always claimed to be proud of his Algerian heritage, he more clearly identified with the mixed ethnic world of La Castellane and the cosmopolitanism of elite football. He had refused to take a position with regard to the ongoing Algerian conflict, much to the dismay of many Kabyle Amazigh activists with whom I worked, who wanted him to come out more clearly in support of Tamazight language and culture. Coaches and players on the Algerian side were more indulgent, first and foremost respecting his playing ability. When asked by journalists before the match about his ultimate loyalties, Zidane acknowledged his hybrid background but side-stepped "political" questions and suggested that he would play his hardest but would be happy with a draw (Dubois 2010: 205).

Given this overdetermined set of expectations, it is not surprising that the match did not proceed as planned. Ultimately play was stopped midway through the second half, with France ahead 4–1, as dozens of young men and women invaded the pitch draped in Algerian and Moroccan flags. Many observers, and even some of the French players, interpreted this as a disastrous demonstration of disrespect, as a failure of integration and civility, and as a sign that reconciliation may not indeed be possible after all. But perhaps one might more fairly emphasize the exuberance and passions of those who took to the field, showing their desire to participate in a spectacle in which they had been positioned as passive observers of a staged affair. As much as they loved football and idolized the players on the pitch, they could not merely sit and watch the performance of a supposed reconciliation by privileged professional politicians and athletes. They too were the nation, living embodiments of the intertwined histories of France and Algeria, in all their sociopolitical complexities, colonial pasts, and postcolonial ambitions. The stage of postcolonial politics was ultimately theirs.

However, the lingering French narrative of the event is not of exuberant binationality, but of a divided nation, encapsulated not by how the match ended but by how it began, with spectators hissing during the playing of "La Marseillaise," the French national hymn. For years, right-wing pundits had evaluated the loyalty of French footballers of color on the basis of whether or not they visibly sung the national hymn at the start of matches, with Zidane himself being singled out for criticism. Actual practice varied quite widely among the players. Some like Zidane preferred to sing to themselves and insisted that they showed their patriotism through their sporting accomplishments, not their singing performances. Others like Karembeu considered "La Marseillaise" to be a war chant and refused to sing it on principle because his homeland, New Caledonia, was still colonized. Still others like star defender Lilian Thuram, who like Anelka was born in France to parents from the Antilles, embraced the public singing as part of a wider, outspoken political engagement to demonstrate that Frenchness was an achieved not ascribed identity, made manifest through ongoing actions and not predetermined by one's religion or the color of one's skin. While Zidane generally sought to efface his presence off the football pitch, Karembeu and Thuram drew on their celebrity status and used the national football stage to try to effectuate political change.

The hissing during the playing of the national anthem, attributed to local *banlieue* youths with a Franco-Maghrebi background, drew a similar line of critique from anxious observers of France's precarious multicultural nationalist narrative. Its repetition at subsequent friendlies at the Stade de France against Morocco in 2007 and Tunisia in 2008 underlined for some a veritable crisis of postcolonial France. Hissing the national anthem of an opposing side may come off as disrespectful from the idealisms of sporting civility, but, as Platini—then president of the European football governing body UEFA—insisted after the Tunisia match, it has long been common practice: "In all stadiums, all anthems are hissed ... I remember the Marseillaise hissed, [as well as] French [spectators] hissing other anthems" (Taïeb 2010: 184). But for conservative politician Philippe de Villiers, "to hiss [during] the Marseillaise is to hiss and insult France." The minister of sports, Roselyne Bachelot, announced that "any match where our anthem in hissed will be immediately stopped and all government members will leave the sporting venue" (Gastaut 2010b: 119). The 2003 law making it illegal to "offend the dignity of the Republic," including offending the flag and the national hymn, passed with support from conservative *and* socialist politicians alike, precisely in response to the France–Algeria match. The French nation required protection from the verbal signs of its postcolonial citizenry, suspected of not having internalized proper patriotic feelings.

HEAD AND HEART

If the pitch-invading spectators took the proverbial stage from Zidane in 2001, he permanently reclaimed it five years later. On July 9, 2006, Italy and France met in the World Cup final in Berlin, Germany. While both countries had won recent World Cups, the presence of France in the final came as a surprise. In the 2002 tournament, its campaign to retain the World Cup after victory in 1998 was a disaster. France exited in the first round after losing 2–0 to its former colony Senegal, whose players were nearly all based professionally in France. France subsequently did well in the preliminary rounds of the 2004 European Championships, but went out in the quarterfinals to a defensive-minded Greece, who went on to win the tournament. In the 2006 World Cup by contrast, France made a very poor showing during the preliminary matches, barely sneaking into the knock-out rounds. Before its victory over Spain in the first knock-out round, most French fans and experts had all but written off the chances of *les Bleus*. Searching for scapegoats, commentators from the political far right once again settled on the fact that the majority of the team's players were men of color and nonrepresentative of the French nation (Forcari 2006: 10). Zidane, who had come out of retirement to play one last tournament, was particularly singled out for criticism, both for his lackluster play and, more egregiously, again, for not enthusiastically singing "La Marseillaise."

However, after brilliant performances against Spain and then Brazil— in which Zidane was remarked to have been the only "Brazilian" on the pitch in terms of his display of creativity and virtuosity, qualities normally associated with South American football (Delerm 2006) —and a gritty victory over Portugal, in which he scored the only goal (from a penalty), Zidane had suddenly emerged as a renewed national hero, and expectations of a French victory charge led by Zidane were running high.[13] Such expectations were nearly fulfilled deep in overtime when, with the match locked at 1–1, Zidane redirected a header toward the goal in nearly identical fashion to the way he had scored the winning goal in 1998, with the ball only to be brilliantly saved by the legendary Italian goalkeeper Gianluigi Buffon. Several minutes later, with only ten minutes to go in the match and a penalty shoot-out looking inevitable, Zidane—in a spectacular gesture that will remain indelibly linked to the 2006 World Cup and Zidane's lasting legacy—seemingly and inexplicably lowered his head and felled Italian defender Marco Materazzi.

In the weeks that followed, Zidane's headbutt (*coup de boules*) became the source of a veritable social drama over race, racism, and violence in France that all but overshadowed France's anticlimactic defeat.[14] On replays, it was clear that Zidane reacted most immediately to a sustained verbal tirade from Materazzi, the exact words of which were subject to much debate, though there was some general agreement that the comments were racist in tenor, with some (including Zidane's own brother) claiming that Materazzi had called Zidane the "son of a terrorist whore."[15] Regardless of the exact words uttered, Zidane's reaction was itself racialized in the press, taken as a sign of his rough-and-tumble upbringing in the *cités* of La Castellane, and of his Algerian "sense of honor" and his Islamic subversiveness (Dubois 2010: 255–56). In a television interview, Zidane later implied that only God knew the truth of his actions. As Guénif-Souilamas has written: "The headbutt transformed the great champion into a simple-minded believer ... Zidane's 'coming-out' as a Muslim 'proved' his irrationality and violence" (Guénif-Souilamas 2009: 212). Far-right ideologues gloated at the downfall of *les Bleus* provoked by the "little hooligan" (*voyou*) "Zidane the African" (Forcari 2006: 10).

In addition to the re-racialization of Zidane, the headbutt was immediately decried by a number of French commentators in the mainstream press (including *L'Equipe* and *Le Monde*) as setting a bad example for children across the world, and particularly for those from the suburban *cités* of France (see Caussé 2006; Droussent 2006).[16] The criticism was magnified by the recent memory of the *banlieue* uprisings of October and November 2005, in which young men and women of color performed the violence that had long been expected of them, but directed it at precisely those institutions of the state and its coercive apparatus from which they had long been marginalized. And it eerily recalled the theater of the 2001 France–Algeria match. Accordingly, the headbutt was read by many as a de facto act of sabotage of French national dreams and an index of Zidane's suspect loyalty to the French nation—and via him the suspect citizenship of all Muslim French and other men and women of color.

But as much as Zidane's headbutt was condemned, it was also admired and embraced, as much for its own technical mastery ("What a headbutt!") as for its implied affect. For a number of Algerian interlocutors, it was finally a sign of his Algerianness, of his Kabyleness in particular, of a hot-headed riposte to Materazzi's verbal challenge, as a legitimate defense of masculine honor predicated on the defense of female kinfolk. It reconfirmed Zidane's masculinity for those Algerians who had previously disavowed Zidane's success and criticized him for being a "virtual Arab" (*'arbi mzowar*) or the "king of France" who had turned his back on his natal culture and allowed himself to be deployed by the French state as an example of integration (Mandard 2006).[17] A simplistic reading, perhaps, but a candid domesticating gesture that preluded Zidane's subsequent homecoming to his father's village in Kabylia—his first trip to Algeria.

More concretely, the headbutt has been materialized in the Berberophone French-Algerian artist Adel Abdesemmed's now infamous 5 meter bronze sculpture *Coup de tête*, originally displayed in front of the Pompidou Center in Paris, subsequently set up on the corniche in Doha,

Qatar, as part of their public build-up to the 2022 World Cup. Qatar is not only a center of the sports media industry in the Middle East and North Africa, but also host to an increasingly large contingent of North Africans working in sporting professions (see Amara 2017). The statue was later moved out of the public view into the Mathaf Modern Arab Art museum, later to be silently sold to a private French collector. The installation is but the most spectacular contribution to an entire industry of artistic, literary, audiovisual, and scholarly productions generated by Zidane's *coup de boules* (Dine 2010; Dubois 2010: 251), the ramifying afterlives of a fleeting moment of footballing drama that have only added to the deification of "Zidane-as-Adonis ... a mute star who speaks only with his body" (Guénif-Souilamas 2009: 216).

In spite of this quickly unfolding legacy, Zidane was nonetheless called upon to apologize in the immediate aftermath of the event. Zidane did issue something like a public apology to the "children" who had seen his final performance, but he refused to regret the action itself. With a final bow to his admiring fans during a subsequent visit to the Elysée presidential estate, Zidane was promptly forgiven by Jacques Chirac and the other dignitaries assembled. Such a ritual recapitulated the racial and spatial divide—what Etienne Balibar (2004) terms "apartheid"—between those from a postcolonial immigrant background, suspected of being unpatriotic and who must repeatedly apologize for their presence (Sayad 2004: 252, 290), and those with "governmental" or "managerial" belonging (Hage 1998) empowered to accept and forgive. As I have emphasized throughout the book, this racialized divide is in no way stable for either the privileged or the marginalized, but must be continuously made and remade—or, as Judith Butler claims, following J.L. Austin (1962), "performed" (Butler 1990)—through public, illocutionary words and deeds that have pragmatic effects. Zidane—as "[n]either completely civilized or uncivilized ... [n]either completely white nor black" (Guénif-Souilamas 2009: 216), as an immortal sporting demi-god but also a man of uncontrollable passion—stood as a liminal figure within this racialized dynamic. Yet, even so, his room for subjective self-fashioning has remained very constrained within the limits of postcolonial nationalism. The current coach of Real Madrid, he appears much more at home as a cosmopolitan professional footballer than as the public emblem of the impossibilities of French-Algerian reconciliation.

THE LIMITS OF PROFESSIONALISM

Professionalism, however, can itself be the source of national anxiety, as demonstrated by *les Bleus* tragic farce—what American soccer journalists comically coined *le meltdown* and French media simply dubbed the "fiasco" or "debacle"—of the 2010 World Cup in South Africa, in which Anelka would play a starring role. Their under-performance was a farce not simply because the team, containing players from the top professional clubs in world football, failed to win a game or score more than a single goal (and that in their final defeat, to the host nation). Nor because of the entire circus of scandals and affairs surrounding the campaign, from revelations about players consorting with underage prostitutes; to the junior sports minister Rama Yade questioning the team's expensive hotel while herself being scheduled to stay in an even more posh one; to accusations that Zidane encouraged players to mutiny against their lame-duck coach Raymond Domenech; to the halftime tirade launched against the latter by Anelka and his subsequent dismissal from the squad; to the training strike led by captain Patrice Evra in solidarity with Anelka; to President Nicolas Sarkozy making the drama a matter of state by summoning veteran striker Thierry Henry to an emergency meeting with his ministers while France was in the midst of a labor strike. Nor did the farce merely lie in the subsequent scapegoating engaged in by the French media and public, alternately pointing the finger at an incompetent and arrogant Domenech, an unprofessional FFF, or the millionaire players who were deemed to care more about their "bling" than the national jersey. Nor even because much of this scapegoating took on thinly veiled racial overtones against a team that included a large number of footballers of color, many of whom grew up in the *cités*.

Rather, what was truly farcical, if not tragic, about the "fiasco" and its racialization was just how absolutely predictable, repetitious, and trite everyone recognized it to be, and yet how much social traction it nonetheless continued to have. The team's failure was anticipated by commentators, and the rift between players and the French spectating public occurred long before the first ball of the competition was kicked (see Lesprit 2009). Anxieties over a postcolonial crisis in national identity exemplified by the selection of the national football team literally repeated racist clichés from decades past, with Finkielkraut himself reiterating his 2005 comments about the team being "black–black–black" in a radio interview with Europe 1 on June 20, 2010 in the immediate wake of Anelka's dismissal. Contrasting the team with the "Zidane generation" of 1998, he qualified it as a "gangsta (*caillera*) generation," as a "gang of hooligans (*voyous*) whose only morality is that of the mafia," thus deploying the same demeaning language as the then interior minister Sarkozy had in the midst of the 2005 violence. Rather than signaling the ethno-racial unity of a new, multicultural France, the team offered a "terrible mirror" of a society divided by "clans," "ethnic and religious divisions," and, above all, "arrogant and unintelligent" individuals.

It is precisely Finkielkraut's theme of social "disunion and decline" (déliquescence) that provided the tragic traction for such outrageous comments and underwrote the farcical politicization of a largely scripted sporting spectacle. The 2005 violence, the ongoing internal "war on terror," and the 2008 economic crisis and subsequent labor unrest once again raised the perennial question of "whither postcolonial France" and encouraged the mythologization of the 1998 victory as a utopian moment of multiracial harmony. The 2010 World Cup "debacle" occurred precisely in the wake of President Sarkozy making "national identity" a political priority and the focus of a new ministry, thus fostering a vociferous public debate over what constituted the fundamental values of Frenchness. It likewise followed shortly after his successful campaign to bring the European Championship tournament to France, during which he drew on a long-standing discourse of national integration through sport, claiming that football would be France's response to the global economic crisis and that it would reunite the nation. That the players seemed to act as a set of "narcissists," overpaid "mercenaries," and "immature caids" rather than as a unified, socially aware "team" worked precisely against this idyllic proposition and recalled too easily the immoral financial traders with their inflated bonuses, as anthropologist Christian Bromberger insightfully noted (Mouillard 2010).

As with financial markets, what was being demanded of both the French team and the French nation was transparency. Sports journalists accused Domenech and the FFF of running a closed shop. For all the talk of lack of team unity, the players were roundly criticized for not talking to the media, for maintaining a collective silence, and for being more concerned about the "traitor" who informed the media of Anelka's screed than the fact that he disrespected his coach. Their remaining on the team bus with the shades drawn during the training strike rather than exposing themselves on the practice field invoked decades-long racialized fears over the ethnic enclaving and cloistering of young women in the cités. For Finkielkraut, their actions represented the esprit des cités rather than the esprit de la Cité, of enlightened civilization. Pundits portrayed the players as having their "headphones over their ears," and the dismissed Anelka was photographed leaving the airport in a hoodie and dark sunglasses—images that recalled the face veils (burqas) that Parliament had been considering banning from public spaces. To be truly French, in other words, meant to be visible, to communicate through their exterior appearance and comportment inner nationalist sentiments. It was the logic of laïcité transported to the international football pitch.

CONCLUSION

What is ultimately at stake in French football politics is how players of color should properly perform national belonging under the public gaze. As public figures on a global platform, they are expected to hypercorrect the supposed deficits of belonging with which they were saddled by their postcolonial background. They are expected to sing the national anthem aloud, respect the team colors, and even celebrate the goals they score with appropriate decorum. They are expected to show proper solidarity and discipline, putting the team and the country above their person. Such visible signs would be proof of their heartfelt allegiance, their true commitment to a France to which they should be grateful for the opportunities it has provided them and their families.

But, ultimately, as Paul Dietschy has concluded, "the contemporary football player is first of all an immigrant worker" (Dietschy 2010: 25), constrained to migrate for professional employment, forced on occasion to change team and sometimes even country. They are necessarily individual journeymen, proud of their craft, whose ultimate object of production is their own future, both personal and professional. While some like Thuram and Karembeu parlayed their playing careers into public politics, understanding their celebrity status as a platform from which to take voice on behalf of other French men and women of color, many others like Zidane and Anelka, while more than aware of their racialized position, simply wanted to play football and let their goals speak for themselves. Like their teammates, they can get caught in the moment, drop their professional decorum, and, in joy or anger, act as impassioned men, headbutting their opponents or saluting their friends. The tragedy is how quickly such gestures become racialized and politicized, attributed to their Muslim faith and spun through a web of Islamophobic anxieties that are ultimately more about whither postcolonial France than about anything to do with the players themselves. For, in the end, they want to be singled out for their individual skills *qua* footballer, not *qua* black or Muslim footballer. As national teammates, they are "just French" (*Français tout court*), as Nasri put it in a 2010 interview in *L'Equipe* (cited in Boli et al. 2010: 11). Or, as Thuram averred, echoing Fanon and anticipating the slogan that was born of the *Charlie Hebdo* attack, "I am a black Frenchman, but I am a Frenchman" (*Je suis un Français noir, mais je suis un Français*) (Blanchard 2010: 131).

6

Tracing Places
Parkour and Urban Space

In the 2004 action-thriller, *Banlieue 13*, the film's writer and producer, Luc Besson, imagines a postcolonial urban dystopia extrapolated from present French republican anxieties. As we have already seen, since the mid-1970s, state planners, politicians, and media pundits have worried that the modernist, rationally planned housing estates (*les cités*) designed in part to house immigrant families have become dilapidated spaces of radical sectarian otherness marked by unemployment, criminality, ethnic enclaving, and potential terrorism. Successive French governments have increasingly approached this failed urban scheme as a policing problem, interpellating the multiracial inhabitants of the suburban *cités* as preternaturally violent, prone to rioting, and a threat to fundamental French values. In Besson's world, the military-corporate state has taken the logical next step to current policies of securitization: walling off the districts, establishing armed checkpoints, and even plotting their eventual destruction.

For the 2009 sequel, *Banlieue 13: Ultimatum*, these thinly veiled references to apartheid South Africa and the occupied Palestinian territories are coupled with an allusion to post-invasion Iraq, as a corporate giant named "Harriburton" has infiltrated the government and convinced it to bomb the district in question so that it can procure the reconstruction contract. As in the first film, an incorruptible martial arts expert and police officer (played by Cyril Raffaelli) must team up with an agile, local jack-of-all-trades (*bricoleur*) (played by David Belle) in order to outwit the military and corporate bad guys and save the *banlieue* from destruction. For the sequel, they must organize the five heavily armed gangs that divide up the housing projects along ethno-religious lines and control the underground economy (which includes supplying the French bourgeoisie with illegal drugs): the "Africans," the "Arabo-Islamic fundamentalists," the "Asians," the "Gypsies," and the "Skinheads." It goes without saying that, once these racialized groups put down their weapons and set aside their internecine conflicts, they are able to out-smart and out-kick the bad guys, unveil the evil corporate plot to the well-meaning

French president, and save their fellow *banlieue* inhabitants. But, in an unexpected twist, the gang leaders agree to go through with the destruction of the district's housing projects, provided that they themselves can plan their rebuilding as an unwalled, integrated community consonant with the true color- and class-blind republican values of *laïcité* and political liberalism.

Banlieue 13: Ultimatum is clearly derived from and functions as the logical culmination of a "*banlieue* cinema" that since the mid-1990s has portrayed the French housing projects as spaces of perpetual conflict between the police and multiracial youths.[1] As the third Besson-produced vehicle for parkour, an urban, gymnastic, athletic practice innovated by David Belle, the film offers a showcase not only for his talents, but also for parkour's ethic of bodily, moral, social, and ultimately racial regeneration. Belle and his male teenage friends from the Parisian suburb of Lisses first started practicing parkour in 1988, but the sport only gained national and quickly international attention in the early 2000s thanks to Besson's film *Yamakasi: Les samouraïs des temps modernes* (2001), named after the group Belle founded. This was followed by a BBC commercial featuring Belle, several documentaries and advertisements starring fellow Yamakasi Sébastien Foucan, and a very active online community united by bulletin board and YouTube postings.[2] Parkour is now actively practiced primarily by young men across much of the globe, with especially active communities in Britain, Russia, the United States, Australia, Japan, China, and just about anywhere that concrete dominates the built environment.

There is much to be said about transnational parkour as a "subversive discourse" (Fuggle 2008), an "anarcho-environmentalist movement" (Atkinson 2009), a "kinetic utopia" (Ortuzar 2009), and a playful liberation from the constraining socio-spatial forms dictated by modernist architecture and statist urban planning (Thomson 2008). As an urban critical practice, it can trace its antecedents to earlier philosophical movements and urban practices like early-nineteenth-century American transcendentalism (Atkinson 2009: 176–77), fin-de-siècle *flânerie* (Benjamin 1978: 156–58; see also Ortuzar 2009: 60), the *dérive* as a Situationist practice of psychogeographic experimentation (Debord 1981b; see also Thomson 2008: 253), or contemporary philosophical expressions of "nomadology" (Deleuze & Guattari 1987; see also Mould 2009: 741–42).[3] In general, parkour might be seen as a spatial appropriation and remapping, a "pedestrian speech act" or "poem of walking" in Michel de Certeau's idiom (de Certau 1984: 98, 101), that narrates, comments upon, and eventually critiques the limits and possibilities of the panoptic worlds constructed by late capitalism—all, of course, at high speed and with innumerable rhetorical flourishes. Parkour has a decidedly playful quality; it reinserts bodily pleasure (*jouissance*) into the drab, "striated," postindustrial urban landscape of office buildings, shopping malls, parking lots, and housing projects—its preeminent sites of practice and play (see Atkinson 2009: 182).

In this chapter, I will approach parkour as first and foremost a postcolonial discipline through which certain French men and women of color seek to become embodied agents in transforming the racialized, dilapidated built landscapes of the *cités* into a home in which they can flourish both psychically and materially. I emphasize parkour's roots in the *parcours du combattant*, or military obstacle course, innovated by the early-twentieth-century physical education theorist Georges Hébert—David Belle's acknowledged textual inspiration—and practiced by Belle's father Raymond during his counterinsurgency training in late-colonial Indochina. But I also pay attention to the exuberant, creative acts of self-making in which parkour practitioners (*traceurs*) engage through their unscripted movements. Such tensions between the playful and disciplined dimensions of parkour—akin to Roger Caillois's distinction between *paidia* and *ludus* (Caillois 2001: 13) in human play more broadly—have marked both French parkour since its founding and are largely at the root of today's splits within the global parkour community, between Belle and Foucan themselves as well as between mainstream parkour and Foucan's Urban Freeflow movement.[4]

Attending to parkour's *banlieue* context allows us to see how masculinized bodies and spaces of the *cités* have proven to be especially salient sites for French colonial intervention and more recent postcolonial anxiety. Built in the midst of the French–Algerian war, the suburban *cités* have been spaces for the containment and surveillance of marked, lower-class, immigrant and postcolonial subjects punctuated by moments of police violence and mobile, guerrilla riposte. If *Banlieue 13* surely engages in cinematic hyperbole, the parkour it features cannot be separated from the spatial and racial tensions over the future of postcolonial France that it vividly depicts. As in the film's conclusion, parkour, as a disciplined mode of playfully respatializing the *banlieue* by those marginalized by French modernity, points to an embodied form of postcolonial urban agency and engagement (Harvey 2000: 233–55). It models active urban citizenship defined through movement and makes claims to civic participation in the making of mobile "counter-spaces" (Lefebvre 1991: 383), enacting what Lefebvre (1996) called the "right to the city" (*droit à la ville*), or Etienne Balibar (2004: 31–50) more recently has termed "the right to belong" (*le droit de cité*).[5] Parkour, as it is practiced in the *quartiers populaires*, interrogates what it means to be a citizen (in the literal sense) for those French men and women of color whose embodied and affective loyalty to the French nation is under constant skeptical scrutiny.

THE *MÉTHODE NATURELLE* AND RACIAL REGENERATION

As any viewer of the 2006 remake of *Casino Royale* knows, parkour involves climbing, jumping, vaulting, and running through urban space, tracing routes less traveled in the name of speed and efficiency—gestures performed in the opening sequence by Foucan himself as he dramatically flees from James Bond. Practitioners of parkour refer to themselves as *traceurs*, as layers of routes, cartographers of built space through their movements (Fuggle 2008: 215–16). They call their sport, or "postsport,"[6] *l'art du déplacement* ("the art of displacement"), emphasizing the ultimate goal of moving, in Belle's own words, "from point A to point B regardless of what is in the way" (quoted in Mould 2009: 748). In the 2002 short promotional film for BBC One known as *Rush Hour*, which launched David Belle to international fame, Belle's leaps from rooftop to rooftop are contrasted with the gridlocked traffic on the city streets below. Parkour thus refigures the built environment as a three-dimensional vector space, and *traceurs* present themselves as the low-tech, creative *bricoleurs* of human movement through it. Unsurprisingly, tropes of freedom, flight, and fluidity mark parkour rhetoric, with *traceurs* likening themselves to "water flowing over rocks" (Atkinson 2009: 190).

But such metaphors of mobility are everywhere tempered by a discourse of discipline. *Traceurs* in both the *cités* and elsewhere advocate mastery and self-mastery (Ortuzar 2009: 56). They microscopically study the various obstacles they seek to overcome, noting their subtle contours much as the way a climber investigates a rock face "problem" before lifting a foot. They engage in ascetic modes of self-creation, devoting hours every day to rigorously training their bodies in strength and stamina (Atkinson 2009: 189). And they break down their free-flowing movements into particular techniques—the "tic tac," the "cat leap," the "precision jump," and so forth—that they practice repeatedly at increasing scales of difficulty and risk. Before Belle attempted the spectacular 23 foot jump featured in the *Rush Hour* video, he and his Yamakasi crew spent years learning to safely fall off the railings and park benches of suburban Lisses.

This real-world method of physical training and the particular techniques of the body that *traceurs* master are lifted straight from the pages of Georges Hébert's encyclopedic five-volume tome, *L'éducation physique, virile et morale par la méthode naturelle*, published during the

1930s and 1940s but developed from earlier studies dating back to 1912.[7] Across his corpus, Hébert strongly promulgated physical training for material, social, and moral utility rather than entertainment, adopting the motto *être fort pour être utile* ("being strong to be useful"). With this goal, he rebuilt the physical education ("gymnastics") that had been incorporated into French public education since 1854 (Vigarello 1978: 155), identifying ten basic sets of "natural" movements: walking, running, jumping, crawling, climbing, balancing, lifting, throwing, defending (*défense*), and swimming. Through anatomical study and direct observation, he recorded the numerous variations of the ten movements, providing visual illustrations and step-by-step training exercises for each—a veritable manual of what would become basic parkour techniques.

According to Hébert, the basic forms had been lost in a twentieth-century France addicted to motorized transportation, comfortable shoes, soft beds, and hot running water—where athletics had been degraded by mimicking Anglo-Saxon "sports" (particularly football and rugby) organized for commercial spectacle and played in the artificial environments of stadia, gymnasia, graded tracks, and manicured fields (Hébert 1946: 35–46).[8] Only the remaining "indigenous peoples" (*peuplades indigènes*)—the "little savages" (*petits sauvages*) of French colonial Africa, Polynesia, and the Antilles, where Hébert had been stationed as a French naval captain and later traveled widely—maintained these natural movements in vestigial forms (Hébert 1949: vi, xv).[9] Only through reviving these primitive techniques, practicing them in natural environments, and refocusing physical education on the social good, could French civilization regain its virility. As Hébert concluded his 1925 manifesto, *Le sport contre l'éducation physique*, the goal of athletics should be to make men, not champions, in order to "regenerate the race" (Hébert 1946: 134).

Hébert's concerns with racial regeneration, moral improvement, and the masculinization (*virilisation*) of decadent civilization (ibid.: 47) were widely shared in early-twentieth-century France. The "national humiliation" of the 1871 defeat in the Franco–Prussian war and the loss of Alsace-Lorraine convinced many observers that the French body politic had become infirm. Drawing on the Prussian institution of the *Turnverein* (gymnastics union), secular and Christian gymnastics movements arose in France with the explicit goal of strengthening the (masculine) national body and race (Holt 1981: 52). Hébert (1946: 88–89) reserved his praise for these movements alone. Like Hébert, other ideologues looked to the colonies as a site for the rejuvenation of the French race. In particular, French Algerian writers of the same period, including Louis Bertrand and Robert Randau, proposed that the hot sun of Africa and the proximity of primitive peoples could lead to the salutary "re-barbarization" of over-civilized France (see Graebner 2007: 27–106; Lorcin 1995: 196–213). Increasingly, the colonial periphery was represented as the training ground where metropolitan boys could become imperial men, and sport played a central role both in the preparation of colonial officers and in the enactment of France's imperial self-aggrandizing *mission civilisatrice*.[10]

Eventually, Hébert's "natural method" became incorporated into French military training. During World War I, Hébert had been charged with renovating physical education instruction in army basic training camps, but after the war, much to Hébert's chagrin, the military abandoned these methods and returned to competitive sports and public spectacles (Hébert 1946: 118–19). Yet, among the colonial military forces, Hébert's ideas found more traction, particularly in the widespread deployment of the *parcours du combattant* obstacle course based on Hébert's basic movements in natural settings. The obstacle course became an essential element in the post-World War II counterinsurgency training being developed in the face of rising anticolonial nationalist movements in Africa and Indochina. David Belle's father Raymond received such training as a teenage orphan in 1950s Indochina, raised by soldiers on a military base in upland Da Lat, Vietnam (Atkinson 2009: 172). After the fall of Dien Bien Phu, Belle *père* repatriated Hébert's methods to Paris, where he incorporated them into the training and fitness regimes of the elite fire rescue (*sapeur-pompier*) unit in which he served. In what serves as a central moment in the origin myth of parkour, Belle *père* famously put his aerial skills to the test in 1969, when he dangled off a hovering helicopter to remove a Vietcong flag that antiwar protesters had mounted on top of Paris's Notre Dame cathedral. For David Belle, his father represented the epitome of the restored virility Hébert had desired, putting his athleticism to work for the moral good of society. David would later incorporate precisely this bodily ethic and social philosophy into postcolonial parkour, adapting the military obstacle course to the concrete, suburban setting in which he lived.[11]

URBANITY AND EMBODIED CARTOGRAPHY

The wars of decolonization were likewise the setting for the construction of the built urban and suburban forms that constitute parkour's new natural environment. Colonial cities like Da Lat, Algiers, Antananarivo, and Casablanca functioned as "social laboratories" for urban planners experimenting with the norms and forms of the French modern, as Paul

Rabinow (1989) and Gwendolyn Wright (1997) have discussed.[12] In a last-ditch effort to win over the hearts and minds of the indigenous population in the face of anticolonial insurgency, state planners in postwar French Algeria, under the leadership of governor general and anthropologist Jacques Soustelle, devised a set of policies known as *intégrationisme* that notably included the construction of modernist projects on the Algiers periphery to rehouse inhabitants of the overcrowded and unpoliceable Casbah and surrounding shantytowns (*bidonvilles*) (Le Sueur 2005; Shepard 2006).[13] As urban historian Zeynep Çelik (1997: 8, 192–93) notes, these schemes became the model for the *cités* later constructed on the outskirts of Paris and Lyon, similarly built to rehouse the urban poor and more specifically to relocate Algerian immigrant workers from the shantytowns of Nanterre and Noisy-le-Grand—which had become sites for organization, recruitment, provision, and fundraising for the National Liberation Front (FLN)—as well as provide housing for many of the nearly one million poorer French citizens (Jews, *harkis*, underclass *pied-noirs*) later "repatriated" from Algeria in the early 1960s (see Haroun 1986; Lallaoui 1993; Sayad & Dupuy 1995).

As early as 1952, the French state established a National Corporation for the Construction of Housing for Algerian Workers (SONACOTRA) with the explicit purpose of relocating shantytown residents, first to temporary housing (*cités de transit*) and later to rent-subsidized housing projects (*grands ensembles*) financed through the 1958 Priority Urbanization Zone (ZUP) legislation. Built on the outskirts of Paris, Lyon, and other French cities, with a minimum of 500 units in a combination of high-rise towers and low-rise blocks, the *grands ensembles* balanced imperatives of social mobility and security, circulation, and containment. They were constructed as part of a larger moral reform project, as utopian modernist experiments in hygienic social life, centralizing housing, commerce, education, and recreation in the immediate proximity of the factories in which many residents were assumed to work. In the process, they broke up the ethnic communities that had formed in the *bidonvilles*, mixing residents of different backgrounds and incorporating them into formal structures of state control and increasingly bureaucratized police surveillance.[14]

Such late-colonial metropolitan developments likewise provide an important context for understanding the Situationist movement of the 1950s as an embodied practice of urban critique whose influence parkour retraces.[15] Like Hébert, the Situationists were highly critical of French *surmodernisation* (over- or hyper-modernization), of a technological lifestyle that detached men and women from their physical environment and routinized their movements around the workday (*métro-boulot-dodo*), of a social world reduced to labor, consumer-ism, and spectacle (see Debord 1994). Rather, they called for a "new urbanism" (also called "unitary urbanism") based on freedom and play in an effort to reattach city spaces to human bodies and humane feelings (Debord 1981a; Chtcheglov 1981; see also McDonough 2002: 241–66).[16] Methodologically, they developed an experimental science of "psycho-geography"—"the study of the laws and precise effects of a consciously or unconsciously elaborated geographical environment acting directly on affective behavior" (Khatib 1958)—whose primary methodology of investigation was the *dérive* ("drifting"). Debord (1981b) specifically understood the *dérive* as a rigorous mapping (or perhaps remapping) project whereby pedestrian drifters would intimately explore a delimited spatial field while behaviorally disorienting themselves—"letting go" (*laisser-aller*).

However, rather than simply a form of knowledge production or map-making, the Situationists deployed the *dérive* as a "direct, effective intervention," as a disciplined "form of action" in a larger ludic politics (Khatib 1958). Moreover, it was a politics with potentially violent consequences. Many of the Situationists were themselves immigrants and thus suspect pedestrians on city streets increasingly occupied by state security forces and subject to nightly curfews—particularly for North Africans in light of the anticolonial insurrection in Algeria and the political organizing of the immigrant community by the FLN.[17] Abdelhafid Khatib, for example, was twice arrested and incarcerated in 1958 while engaging in nighttime *dérives* in the Paris open-air market area of Les Halles. Such policing intensified in the years that followed, reaching an extreme on October 17, 1961 with the massacre of Algerians marching through the streets of central Paris to protest against the French–Algerian war.

POSTCOLONIAL CREATIVITY AND VIOLENCE

The *dérive* never caught on as a generalized mode of social protest or playful intervention, though its critical insights were captured in emerging New Wave cinema, particularly in Jacques Tati's boisterous satire *Playtime* (1967), in which M. Hulot drifts through a disorient-ing super-modern Paris on some unspecified bureaucratic errand.[18] Yet the streets of Paris and its environs remained the privileged lieu for ludic—and sometimes violent—politics, most notably in May 1968 but also in periodic confrontations between police and mobile youths from the early 1980s through the May 2005 *banlieue* uprising (see Bloom 2009; Mbembe 2009; Silverstein 2008b; Silverstein & Tetreault 2006).

As I discussed in Chapter 3, French men and women of color living on the urban peripheries have been repeated victims of racist and police violence since the 1970s, and have repeatedly mobilized against it, from the street demonstrations of the 1980s "Beur movement" through the self-defense initiatives of the Mouvement Immigration Banlieue (MIB) of the 1990s to the Party of the Indigènes of the Republic (PIR) today.

Public insecurity in the *banlieues* and other *quartiers populaires* has been exacerbated by rising precarity and a sense of spatial isolation and immobility.[19] Unemployment rates exceeding 30 percent over the last three decades have resulted from the deindustrialization of the urban periphery and particularly the closing of the automobile and manufacturing concerns that had previously recruited immigrant labor and financed the construction of the *cités*. More and more, residents must commute great distances to deskilled jobs in the city centers. Young residents have often found themselves blocked by the public education system that encourages many from a postcolonial immigrant background to follow vocational degrees that are increasingly irrelevant, and residence in the *banlieues* itself can have a further stigmatizing effect on young job seekers. Moreover, the *cités* have been marked by significant physical dilapidation, with many buildings and public facilities suffering from water damage, insulation problems, broken elevators, or worse. The lack of local capital, alongside occasional petty crime and property violence, have brought about the flight of local commerce and the augmentation of heavy-handed policing that has largely criminalized certain everyday practices (such as assembly in the entryways or basements of public housing).

The challenge for French men and women of color in the *banlieues* is to construct meaningful, flourishing lives under conditions of economic privation and police harassment. In part this has involved the development of a healthy informal economy—including a series of gray-market institutions revolving around the drug trade or the fencing of stolen consumer items—for the provision of employment as well as goods and services not otherwise locally available or affordable. Daily open-air markets operate in the shadow of boarded-up shopping centers. Residents with vehicles have created an informal taxi service to carry neighbors to and from transportation centers or places of work, commerce, or entertainment that are generally underserved by public transportation, and thus difficult to access from the *cités*. Through after-school tutoring programs, resident associations constitute a parallel, if severely underfunded, education system that attempts to compensate for the depressed conditions in French schools. The same associations also provide day-care for working mothers and legal advice for local residents.

Indeed, such a parallel structure operates with the tacit knowledge and minimal funding of the French state, which has largely devolved the provision of many such social, educational, and legal services to civic associations (Kastoryano 2002: 101–2).

The response of successive French governments to what is often referred to in the media as the *crise des banlieues* ("the crisis of the *banlieues*"), or more generally as a *fracture sociale* (or "social fracture"), has been twofold (see Silverstein 2006). On the one hand, as we have seen, they have increased police intervention, predicating urban renewal on social and political quiescence. Successive French governments on both the left and the right have increased the numbers of the Anti-Criminal Brigade, CRS riot police, and military gendarmes charged with patrolling the *cités*, augmented in recent years by antiterrorist laws and state of emergency provisions. Since the mid-1990s, the explicitly stated goal has been to "penetrate the milieus of delinquency" (Leclercq 1995), or, in the inflammatory words of the then interior minister, Nicolas Sarkozy, to "power-wash" (*nettoyer au Kärcher*) the "scum" (*racaille*) from the streets.[20] By the time of the 2005 urban uprising, it would not be much of an exaggeration to claim that the primary representative of the French state that a young French man or woman living in a *quartier populaire* was likely to encounter on a daily basis was a police agent.

On the other hand, since the late 1980s, the same governments have responded to the "crisis" of the *cités* through a series of urban renewal plans—leading to the creation of a complex network of national commissions, urbanization laws, educational priority zones (ZEP), and funding programs—designed to reintegrate the neighborhoods in question into national and global economies and transform their inhabitants into productive citizens. These plans reached perhaps their most elaborate form in the conservative prime minister Alain Juppé's 1995/6 "Marshall Plan" (which included the "National Urban Integration Plan" and the "Urban Revival Pact").[21] With the goal of luring young residents from the street economy into the formal economy, the plan delimited hundreds of "sensitive urban zones" (*zones urbaines sensibles*) in which local cultural associations and other nonprofit organizations would receive state subsidies to hire young residents to work in paid internships. At the same time, the plans established a number of "enterprise zones" (*zones franches*) in especially "hot areas" (*quartiers chauds*) throughout the country in order to provide tax incentives to encourage the return of commercial ventures scared away by the rise in suburban violence. As such, like the original Marshall Plan, designed to reconstruct Europe after the end of World War II, Juppé's plan depended on an insertion of capital into de-capitalized areas, though this time, with a neoliberal twist, with local associations and multinational corporations acting as the prime agents of change. Unfortunately, the various austerity measures that have been pursued as a result of France's membership of the European Monetary Union and more recent financial crises have torpedoed these plans of state investment and urban renewal.

One of the consistent features of the variety of urban revitalization projects is the construction of social centers and sports facilities (see Chantelat et al. 1996). Renovated housing projects include central courtyards with football fields and basketball courts, as well as indoor gymnasiums and boxing rings. Various *banlieue* investment programs have targeted the building of sports infrastructures, seeing in them not only a means to prevent violence, delinquency, and drug abuse, but also to defuse the sectarianism and jihadist tendencies pundits fear are spreading among French men and women of color, and Muslim-French residents of the *quartiers populaires* in particular. Such plans have treated sport as a "privileged remedy for contemporary social dysfunction" (Sakhoui 1996: 81), as a means to transform *cité* youth into moral French subjects defined by secular attitudes, a sense of fair play, and a strong work ethic—much as colonial physical education was used to "civilize" indigenous subjects (Gasparini 2008).[22] However, in a postcolonial context of fiscal austerity, the "integrating mission" has operated via the private sector, with the French state soliciting sponsorship for their urban and social renewal programs from Nike, Adidas, Coca-Cola, and other multinational companies.

This recolonization of the *banlieues* by state security and corporate capital has brought forth a number of responses from residents. In particular, the multiracial youth of the *cités* has developed multiple forms of embodied practice to literally take back the streets and claim ownership over the modernist spaces increasingly associated with poverty, violence, and the police. The 1983 March for Equality and Against Racism used mobility and street theater as a particular corporeal engagement through which to protest against the murders and deportations of French men and women of color (Hajjat 2013). Subsequent antiracist marches followed over the next two years, alongside public concerts and the formation of neighborhood organizations calling for the physical and cultural rehabilitation of the *cités*. Older residents (*les grands frères*) established themselves as an alternate model of community solidarity, welfare, and self-policing for areas that public resources had all but abandoned or left to the depredations of corporate profit-making and private security firms (Duret 1996).

As I will discuss in the next chapter, young residents of color developed aesthetic practices to appropriate and domesticate the housing projects and transform them into spaces for freedom and self-expression. Novels and films written throughout the 1980s and 1990s generally depicted the housing projects as sites of isolation and incarceration, with young characters feeling trapped by unemployment, concrete architecture, and the invisible walls of racism and classism that separated the *banlieues* from the city center (see Hargreaves 1997; Hargreaves & McKinney 1997; Rosello 1998; Silverstein 2004a: 184–212). Their ritual moments of evasion, flight, or "letting go" (*laisser-aller*) are inevitably interrupted by parents or police who violently return them to the *banlieue's* striated precincts (see Begag 1989; Charef 1983). More recently, *banlieue* cultural producers have adopted what Robin D.G. Kelley (1996: 136) calls a "ghettocentric" perspective, placing the *cités* and other neighborhoods at the center of their imaginary worlds. This is certainly the case in rap lyrics, as will be detailed in the next chapter. But, more generally, residents have developed local speech idioms, naming practices, and dress styles that distinguish themselves from those living in neighboring housing projects. They have transformed the negative spaces of modernist architecture—cellars, garages, concrete courtyards, and so on—into places of play and leisure. They have marked these and other *banlieue* locales with graffiti and tags, creatively destroying them with "bombs" of spray paint.[23] Indeed, a number of parkour practitioners first developed their climbing and evasion skills as graffiti artists.

Hip-hop thus prefigures parkour's imagery of mobile urban samurais, as well as the tension between free artistry and its inevitable commercialization. The exaggerated scenes of violence and calls for insurrection that featured in some hardcore rap of the late 1990s and early 2000s (Hélénon 1998; Silverstein 2002b)—much like the suburban dystopia of *Banlieue 13*—may be hyperbolic, but they do sell well and reflect the periodic conflicts between local youths and the various state security forces that have progressively occupied the *cités*. Actual violence has followed the same structural logic of mobility and containment, with repeated instances of parkour-like scenes of police chasing young men either on foot or on motorbikes across the urban landscape (Bloom 2009). The tragic endings of a number of such chases have often been the sparks that set off the so-called "riots" mentioned above. In these violent uprisings, mobile groups of young men, armed with the homemade weaponry of baseball bats or Molotov cocktails, target the very modern symbols of their perceived incarceration, including police stations, security-patrolled supermarkets, and their wealthier neighbors' automobiles.

As Kristen Ross (1995) has shown, cars were a central trope for French late colonial and postcolonial modernity, metaphorizing the mobility, freedom, and prosperity promised by the postwar republics, but also the risks of *surmodernité*. For critics and artists like Godard and Tati, automobiles simultaneously signaled the revolt of the younger generation and new social pathologies of anomie.[24] Insofar as most youth of the *cités* have no means to own or access cars, they also become an index of their exclusion from full, active participation in the urbane life of French citizenship. Parkour, in its rejection of consumerist technology and celebration of self-mobility, proposes a more embodied form of social belonging in closer relationship with the built and natural environments. But likewise, in a manner that might ring true to Hébert, in moments of confrontation, young *cité* men also consistently torch the municipal gymnasiums built as part of the urban renewal projects of the last several decades.[25] When interviewed after these incidents, participants attest to the ludic quality of setting fires or confronting the police, but also justify their actions in the name of defending their homes and their families from outsiders. The very state institutions of postcolonial integration have become for them instruments of exclusion and the perpetuation of durable inequality.

PARKOUR AS OCCUPATION

Traceurs, by contrast, may creatively and radically appropriate and domesticate the modernist built forms of the *cités*, but they do not destroy them in the process. Like *dérive* drifters and hip-hop graffiti artists, they develop intimate, embodied knowledge of particular locales, and the routes they trace through these three-dimensional urban territories establish a sense of homely belonging through a mobility otherwise denied them. They explicitly reject rules and ignore "keep out" signs,[26] but they do not engage in any direct resistance of the state— David Belle, after all, trained as a *sapeur-pompier* just like his father, more inclined to put out fires than start them. They trace not only new urban cartographies but postcolonial lines of genealogical descent back through Raymond Belle to Georges Hébert and his colonial program of self-discipline, masculinization, and racial regeneration. Families of the original *traceurs* hailed from across the former French colonial world, including notably West Africa and Vietnam. If the group name Yamakasi derives from the Congolese Lingala word for "strong spirit," it also evokes the Asian martial arts (and particularly the films of Jackie Chan) that they consumed as children.[27] Theirs is a post-Bandung expression of Afro-Asian unity, but one explicitly seeking to morally revive France from within by modeling an intimate, corporeal connection between French men and women of color and their spatial environments. As in the conclusion to *Banlieue 13: Ultimatum*, parkour inverts the modernist urban problem: instead of the French state needing to solve its "*banlieue* crisis*,*" it is the multiracial *cités* which will save France from its corporate-*cum*-security self.

But such grassroots projections of postcolonial unity are tenuous at best. If David Belle seeks the freedom and masculinity denied by the spatial isolation, concrete containment, and racialized policing of the *quartiers populaires*, he does so through a self-consciously ascetic lifestyle and close cleaving to the basic movements of Hébertism. He explicitly polices parkour from the various acrobatic flourishes other *traceurs* have developed across the globe, has codified its movements, and is working to integrate parkour as a recognized sub-discipline of the sport of gymnastics. As a mode of urban practice, parkour for him is a utilitarian modality of efficient movement through space; his urban imaginary runs along straight, albeit unexpected, lines. While in interviews he underlines his philosophical inheritance of Hébert and Debord's critique of consumerism and the "society as spectacle" (Debord 1994), this does not stop him from wanting to "get paid." He has parlayed his participation in various Besson productions into an acting, choreography, and stunt career. While, like Zidane, he generally eschews the public spotlight and seems to prefer the comfort of family and friends in Lisses, his athletic accomplishments and backstory have made him a global brand.

In contrast to Belle's disciplining of parkour, Sébastien Foucan and other former members of the Yamakasi group have cultivated the creative elements of parkour and embraced all the acrobatic tricks that characterize today's skateboarding and rollerblading. They readily incorporate elements from capoeira and other martial arts. Their imagined space is decidedly more curvaceous and individualized, ideally escaping any effort by the state or its citizens to police it. Indeed, Foucan, born in Paris to parents from Guadeloupe, has developed parkour practice into a global sport of "freerunning," with gym classes, retail sportswear, and public performances. Like a neoliberal *bricoleur*, he has entrepreneurially fashioned an occupation out of his embodied skill set and has welcomed the celebrity status he has gained, competing in the British reality show *Dancing on Ice*, and launching a clothing line in the UK. For Foucan, parkour definitely pays.

In these ways, parkour, as simultaneously global spectacle and disciplined movement of racial engagement and national regeneration, actualizes the socio-spatial tensions of late-capitalist postcolonial France. While many French men and women of color have achieved professional success through education and career mobility (see Beaman

2017), for many others growing up in the *quartiers populaires*, those normative lines of social mobility are either blocked or require a level of personal sacrifice unlikely or impossible given their family or living situation. And even those who have entered the professional ranks still have to continually perform Frenchness as an embodied quality of self-presentation, all under the suspicious and anxious racializing gaze of a white public. Navigating this racial and class landscape and building a flourishing life in the context of socioeconomic precarity require equal measures of discipline and creativity. Parkour, in its different guises, corporeally models precisely this struggle. In tracing places, it calls forth a postcolonial France that begins in the *cités* and points to cosmopolitan worlds well beyond national borders.

7

Hip-Hop Nations

On November 24, 2005, the French justice minister Pascal Clément opened an investigation into seven rap groups accused of promoting "incivility, even terrorism," among France's "uprooted, de-cultured youth." Clément's action responded to a petition, initiated by Gaullist deputy François Grosdidier and signed by nearly a quarter of the French Parliament, which came in the immediate aftermath of three weeks of violent confrontations between young residents of suburban *cités* or *quartiers populaires* and the French police, during which 10,000 cars were burned and some 4,800 young men arrested in 280 municipalities across the country (see Silverstein & Tetreault 2006). The rappers cited in the petition were a motley collection of multiracial, hardcore artists, whose offending lyrics Grosdidier had unsystematically collected from the internet with the help of his son. They included some artists (113 and Monsieur R) who were popular stars, others (Smala and Salif) who were less well known, and several (Fabe, Lunatic, and Ministère AMER) who had not performed for ten years or more.[1] What united them, according to Grosdidier, was their endorsement of "antiwhite racism" and "hatred for France" (Kessous 2005).

While the petition was clearly an effort to identify scapegoats for the recent *banlieue* violence—with immigrant polygamy also cited as to blame—the prosecution of French rap artists was not particularly new. Indeed, Ministère AMER had already been found guilty of "provocation to murder" in 1997 for their song "Sacrifice de poulets."[2] Monsieur R (Richard Makela) was at the time of the petition preparing for a civil case of pornography initiated by Gaullist deputy Daniel Mach against the song "FranSSe"—which includes a rape fantasy in which France is presented as a "slut" (*grace*) who should be "screwed to exhaustion," and whose music video includes images of sex acts performed with the French flag by two naked white women called "les Gauloises."[3] Earlier criminal cases had been brought in 1996 against the pioneer hardcore duo Suprême NTM,[4] in 2002 against Hamé (Mohamed Bourokba) of the group La Rumeur,[5] and in 2004 against the mega-popular trio Sniper,[6] all for some version of public abuse, defamation, or incitement to violence against the national police. Their recordings have further been subject to periodic bans from the national airwaves, and, in a number of instances, scheduled concerts have been cancelled by conservative mayors. As in the case of Dieudonné, their words are deemed to endanger the fragile postcolonial French Republic.

What is particularly interesting about Grosdidier's petition, then, is less the threatened prosecution of the artists in question, nor even the implication that their verbal violence abetted physical violence. Rather, it is its explicit racialization of the conflict through its accusation of "antiwhite racism" leveled at the rap artists. In so doing, the petition deployed a language and ethic of antiracism to fight against rappers whose very political project is self-consciously antiracist, namely, to articulate the racial discrimination and institutional exclusion experienced by French men and women of color living in the *cités*. This occupation of a racialized moral high ground dovetailed with the larger law-and-order attitude of the minister of the interior, Nicolas Sarkozy, who in 2003 threatened to prosecute Sniper on similar grounds, declaring their lyrics to be racist and anti-Semitic.[7] Sarkozy subsequently appointed Grosdidier as his party's national secretary for integration, praising the latter for his work in "breaking taboos around the antiwhite racism of certain rappers" (Kessous 2006).

The appropriation of antiracist discourse by the French political establishment represents a significant shift in the ideological landscape in which race and space have become the grounds on which the future of postcolonial France is contested. On the one hand, the move parallels an earlier tactic by Jean-Marie Le Pen, who in the 1980s redeployed the tentative multiculturalist vision of a "right to difference" (*droit à la différence*) within a "plural France," as put forth by the Socialist Party and its client antiracist organization SOS-Racisme (Désir 1985; Parti Socialiste 1981), to argue against integration and assimilation policies as injurious to immigrant (not to mention French) sacrosanct identity, and thus morally repugnant (Balibar 1991; Gallissot 1985; Taguieff 1991; see also Hargreaves 1995: 194–97). The resulting reversion of antiracist organizations to a universalist discourse of a "right to resemblance" (*droit à la ressemblance*) within a putatively race-less France of individual citizens created the ideological trap sprung by Sarkozy and Grosdidier, according to which any discussion of discrimination *qua* racial discrimination is suspected of abetting sectarian communalism, if not racial hatred.[8] Arguably, this tactic of ideological appropriation, alongside the growing security discourse and blame-the-victim orientation of Islamophobic moral panics around French postcoloniality, represents yet another example of the growing acceptance of Le Pen's ideals by the French political mainstream—of the already remarked upon *lépenisation des esprits*, or "Le Pen-ization of the soul" (see Le Goaziou and Mucchielli 2006: 155).

On the other hand, the very use of a racialized language of whiteness in the petition followed Sarkozy's larger policy shift to an American model of social management that combined elements of affirmative action (*discrimination positive*), neoliberal privatization, and neoconservative policies of domestic security. His creation of the French Council of the Muslim Faith (CFCM) and later appointment of a number of Muslim-French government officials like Rachida Dati and the novelist/sociologist Azouz Begag as delegate minister for the promotion of equality indicated a partial shift in governmentality from the treatment of the French polity as an undifferentiated group of commensurate citizens, to its management as a set of incommensurate, or even conflicting, communities. The denunciation of rappers (implicitly of color) as engaged in "antiwhite racism" tentatively projected the French nation as a congeries of racialized political actors, in partial violation of the secular republican model of undifferentiated citizenship.

In what follows, I explore how French hardcore (or "gangsta") rap artists in the first decade of the twenty-first century, in the period around the 2005 *banlieue* uprisings, negotiated this shifting political and ideological landscape of race, and how they put their dangerous words to work in a project of postcolonial sociopolitical change.[9] Drawing on a "ghettocentric" (Kelley 1996) imaginary of local *cité* (or *téci*) belonging, via images largely appropriated from African-American popular culture, these artists project both a micro-local identity and a transnational solidarity across "ghetto" spaces that simultaneously racializes suburban (or *banlieue*) space and spatializes French racial otherness for their multiracial and multiethnic listening publics who cannot be easily reduced to a bipolarity of blackness and whiteness.

From this ghettocentric subject position, rap artists engage in a vehement denunciation of the extant conditions of the social and economic exclusion of the *banlieue* housing projects, deploying lyrical, often sexualized, violence as political critique.[10] In the context of a history of violent confrontations with the police and the progressive securitization of the *banlieues*, and in a situation of ongoing marginalization from the formal political realm, the violence of words and deeds must be understood as an effort of direct political engagement, and becomes often allied with activist projects of social change in which rap artists themselves become directly involved. As Sadri Khiari, the co-founder of the Party of the Indigènes of the Republic (PIR), has written, "rap is nothing less than the sign of the dynamism of resistance of the *quartiers* [*populaires*]; it constitutes still today one of the principal medias through which a strongly decolonial cultural and political tie is formed, among new generations, notably *indigènes*" (Khiari 2009: 117).

In this sense, the *caillera*—the "social bandit" operating outside of the law (see Hobsbawm 1959, 2000)—emerges as a recurrent proto-political figure that hardcore rappers ambivalently avow and disavow, often identifying with it allegorically (if not autobiographically) while bemoaning it as ultimately ineffective in promoting lasting social change.[11] It is precisely this racialized, sexualized, and violently independent subject— literally, the *racaille* whom Sarkozy claimed that he was going to "power-wash" (*nettoyer au Kärcher*) from the streets of France during the early days of the 2005 confrontations—who constitutes the abject of secular republican fantasies of race-less citizenship, the constitutive outside for a postcolonial French nation.

But the *caillera* is not the only postcolonial subject politicizing the *banlieue*. In this chapter, I contrast gangsta representations of hyper-masculine "ghetto patrimony" to a different musical dimension of the postcolonial *banlieues*: an emergent Islamic hip-hop project that has emphasized love and hope over hatred and despair, and that has sought to cultivate flowers of peace in the harsh concrete of the *banlieue* "ghetto." In contradistinction to many hardcore rappers of the 1990s and early 2000s, pious Muslim hip-hop artists have grounded their sense of identification not only in the hyper-localized settings of the *cités* but also in transnational geographies of Islamic humanism. In exploring how these ambivalent identifications are negotiated by gangsta and Sufi rappers with different thematizations of love and hate, peace and violence, I detail how postcolonial space is sonically racialized, and how race is lyrically spatialized in the *cités*. The result, I argue, is a broader political project to structurally reconfigure the *banlieue* into an embodied Islamic environment mediated by word and sound-image, by social engagement and collective organization.

GHETTO PATRIMONY

The contemporary constitution of the French *banlieue* as a site for post-colonial hip-hop interventions and Islamic cultural production has required the appropriation over the past several decades of a racialized space explicitly established to "integrate" French men and women of color and eliminate the cultural practices, social solidarities, and religious publics deemed incompatible with *laïcité*. As I have discussed, aspirations of social mobility have proven to be little more than utopian for many of those who have grown up in the housing projects. Unemployment and relative socio-spatial isolation have produced a sense of collective hardship (*galère*) and disenfranchisement. Quotidian police stops combined with periodic confrontations between young residents and the police have augmented a sentiment of low-intensity "hate" (*la haine*) for the French "system" as a whole. This drab built environment creates an aura of audiovisual banality that is repeatedly thematized in fiction and songs authored by *banlieue* residents. The gray concrete (*béton*) comes to symbolize a life of immobility and repetition, generally contrasted with an imagined elsewhere of bourgeois pleasure or their parents' homelands (see Charef 1983; Kettane 1985: 36–38).[12]

In addition to the gray-market economic ventures, grassroots social service, and insurgent architectural modifications discussed in the last chapter, residents embellish the discordant *cité* soundscape of traffic, car alarms, construction, and vocal arguments—an acoustic environment faithfully recorded in Jean-Luc Goddard's avant-garde film *Deux ou trois choses que je sais d'elle/Two or Three Things I Know About Her* (1967)—with recorded or improvised musical forms of different genres played from portable stereos for small groups of listeners or, on occasion, blasted from apartment windows for all to hear. For those youths of color often excluded from private nightclubs, courtyards, entryways, and basement venues become privileged spaces for building a social life mediated through sound.

Hip-hop in particular has been a salient musical form for particularly young men (and some young women)—as both producers and listeners—to comment on life in the *cités* and re-spatialize the *banlieue* as a site for collective action and individual fulfillment.[13] If the French state has contributed to the development of the French hip-hop industry through quotas on radio airplay promoting Francophone musical production, and if record labels have commoditized images of violence and sentiments of "hate" for their own profit (Silverstein 2002b), hip-hop artists and their listeners have nonetheless constituted a counterpublic for commentary and critique on postcolonial France.

By and large, hip-hop artists embrace the entrepreneurialism of their ghettocentric musical ventures through the adoption of figures of street lore: pimps, drug dealers, and other economic opportunists operating on the margins of legality. In general, the *caillera* persona has come to dominate the self-presentation of many male rappers, through their autobiographical boasts, their dress, their gang-style poses and gestures, and the images and sounds of violence in their songs, videos, and cover art. A case in point is the group 113.[14] The group has serially represented itself in song as a gang of "marginal" figures "outside the law,"[15] as "fugitives ... presumed to be dangerous,"[16] and as "street niggaz (*négros*), *ruff* in spirit and 100 percent insubordinate (*insoumis*)."[17]

This situational alliance with the "street" and its boastful claims of thug life are supplemented by rap artists' ghettocentric orientation in their self-organization and symbolic economy, and by their emphasis on local postcolonial identification and action that transcend intervening diacritics of race, ethnicity, and religion. As the artist Lunatic avowed, "If I rap, it's one for the street, two and three for the cash."[18] Rappers thus engage in what Michel de Certeau has termed "spatializing practices" (de Certeau 1984: 96), constructing alternate social totalities and subjectivities on the embers of built and dilapidated *banlieue* forms, endowing them with separate frameworks of value and hierarchy than those projected by the integration projects of the French nation-state (see Castells 1983: 73–96). For de Certeau, such forms of appropriation amount to contemporary equivalents of "poaching," with rap artists making a living through the reinvention and re-aestheticization of everyday *cité* life—living, as de Certeau would have it, "on the property of others" (de Certeau 1984: xii).

Elsewhere I have discussed the rappers' re-aestheticization of everyday *cité* life in terms of the organization of posses, graffiti tags, and the use of local imagery and identifiable figures in song lyrics, shout-outs, and album cover art (see Silverstein 2002b). In this chapter, what I am interested in is the rappers' invocation of a common *banlieue* culture or *patrimoine du ghetto* which supplements (and in some cases replaces) racial, ethnic, or national identification. This transcendent "ghetto heritage" is largely expressed through a gendered kinship idiom in which their age-mates (regardless of cultural or religious commonality) are addressed as classificatory "brothers" (*frères* or *reufs*) and "sisters" (*soeurs* or *sistas*), and the larger community—whether a particular housing project, or the entirety of postcolonial France—as their "family" (*famille* or *mi-fa*) or "clan." The fraternity they invoke through this idiom is explicitly contrasted with the *fraternité* of the French national triptych, which they depict as racist and hypocritical. As La Clinique rapped in 1998, "That is France: liberty to shut up and be deported (*fermer sa gueule et prendre son charter*). Equality for whom? My fraternity starts with my brothers."[19]

In these ways, the invocation of familial belonging and community solidarity proposes local patriotism at various scales of inclusivity in the place of national identity. The group 113 refers to Vitry-sur-Seine as "my nation" (*ma patrie*),[20] and Assassin famously claimed, "My only nation is my posse ... The flag of unity is planted in the 18th".[21] At the same time, rap artists seek to transcend hyper-local identifications of race or space and envision a mode of ghettocentricity in which different living experiences in the *quartiers populaires* are treated as commensurate and the basis for a unity of struggle. In collaborations between artists from different regions they shout out to their different constituencies, implicitly calling for a transcendence of their differences. As Sniper rapped in their controversial song, "La France":

> In all the *cités*, we stand together
> When we get kicked in the balls, we stand together
> Negroes (*négros*) and wogs (*bougnoules*), we stand together.[22]

Ghetto patrimony thus calls forth a form of pan-*quartier* solidarity to confront racial discrimination, police harassment, and state violence— themes repeatedly invoked in gangsta rap much as they are in so-called "*banlieue* cinema." Hardcore rappers both memorialize the victims of police violence and imagine violent retribution. The language of hate, violence, and revenge pervades the work of many commercially successful *banlieue*-based hardcore groups including Assassin, Diam's (*sic*), Ministère AMER, Sniper, and Suprême NTM, among others, who dream of "sacrificing" police officers, "exterminating" politicians, and "setting fire" to the government buildings in which they work.[23]

This imagined violence is often sexualized. On a number of hardcore rap tracks, France is feminized either as a fickle lover, a bad mother, or a whore who should be "screwed."[24] Similarly, Sinistre metaphorizes France through the nationalist imagery of "Marianne," but instead of deploying her as a symbol of radical egalitarianism, she is represented as an icon of hypocrisy and racism.[25] Sinistre wonders:

> Does she really love me? ...
> Is it worth it that she loves me? ...
> Does France love me?
> In spite of me and my housing project?

By the end of the track Sinistre decides that the expressed "love" is only material, good only for sexual gain.

The reduction of love to violence and the embrace of hate in some ghettocentric rap is often allied with calls for revolution in hip-hop discourse. In tracks produced after the *banlieue* revolts of 2005, the young men on the street are generally portrayed as "insurgents",[26] if not "revolutionaries",[27] even if their "pyromania" is regretted as ultimately self-destructive.[28] Hip-hop visions of an uprising starting on suburban mean streets are clearly sensationalized for commercial effect, if criminally prosecuted as explicit incitements to violence. Nonetheless, politically engaged rap artists, like activists such as the PIR, generally have approached violence not as a frivolous expression of a generation of youth in revolt, but as part of a larger, embedded structure of historical marginalization and decolonizing resistance.

ISLAMIC SPACES, ISLAMIC SOUNDS

Gangsta rap, however, is not the only genre of hip-hop, and hyper-masculine violence is not the only response to the experience of degradation and discrimination in the French *quartiers populaires.* Indeed, "peace, love, unity, and having fun" have been persistent themes in international hip-hop from Afrika Bambaataa's pioneering compositions of the early 1980s through the "conscious rap" of KRS-One and others.[29] If, for French hardcore rappers, such ideas tend to be more generally broached in nostalgic invocations of earlier, easier times,[30] for others, they remain salient as an ethical model of self-cultivation and political action. In particular, over the past decade, a vibrant Islamic hip-hop scene has also emerged alongside, and sometimes overlapping with, the hardcore rap described above, deploying a broader critique of the post-colonial French state's racism and hypocrisy toward the imagination of a world of solidarity premised on "love" rather than "hate."

As with other ghettocentric productions, Islamic social worlds in the *quartiers populaires* have historically emerged through a similar process of spatial appropriation and insurgent urbanism. As discussed in Chapter 2, until recently the direction of Islamic life in France—including the management of mosques, the organization of communal celebrations, Qur'anic education, the certification of halal butchers, and the administration of Islamic cemeteries—has largely been under the control of various immigrant cultural agencies operated by North African, Middle Eastern, and West African states (Laurence 2012). While there are today over 2,000 recognized mosques in France, including over 100 establishments with dedicated buildings in the Paris region, the creation of independent spaces for public religious practice is still often an uphill battle. Even those mosques that are eventually constructed are, as we have seen, subject to strict municipal regulation, limiting their size, their architectural form (with only ten minarets authorized throughout France), and their function. Calls to prayer broadcast outside the mosque are prohibited, as they are in much of the world where non-Muslims are in the majority. Although the more popular mosques cannot accommodate the number of worshippers wishing to join in with Friday midday prayers or Ramadan, recent municipal regulations forbid prayer spilling over into public streets or squares.

To fill the demand, thousands of prayer rooms in store fronts or in the basements of public housing buildings—both officially recognized and underground—have been established throughout France, the fruits of protracted efforts since the 1980s by local Islamic associations, charitable organizations, and neighborhood groups to provide alternative resources for self-education and spaces for public expressions of piety (see Kepel 1987: 229–42). These often double as sites for community discussion, private religious education, collective celebration, or simply spaces for (mostly) men to relax and meditate in the transition from work or school to home. Some of these associations and prayer spaces have become rallying points for a variety of Salafi and other reformist Islamist movements, but their ideological orientations depend largely on local communities and the availability of religious scholars to direct them. A number of *banlieue* residents have further joined evangelical groups like the Tablighi Jamaat, an international movement founded in India in the 1920s that engages in missionary *da'wa* (invitation).

As we have seen, such developments of Islamic counterpublics have prompted repeated moral panics over the feared existence of a transnational jihad linking Muslim-French citizens in the *cités* to Afghanistan, Iraq, Syria, and beyond—panics that have led to heavy surveillance, policing, and the imposition of legal regulations on Islamic expression and practice. While state attempts to create a "French Islam" (*Islam de France*) around the CFCM and the Islamic Cultures Institute (ICI) have artificially privileged certain foreign-trained male actors and excluded local pious women (Davidson 2012; Fernando 2014), they have in the meantime given voice to a rising number of Sufi orders (*tariqat*) like the 'Alawiyya and Boutshishiyya discussed in Chapter 1, groups seen by French state officials as less threatening.

Sufism has long been a central site of state interest and knowledge production in France, with early translations, commentaries, and studies of Sufi texts going back to the seventeenth century. Interest continued in the colonial era, with colonial officers surveilling North and West African Sufi lodges (*zawaya*) as potential vectors of resistance while simultaneously promoting rural, "popular" religious practices as more pliable than urban Islamic institutions and as a counterweight to the Islamic reformism of the nationalist movements. Meanwhile, twentieth-century intellectuals like René Guenon embraced the esoteric and quietist dimensions of Sufism, assimilating them into a universalist theology or "sacred science" (see Sedgwick 2004). In general, Sufism has appeared more compatible with *laïcité* because of its inward-looking spirituality, its emphasis on the personal and emotional rather than the public and political. Among Muslims in France, Sufism has been historically prominent as a parallel mode of social organization, particularly uniting West African Muslims on both sides of the Mediterranean through material and spiritual exchanges fostered by the Tijaniyya, Muridiyya, and Gnawa orders (Kane 2008; Kapchan 2007; Salzbrunn 2002). Since 1990, France has further become an important node in a transnational Sufi revival, particularly through the Lebanese al-Ahbash, the Turkish Gülen, the Algerian 'Alawiyya, and the Moroccan Boutshishiyya movements, which have taken on expanded political roles in their respective home countries, and have increasingly devoted explicit attention to the Muslim diaspora in Europe (see Skali 1999: 18).[31] These anti-extremist groups have a strong educational mission, have published a number of Islamic references in French, and have a widespread online and physical presence across the French urban and suburban landscape.[32] They promote music and the arts as tools of devotion and community building, and specifically recruit among artistic and cultural producers in France.

Increasingly, these Sufi groups have allied with the French state to promote a "French Islam" that is politically moderate and explicitly avows an ideology of "living together" (*vivre ensemble*) across ethnic, racial, and religious borders. In 2006, the Paris municipality worked with Moroccan ethnomusicologist Faouzi Skali of the Boutshishiyya movement to create the ICI, a public center for artistic exhibitions and musical events. The ICI secured €22 million in funding from Paris mayor Bertrand Delanoé to build two state-of-the-art, glass-and-steel facilities, all in support of the "spread of a modern, secular Islam."[33] It is located just blocks away from the French storefront headquarters of the Association of Islamic Charitable Projects (AICP), the international outreach arm of the al-Ahbash movement that likewise deploys musical education to "preach moderation."[34]

If the ICI represents a concrete manifestation of a Sufi revival in the heart of Paris, the spatial imaginary of French Sufi adepts extends into the *banlieue* peripheries as well. On the one hand, Sufi mysticism, as it has been primarily practiced in France as an interiorized, individualized pursuit, is arguably less dependent on the establishment of a purified (*halal*) physical environment than other Islamic traditions or movements. If worshipers do regularly gather for collective meditation (*dhikr*) or in celebration of holidays, they can adapt any number of spaces for the purposes, from municipal community centers to storefront association locales to an adept's private apartment. What sanctifies these spaces are the words and music of devotion, the sounds of divine love expressed in human form (see Kapchan 2009).

On the other hand, Sufis remain attuned to the socio-spatial worlds adepts inhabit. Indeed, opening one's heart to divine grace involves learning to truly see and listen to one's surroundings, to perceive deeper structures beyond superficial appearances. For French men and women of color, whether born Muslims or not, Sufism provides a way to think out of the racializing constraints of Islamophobia and *laïcité*, connecting them to adepts across the globe. For the number of hip-hop artists who have begun to follow the Sufi path, this also means taking a step back and reassessing their fetishized relationship to the cruel authenticity of the *cité* street. In so doing, they conjoin their invocation of divine "love" (*mahabba*) with an articulation of a "ghetto patrimony" that is neither sectarian and violent, nor deterministic of their identity or future aspirations.

SUFI RAP

Perhaps the most publicly recognized French hip-hop artist to embrace Sufism is the rapper, spoken-word poet, and author Abd al Malik.[35] Born in 1975 as Régis Fayette-Mikano to Catholic Congolese parents, Malik grew up in a rough public housing project in the Neuhof suburb of Strasbourg. As he explains in his autobiography, *Qu'Allah bénisse la France* ("God bless France") (Malik 2004), subsequently turned into a feature-length film, he lived a double life as a pickpocket and drug dealer, on the one hand, and a brilliant student of philosophy and literature, on the other.[36] Following his brother's lead, he converted to Islam as a teenager and started rapping as part of the group New African Poets (NAP), made up of other Neuhof youth. After an extended period devoted to *da'wa* with the Tablighi Jamaat, Malik broke with the evangelical movement and flirted with Salafi revivalism, before finally finding his path among the Boutshishiyya, devouring Skali's writings and pledging himself a disciple to the order's then Morocco-based leader Sidi Hamza in 1999. Since then, Malik has embarked on a solo career with five successful albums of spoken-word poetry, three published books, and one film to date.[37] In addition to numerous musical and literary prizes, Malik was decorated as a knight (*chevalier*) of the arts and letters by the French Ministry of Culture in 2008, and has been named the official patron of the ICI.

Malik charts a complicated route between avowals of authenticity and co-optation by state institutions, setting himself up as a liminal figure capable of presenting street aspirations in palatable form to a mainstream French audience, while also translating the positive values embedded within French liberal values to *cité* youth and other French men and women of color inclined, for good reasons, to distrust them. Malik's written and sung texts present a didactic tale of religious conversion from the outside in, from the violent words shouted on the street to a state of inner peace and harmony, from hate to love. If NAP's first album, *La racaille sorte 1 disque* ("The gangsta releases a record"), relied on harsh gangsta rap sounds and equally raw themes of life on the streets,[38] their next, *A l'intérieur de nous* ("Within us"), featured Middle Eastern ornamentation and soft R&B harmonies sung by Malik's wife Wallen (Nawel Azzouz).[39] Instead of the scenes of urban decay featured on most hardcore French rap albums, the cover art depicts an interior space, with the three rappers' chest cavities revealed in an x-ray, and an Islamic star and crescent superimposed over Malik's heart. Malik's first solo album confirms this spatialized thematization of love, borrowing the title, *La face à face des coeurs* ("Heart to heart"), from Skali's treatise on Sufism (Skali 1999) and featuring a cover photo of Malik revealing his heart behind his jacket and tie.[40] Commenting on this trajectory, Malik later wrote:

> In spite of the celebrity that [our first] album brought us [i.e. NAP], our failure was already certain … We had always tried to prove that we were the purest, the deepest … In music as in life, the point is not to transcribe a mentality or a moment, but to simply translate the language of the heart. (Malik 2004: 175)

In his autobiography, Malik narrates his upbringing in the *cités* of Neuhof and later the Parisian suburb of Plessis-Robinson as an internalization, but ultimately rejection, of a sense of "desolation" and "internal misery" (ibid.: 81). He describes in stark terms the harsh socio-spatial environment of the *quartiers populaires* characterized by social precarity, unemployment, delinquency, and "real and exaggerated (*fantasmée*) insecurity" (ibid.: 14–15), but also underlines the vibrant family and communal life there, the moments of joy and togetherness across lines of race and ethnicity—a true "multicultural mosaic" (ibid.: 14). In a later book that is a plea for urban peace—in English translation it is titled "The *banlieue* war will not occur"—Malik summarizes these reflections with an imagined dictionary entry for "*cité*":

> A lie. A promise of a better future for the most deprived, but which has turned into a nightmare, into a ghetto. A compost heap (*terreau*) of urban anger. And, although a real *joie de vivre* can prevail, its inhabitants often suffer from the weight of a destiny that seems insurmountable, as if they were all living in an open-air prison. (Malik 2010: 41–42)

Ultimately, for Malik, the true tragedy for many young French men and women of color is that one's ghetto patrimony is taken as spatial predestination, that the drabness of housing-project architecture determines a featureless life: "The drama of the *cité* is determinism, the belief in an inescapable destiny" (Malik 2004: 81). Internalized, such a foreboding is transformed into paralyzing anger:

> Fear, rage cloistered me in hate,
> Sowed this seed, brought forth misfortune.
> So many ups and downs, enabled by rancor,
> And hate multiplies, I am its prisoner.
> Bit by bit we see that this only leads to pain.[41]

The challenge, for Malik, under these conditions, is to recognize the poetry of life and find one's solace in an interior space of divine peace:

> One should be careful when one uses words,
> The speech of the people the language of the street,
> Because from beauty can flow absolute ugliness.
> In trying to be of the street one becomes a sewer.[42]

Malik's own lyrics are explicitly poetic, sung over light melodies from French *chanson*, jazz, and pop R&B. Malik likewise encourages his listeners to recognize and cultivate the beauty of life in the *cités*, to reject fatalism and hatred, and to embrace hope and love.

> France is beautiful, you know it's true we love France ...
> France is beautiful; look at all those beautiful faces mixed together,
> That's heavy (*ça c'est du lourd*).
> And when you insult this country, you insult your country,
> In fact, you insult yourself.
> We need to rise up, we need to fight together.[43]

Jeanette Jouili has interpreted Malik's emphasis on interior spiritual revitalization as a "patriotic" upholding of French secular republican values, though one that reimagines the French nation as an "affective community bound by feelings of love" rather than a rational public sphere of dispassionate citizens and stakeholders (Jouili 2013: 72). In a recent work, Malik explicitly avows *laïcité* as a fundamental aspect of French life:

> Religion should no longer be the potential enemy of the Republic but its major ally ... Religion lived in the private sphere, shared, questioned, discovered with others, should become a school for peace

… Our Republic must be strong on this count. Intransigent to all attempts to appropriate or deviate from the sacrosanct rules of *laïcité*. (Malik 2012: 223–24)

But for Malik this is ultimately not simply a matter of state policy, but of self-recognition and personal effort that starts on the streets of the *cité*. In the end, Malik believes the spiritual and communal renewal of France will take place by French men and women of color living in the *quartiers populaires*:

The *banlieue* will perhaps tomorrow become the place for the beginning and the end of the quest of all those who seek lost peace. These areas, which are accused of being at the source of all the evils that bring gangrene to our society, will perhaps be the place where all come in search of salvation. (Malik 2010: 167)

Not all Muslim-French hip-hop artists or activists, of course, share Malik's optimism or avowed love of France or its secular values. Indeed, Malik has been roundly criticized for his patriotism and for his co-optation and deployment by the French state (see Denis 2008). Médine (Médine Zaouiche), a French-Algerian rapper from Le Havre who mixes the strident sounds of hardcore rap with a vehement and didactic lyrical critique of imperialist violence and global Islamophobia, particularly calls him out for failing in rap's ethical duty to resist racializing norms, likening Malik to a "Swiss guard, ostensibly an engaged combatant but who never calls for struggle" (Boniface & Médine 2012: 52). With a shaved head and prominent beard, and often photographed with a raised clenched fist, Médine lionizes Malcolm X and Black Power militancy, calling himself an "Arabian Panther".[44] Where Malik promulgates nondenominational spirituality and interfaith dialogue, Médine underlines his Islamic specificity in his stage name (French for the city of Medina), and in his albums' themes, imagery, and format. For example, Medine releases his music through his production company Din Records (*din* meaning "religion" in Arabic), and the "i" in "Din" and in "Médine" are graphically rendered in the form of a minaret. And unlike Malik, he makes no attempt to translate this piety into the terms of *laïcité*: he leaves religious terminology in its original Arabic, dates his albums according to the Islamic *hejira* calendar, and designs his CD booklets to read from right to left as if they were written in Arabic. He thus ultimately grounds his artistic critique in the broader space–time of Islam.

At the same time, as Jouili (2013) has emphasized, Médine maintains a localized engagement in contemporary postcolonial France. Nearly every song includes references to current events and French figures that his French listeners of color will clearly recognize, and to which they might relate. Médine's consistent pedagogical theme is to encourage his audience to understand their ghetto patrimony as part of a broader structure of power and domination. He has conjoined this didactic effort with his work as one of the founding members of the PIR, on whose behalf he offers concerts. And he has stood side-by-side with Dieudonné and Tariq Ramadan, appreciating their provocation, critique, and self-reflective analyses (Boniface & Médine 2012: 192, 202). For all of this, he has been criticized as a fundamentalist and intolerant reactionary, an enemy of French secular republican values (see Fourest 2015). But his call is as much for interior spiritual renewal as exterior political change. Although his second album is entitled *Jihad*, the subtitle is "the greatest combat is against oneself," thus joining Sufi adepts in referencing the "greater" or "spiritual jihad" (*al-jihad al-akbar, al-jihad al-nafsi*), not military force. On the final track, Médine continues:

> Those who choose the military solution,
> Haven't they seen that they use us more than they help us ...
> For whites, blacks, and those of immigrant heritage,
> My riches are cultural, my combat eternal.
> It's the one within me against my evil self.[45]

Thus it is of little wonder that, despite their differences, Médine and Abd al Malik actually have collaborated, notably on Médine's first album, a multi-artist reflection on the challenge to Muslims everywhere of the September 11 attacks.[46] Over the years Médine has worked on various collective musical-*cum*-political projects with a large number of Muslim (and some non-Muslim) hip-hop performers, including a number associated with hardcore rap like Diam's, Kery James, Monsieur R, Rim-K (of 113), Salif, Sinik, and Sniper. Several of these were converts or reverts to Islam, notably Diam's (Mélanie Georgiades), who converted to Islam in 2008, but also Akhenaton (Philippe Fragione) of IAM and Kool Shen (Bruno Lopes) of Suprême NTM. As discussed earlier, rap collaborations often cross religious lines, with groups like 113 and Sniper including both Christian and Muslim artists. Religiosity, when invoked in lyrics, tends to be framed as a nonsectarian submission to God, and even these particular Islamic themes are presented inclusively and in explicit opposition to France's official discourse of *laïcité* (Molinero 2011; Silverstein 2012; Swedenburg 2015).

Of these various artists, Kery James has been probably the most prominent in conjoining invocations of ghetto patrimony with Islamic humanism.[47] Like Abd al Malik, this self-proclaimed former street thug and hardcore rapper of Guadeloupean descent from the pioneering hip-hop group Idéal J and later Mafia K'1 Fry subsequently converted to Islam and embarked on a solo career dedicated to inner reflection. In 2002, James organized a mega-concert in the Stade de France soccer stadium in suburban Saint-Denis under the theme of "urban peace" and featuring dozens of hardcore groups including 113, Fonky Family, and Sniper, with stark freestyle compositions brought together in explicit invocations of antiracism, solidarity, and inner peace.[48] Two years later he produced a collective album with a similarly diverse group of artists, produced by the al-Ahbash association Savoirs et Tolérance and interspersed with Sufi worship songs sung by the Sufi movement's choral ensemble.[49] The album had the explicit message of "bringing to light Islam's teachings of peace, fraternity, patience in the face of injustice, generosity, and other human qualities".[50] Its sales proceeds were slated to open a Muslim cultural and artistic center in the Parisian *banlieue* of Gennevilliers (see Médioni 2004).

CONCLUSION

Overall, in spite of differences of style and approach, the didactic musical efforts of Abd al Malik, Médine, and Kery James point to new avenues of affiliation, imagination, and critique for Muslim French and other men and women of color, one that conjoins an authentic affirmation of the postcolonial struggles within the *quartiers populaires* with an effort to build an interior space of love and peace that transcends the racialized spatial limitations of the *cités*. Islam provides a rich semiotic code through which to interpret the trials and tribulations of *cités* life. It outlines a framework of belief that allows singers and listeners to contextualize their current struggles within a longer collective history and situate their wanderings along a more consequential personal path toward God. It offers poetry and musical forms that enrich their artistic endeavors and appreciation. In this regard, Islamic sounds and themes supplement the African rhythms and Caribbean reggae motifs within French hip-hop that have long called *banlieue* audiences' attention to ongoing issues of slavery and colonialism, to the continuity of what they call "Babylon." Muslim-French rappers and hip-hop artists broaden *caillera* personae and ghettocentric perspectives appropriated from US gangsta rap. Their efforts thus parallel and are intertwined with the adoption of various Islamic perspectives—including Nation of Islam and Five Percent tendencies, but also mainstream Sunni and Sufi varieties—by a number of African-American hip-hop artists (Aidi 2014). While it is unclear whether the *banlieues* will truly become the site of reconciliation and salvation for postcolonial France as Malik imagines, he and other Islamic rap artists have nonetheless positioned themselves and their audiences of color as agents of change and voices for a future society that is spiritually and politically connected well beyond the strictures of its *banlieue* walls, its secular republican norms, and its Islamophobic anxieties. However, in the process, they have not in any way dulled their critique or pacified their dangerous words. To the contrary, the sharpness of their expression and vehemence of their condemnation—like the burning cars lit by *cité* youth—is what makes those insulated from social and economic precarity take notice, forcing them to confront the institutional racism and Islamophobia that still structures postcolonial France.

Conclusion
Postcolonial Love

In the heat of the 2005 urban uprisings, the footballer Lilian Thuram and then interior minister Nicolas Sarkozy exchanged verbal barbs in a public debate about the causes and conditions of the exclusion felt by young French men and women of color living in the *cités*. Sarkozy had famously written off the unrest to the petty delinquency and violent tendencies of the "*racaille*," essentially the misogynist *garçon arabe* who purportedly refuses to accept liberal and secular republican values. Thuram, who was born in Guadeloupe but grew up in the northwestern Parisian *banlieue* of Bois-Colombes, took the comments personally and suggested that there were deeper, structural roots to young men's sense of alienation. Sarkozy retorted that "liv[ing] in Italy with a [large] salary… [Thuram] certainly has a nostalgic vision of what life was like in the *banlieues* when he lived there" (Lebegue et al. 2005). Conservative presidential candidate Philippe de Villiers, in a subsequent RTL radio interview, similarly dismissed Thuram: "It's always curious to see millionaires give social lessons. Footballers are made for playing football" (cited in Artiaga 2010: 170). Thuram resisted such censorship and continued to give voice to those, like himself, who had grown up suffering from racial discrimination and socioeconomic precarity. During a May 2006 television program, he insisted, "People ask the question: Do the people who live in the *banlieue* love France? Of course they love France."[1] As Laurent Dubois (2010: 239) notes, Thuram then went on to ask whether France loves them.

This book has been very much about French men and women of color like Thuram and those who took over the *cité* streets in 2005, who have refused the path of "exit," as Marwan Muhammad (2017) has termed it (following Hirschman 1970), but can neither easily submit themselves to uncritical "loyalty" and unreciprocated love, and instead have taken "voice" to insist on their say about the future of postcolonial France. Sometimes those voices, like Thuram's, are loud, strong and analytical, and even if dismissed, are at least heard. Sometimes, like Fadela Amara (2006) or Abd al Malik, they speak squarely in the language of *laïcité*, and even when profoundly critical of postcolonial France's failure to live up to its liberal ideals their voices resonate more loudly in the mainstream public sphere. The voices of others, like Tariq Ramadan or

Dieudonné, even when also drawing on French rhetorical and philosophical traditions, can only be heard by the broader (white, bourgeois) public as hate speech, anti-Semitism, or at best double-talk; they nonetheless establish resonant counterpublics that mainstream observers find decidedly threatening. But in many other cases the "voices" of Muslim French and other men and women of color do not articulate in clearly intelligible phrases, but take the form of ambiguous noise, gesture, dress, action, or even silence. Not singing or even hissing during "La Marseillaise," not observing a minute of silence for the victims of the *Charlie Hebdo* attacks, wearing a *hijab* (perhaps fashionably emblazoned with the colors of the French flag), making a *quenelle* arm gesture, or setting fire to a car all tend to be taken as aggressive refusals of national belonging and even as a violent hatred of France. What would it mean, however, to instead take them as eminently French articulations of a much more ambivalent set of feelings? How might we see them as embodied performances of a postcolonial France in the making?

In this book I have focused on the affective and embodied dimensions of contemporary national anxieties and grassroots engagements over France's future. Songs of Islamic devotion, joyous football pitch invasions, and parkour tracings of urban space all constitute creative expressions of postcolonial French identity. They both mark the collective corporeal presence of French men and women of color within the metropolitan landscape while also connecting them to others well beyond France's borders. They become the bases for group solidarity that transcend subsidiary diacritics of ethnicity and religion while at the same time not erasing the various particularities that define social personhood. The activists, artists, athletes, and authors of color about whom I have written generally do not view their racialization as a sign of the pathological failure of the French Republic to assimilate its subjects into liberal ideals of secular citizenship. They rather presume the secular Republic to be always already racialized, and take voice and action to fight against the institutionalized inequality, discrimination, and violence that such racialization has so far entailed. And they call for—indeed project themselves into—a future postcolonial France defined as much by Muslimness and blackness as whiteness. Such a France they could love, because indeed such a France would fully include and love them.

By way of conclusion, in this chapter I explore a few of the various ways in which Muslim French and other activists and authors of color have responded to the repeated demand to perform the proper sentiment of national allegiance, to love France or leave it. I focus particularly on the Party of the Indigènes of the Republic (PIR) and their call for an ongoing decolonizing revolution that would be both institutional and affective. Indeed, drawing on anticolonial and civil rights antecedents such as James Baldwin, Aimé Césaire, Frantz Fanon, Martin Luther King, Malcolm X, Albert Memmi, and Abdelmalek Sayad, they link material transformation and spiritual renewal, and like them insist that the onus for change rests with the broader society, and that men and women of color ("the decolonial majority") should not have to accommodate themselves to or find their place within an already racialized France. Postcolonial love is something which the white world must learn, and which it must learn fast.

NATIONAL AFFECT

In this book I have explored recent moral panics in France around Islamic veiling, conversion, and "radicalization," in addition to broader national anxieties about *banlieue* violence, misogyny, and anti-Semitism, and the artists and athletes who seem to articulate it, which have been largely interpreted by the French state and media as expressions of the disdain, indeed hatred, of Muslims and other French men and women of color for French secular values and French culture more broadly. Such interpretations have motivated both restrictive forms of policing and surveillance, as well as demands for Muslims to demonstrate their national loyalty in verbal and embodied forms. These demands have been historically premised on a projection of those from postcolonial immigrant backgrounds as normatively docile subjects, as quiescent guests who will eventually assimilate themselves into professional or class-based interest groups. While the 1983 March for Equality and Against Racism and the larger civil rights movement of young French men and women of color— who demonstrated themselves to be agentive political subjects and not just the passive objects of state projects of "inclusionary exclusion" (Partridge 2012)—pushed back against those fantasies, the French state quickly worked to co-opt their energies via an ideology of managed multiculturalism (see Hage 1998), constituting what Sadri Khiari (2009) has called a "colonial counterrevolution."

More than ever, *laïcité* has become the language of postcolonial domination in France, inscribed as a set of normative republican values of citizenship premised on a direct relationship between individual subjects and a providential state, theoretically unmediated by intervening cultural or religious values or ascriptions. The secular republic imagines itself, in Ernest Renan's classic term, as a "daily plebiscite" (Renan 1990: 19), a Habermasian public sphere par excellence in which liberal individuals endowed with rights and subject to civic responsibilities freely choose to participate in a rational, dispassionate manner. While there is a nontrivial degree of triumphalism within French republicanism as a world historical overcoming of aristocratic privilege, as a global emancipation from human unfreedom, as a universalist transcendence of sectarian particularisms—ignoring, of course, the French Republic's own imperialist genealogy and complicity in the reproduction of various forms of inequality in the name of its "civilizing mission," as Talal Asad (2003), Ann Stoler (2016), and Gary Wilder (2005), among others, have traced—there is also, as we have seen, a profound anxiety that the secular republican ethic is precariously vulnerable, forever imperiled by the intrusion of apparently illiberal (read Islamic) subjectivities burdened by obligations to other authorities legitimated by other sources, bearing private passions rather than rational dispositions.

And yet such a self-aggrandizing projection of liberal values is shot through with hypocrisies that misrecognize all the ways in which it itself is premised on nondiscursive, embodied sentiments. Why, for instance, is the emancipation of Muslim-French women measured by their sexual availability? Why has the defense of *laïcité* taken such an impassioned form? If the secular state supposedly supersedes the church, and faith is but a private concern, why are revelations of conversions of "white" French men and women to Islam taken as a threat to the public order? To what extent does liberalism contain within it its own moral, aesthetic, and affective register (Berlant 1997)?

In Chapter 5 I discussed the ways in which organized spectacles of mourning and triumph—whether in the form of the republican marches in the wake of the *Charlie Hebdo* shootings, or victory parades of the national football team—have been central to the reproduction of the French nation as a living, felt collectivity to be internalized by citizens. French men and women of color have been particularly scrutinized in these settings, and expected to hyper-correct their public self-presentation in their heartfelt singing of national hymns or their avowals of "Je suis Charlie." But the surveillance of national identification and loyalty generally addresses more banal, quotidian performances of attitude and affect. As Abdelmalek Sayad (2004) critically analyzed, Algerian immigrant laborers in France, like other subservient racialized or colonial subjects, were expected to adopt a polite posture of self-effacement, with any display of prideful stature consistently countered with punishing violence by police or other self-appointed managers acting on behalf of the (implicitly white) nation-state. The more recent and no less violent policing of Muslim-French affect reads signs of respect in speech and gesture, particularly among those born or raised in Europe, as indexes of loyalty to national projects. As Susan Terrio (2009) reports in her ethnographic work on youth courts, young Muslim-French citizens are literally judged for their dress and their address, for whether they use the formal *vous* or informal *tu* pronouns when speaking to the bench, for whether their clothing, expressions, and posture are appropriately respectful to state representatives. Trica Keaton (2006), Julie Kleinman (2016), and Chantal Tetreault (2015) likewise show how the classroom presents a similarly symbolically dense context in which teachers and principals likewise assess pupils' attitudes in terms of affective registers of seriousness and respect, reading pupils' defiant performances, usually actually addressed to their teenage peers, as signs of incipient incivility—leading to potentially significant consequences for the young men and women's educational futures.[2] Whether students present as appropriately serious in quotidian educational rituals, or as adequately sorrowful during lessons on the Holocaust, has, as we have seen, been the subject of repeated jeremiads by French national teacher unions and alarmist warnings of "lost territories of the Republic" (Brenner 2002). This of course has been amplified in the case of public celebrities of color like footballers, doubly scrutinized for their conduct, and projected as examples for others on how to be correctly French. Note in particular how Zidane's contrite public apology for setting a bad example with his 2006 headbutt was followed by a presidential pardon and expression of gratitude for past service, all of which followed a ritual form as if he had committed a veritable act of treason.

From the identitarian position shared by many National Front politicians and voters, such failures of national affect were only to be expected. How could one truly *feel* French if one was not integrally rooted in the blood and soil of the Catholic rural heartland (Holmes 2000)? Such evocations of a "true France," as Herman Lebovics (1994) has argued, have since the late-nineteenth century played a minor but deeply resounding theme to the dominant notes of secular republicanism. But Islamophobia is precisely where culturalist and republican arias of France resonate. If secular fundamentalists continue to have faith in the integrating mission of the republican state, and indeed require a certain number of exceptional Muslim subjects like Fadela Amara to publicly convert to *laïcité*, they harbor deep suspicions that Islam, unregulated by state intervention, can provide a fertile ground for the cultivation of liberal subjectivity and rational dispositions. Islamic conversion and "radicalization" are not only taken as the failure of the French state to provide sufficient material resources or fulfill some primordial need to identify, but as an outright betrayal of French cultural values. To many mainstream observers, the creative acts of self-making entailed with religious conversion (see Özyürek 2015) come off as civilizational animus, as the irrational hatred of "our way of life," as at best a derivative and reflective "antiwhite racism." "France, love it or leave it," emerges as the oft-repeated response on both the Right and the Left who seem to conspire to make an imagined "clash of civilizations" a self-fulfilling prophecy.

In the 1990s the dominant affective register of resistance to racial, spatial, and religious discrimination did indeed seem to be hate. As portrayed in Matthieu Kassovitz's film *La haine* (1995), but also in some of the gangsta rap lyrics analyzed in the last chapter, cycles of police killing of young French men and women of color followed by anti-state insurrections, followed by further violence against local youth seemed to be spiraling out of control, making everyday *banlieue* life unbearable, offering only precarious futures, and leaving little hope for social reconciliation. Despair (*la galère*) was the prevalent sentiment expressed to sociologists who made the *banlieue* housing projects the site of their ethnographic research (see Dubet 1987; Dubet & Lapeyronnie 1992). Younger residents of color felt abandoned by the state, without the same job prospects as their parents, suffering under crumbling housing, educational, and commercial infrastructures. "France" made its presence felt primarily through the police and other disciplining authorities. As Thuram implied, many found it hard to love France when it treated them with suspicion and spoke in the language of violence.

But, as discussed in the last two chapters, out of despair and abandonment often come creativity and even joy. For all the spatial isolation, physical dilapidation, economic precarity, and institutional racism, residents have transformed their living environments in the *quartiers populaires* into thriving spaces of kin solidarity and artistic innovation. Hip-hop, as we have seen, has been a particularly salient aesthetic practice especially for young men of color to comment on life in the *cités* and re-spatialize the *banlieue* as a site for collective action and individual fulfillment. Through dance, graffiti, and music-making, they have elaborated on, and even commoditized, their sentiments of "hate" for their own self-reflection, and sometimes for their own profit. They have appropriated the negative portrayal of them as "scum" (*racaille*) into a positively entrepreneurial, if hyper-masculinist, image of the "gangsta" (*caillera*) who, in the words of Monsieur R, is willing to "put on the hood" if that is the menacing role society expects him to portray.[3] Such imagery underwrote calls for political unity, even revolution, particularly in the wake of the 2005 urban uprisings. While French politicians brought repeated court cases against rap artists for incitement to violence, antiwhite racism, and hate speech, the artists themselves narrated the insurrection through a French revolutionary vocabulary, painting the young men rising up against the police as a new generation of *sans-culottes*, if surely inspired by the history of Black Power and anti-colonial resistance as well.

REVOLUTIONARY LOVE

However, as we saw in the case of Abd al Malik, Kery James, and other Muslim-French rappers from the first decade of the 2000s, revolutionary anger and resistance to racist exclusion need not be framed in the gendered language of hatred and violence. Indeed, Muslim and other artists, activists, and intellectuals of color across France and beyond are similarly deploying a language of love to talk back to racism and Islamophobia. Among them are Marwan Muhammad, a former financial professional and current director of France's Collective against Islamophobia in France (CCIF). As he reveals in his autobiography, his moral education also began through hip-hop, as a DJ inspired by Kery James and other Muslim-French and American rappers committed to "social emancipation." "Frequenting the hip-hop world allowed me to gauge the ethical coherence of the artists and refine my moral sense, just at the time as I was deepening my religious attachment" (Muhammad 2017: 43). Such sensibilities pushed him to further engage in the struggle to combat anti-Muslim racism and fight for a "diverse and fraternal" France, "where everyone can continue to live together in peace … and true equality" (ibid.: 147). Muhammad fears that nonreciprocal nationalist demands of "France, love it or leave it" will simply amplify a contrarian sentiment of ghettocentric disengagement: "France, love me or I'll leave." As I mentioned in the Introduction, for Muhammad:

> It is on this ground [of love] that is determined the future of not only Muslims, but of the whole of French society, in its capacity to innovate and renew itself, to be true to what it wishes and pretends to be: a country where everyone can find their place, whatever their trajectory, their origin, their religion, or their beliefs. (ibid.: 232)

A similar humanistic perspective is articulated in the autobiographical poems of Mohamed El Bachiri, a Belgian Muslim whose wife Loubna was killed in the March 2016 Brussels attacks on the metro system where he works as a train driver. The poems, which El Bachiri tapped into his smartphone during countless sleepless hours, are poignant in their visceral sorrow and pain, caused as much by Islamic State militants as by the Islamophobes and racists who have long denied him and his family a true sense of home in Belgium. But they also express a broader appreciation for the "atmosphere of brotherhood, peace and love" (El Bachiri

2017: 21) he experienced in Catholic school or more broadly during the Belgian holiday season. At each step of the way, the poems counter his crisis of faith and loss of purpose after Loubna's death, even his occasional surging anger and hate, with evocations of heartfelt devotion.

> Love, that which drives me, lets me live and live on.
> Love, the foundation, the pedestal upon which all faiths must stand.
> Love, the source from which all people should be able to draw.
> Love, the beginning of all blossoming.
> Love, the refuge for those choking on their tears.
> Love, the embracing of an unknown soul. (ibid.: 90)

In a prose poem entitled "Jihad," he re-discovers his faith as an affective struggle:

> I vow to reply to this injustice, as an homage to who Loubna was and always will be, and as an act of respect, admiration and love toward all my human brothers and sisters ... In the ordeal I have to go through I feel more like a "jihadist" than the greatest warrior. I am a jihadist for love. Don't ask me to hate, I would rather die! (ibid.: 76)

In the "final strophe" of the short book, he acknowledges the privilege of his struggle, that the tragedy gave him a voice many others are denied:

> I the metro driver,
> was a Muslim like so many of the others
> you never hear
> you never see
> But of whom there are oh-so many. (ibid.: 92)

His plea is for a Belgium where the voiceless can be at least felt, if not heard, and where they can truly, unconditionally love and be loved.

Invoking love as the affective ally of peace and the response to war and hatred constitutes a powerful critique of institutional racism and social injustice, a critique grounded in Islam but with wide postcolonial resonances. The founding moment of the Black Lives Matter movement in the United States was a Facebook post by Alicia Garza in the wake of the summer 2013 acquittal of the killer of Trayvon Martin, entitled "A love note to black people." Expressions of and demands for unconditional love underwrite many Black Lives Matter protest actions. At Reed College in Portland, Oregon, where I teach, student activists of color grouped together as Reedies against Racism have, since 2015, similarly repeatedly called on faculty and the administration to love their students of color unconditionally, and they decry any disciplinary action against or lack of academic accommodation for protesters as love's opposite: "white supremacy." As Robert Stam and Ella Shohat (2012) have brilliantly argued, contemporary racial projects, postcolonial discourse, and identity politics need to be understood within their transnational frame, which connects France and Belgium across the "postcolonial Atlantic" to the United States and Latin America (see Aidi 2014).

In France, the PIR has similarly critically engaged love as a national and counter-national affective register in their call for political agency among French men and women of color.[4] In this sense they understand themselves as picking up the baton from the 1983 march, with their own 2005 march originally planned to mark the twentieth anniversary of the earlier event. Even more explicitly than the 1983 marchers, who articulated their critique of racism via a liberal discourse of civil rights (Hajjat 2013), Houria Bouteldja, Sadri Khiari, and their PIR collaborators explicitly oppose liberal universalism with what they call "decolonial thought." While rejecting Marxism's Enlightenment and colonial genealogy, they—like Césaire, Fanon, and other anticolonial forebears—conjoin a broadly Marxist (indeed Nasserist) analysis of structures of inequality with a strategically essentializing celebration of black and Muslim pride and a critique of enduring white and Jewish privilege. They thus position themselves as translators of the inchoate anger of a specifically French marginalized subjectivity, but also embrace a broader public of men and women of color across national borders and level their call for resistance at global imperialism more broadly. As Bouteldja declared at the fifth march of the PIR in 2009, "Whether we are from Africa, the Arabo-Muslim world, the Caribbean, *cité* residents, or simply anticolonialists, we must unite in a common combat in the name of our dignity in France. We must unite to express our solidarity with all struggling peoples" (Afghani 2009). In this sense, Bouteldja has been outspoken in her solidarity and support for Palestinians rights and dismissive of those leftists who refuse to recognize Israel as a violent settler colonial state. Indeed, she begins her recent book with a scathing critique of Jean-Paul Sartre who, in spite of his avowed solidarity with decolonization struggles, supported the creation of a Zionist state. While certainly recognizing the long history of Jewish suffering at the hands of white anti-Semites, she condemns contemporary philo-Semitism as "the last refuge of white humanism" (Bouteldja 2016: 18) and the alibi for continued imperialist violence. "Shoot Sartre (*Fusillez Sartre*)," she concludes (ibid.: 28).

But this violent language is positioned within a larger reflection on "love" as a political instrument. On the one hand, the PIR has explicitly rejected official demands to love France as expressions of institutional racism and Islamophobia. "Loving France," PIR co-founder Sadri Khiari wrote in 2007, "has become a new condition of nationality," with blacks, Arabs, and Muslims taken as "guilty in their nature of a grave offense: non-love" (Bouteldja & Khiari 2012: 122). The correct response, Bouteldja amplified in 2011, is not for French men and women of color to love France, but to love themselves: "We must love ourselves. *We have to love ourselves*" (ibid.: 310, original emphasis). Following James Baldwin, she takes such self-love as a political act in and of itself, and as a necessary step toward the self-consciousness required for true liberation.

On the other hand, for Bouteldja, love is not merely an inward sentimental turn but an external, active engagement with the world. The subtitle of her recent book is "toward a politics of revolutionary love," a term which she attributes to the Chicana activist Chela Sandoval (Bouteldja 2016: 13).[5] I cannot do justice to the intellectual sweep or emotive verve of Bouteldja's essay, but it boils down to a simple proposition, an offer which whites (*les Blancs*) cannot refuse if they wish to retain some level of bourgeois privilege and stave off the inevitable decolonial revolution: You give us love, we'll give you peace. Such a love is not reciprocal; it is one-sided. It requires that whites fully accept French men and women of color and their struggles for freedom and equality as part and parcel of the (trans)national, decolonized "greater We" (*le grand Nous*). Such a love, she specifies, is not about the "heart" as a sentimental or spiritual figure, Islamic or otherwise. It is a love of political transformation.

> In order to realize this love, there is no need to love each other or have pity for each other. All that is necessary is to recognize and inhabit that moment "just before hate", to push it away as much as possible and, with desperate hope, conjure away the worst. That will be the We of revolutionary love. (ibid.: 139–40)

Love is a modus vivendi, an act of political solidarity and mutual recognition, the condition of possibility for a future together.

Not surprisingly, Bouteldja, like Dieudonné (whom she appreciates but condemns for his provocative courting of right-wing figures), has been roundly condemned by French politicians, pundits, and even academics for her uncompromising language. Mainstream public figures have regularly accused her of anti-Semitism, antiwhite racism, and homophobia. Unlike Abd al Malik, Amara, or Memmi, she refuses to criticize the "existential malaise" of postcolonial *cité* residents who reject bourgeois French society and occasionally adopt anti-Semitic rhetoric (Bouteldja 2014). But, in the process, she carefully and explicitly avoids the hate in terms of which such malaise is often expressed. Only by seeking and earning the love of the *indigènes*, only by denouncing white privilege and its material advantages, and only by building solidarity through acts as well as words can a positive transformation of the social order transpire. Only revolutionary love will bring postcolonial peace.

Some readers will no doubt be disturbed by Bouteldja's transmutation of the American civil rights slogan "No justice, no peace" (itself multiply transformed from King to Farrakhan to Black Lives Matter) into essentially, "No love, no peace." The PIR certainly understand the postcolonial struggle of French men and women of color as one for social justice and dignity, but they dismiss formulations that would reduce this to a fight for individual rights. At the close of her book, Bouteldja rejects the Cartesian *cogito*, both subsuming it under the more transcendent "Allahu akbar!" (God is greater), and specifying that while she may indeed be because she thinks, what she is is ultimately a *khoroto*, a simple Arab bumpkin (ibid.: 140). Her identity, like that of France, is always already racialized. Any future postcolonial France must indeed accept this existential fact and move forward from there. And in the face of resurgent nationalist populisms and white supremacism across the globe, moving forward is the only progressive political option. For all their differences, the various postcolonial activists, artists, athletes, and authors surveyed in this book agree on that point. Like them, we have no choice but to continue to hope and strive for social justice, peace, and indeed love.

Notes

INTRODUCTION

1. The classic study of how the experience of German occupation marked the postwar French republics is Rousso (1991). In terms of how it resonated in later conflicts, particularly in the French–Algerian war, see Evans (1997: 31–73) and Prost (2002: 107–24).
2. See Le Sueur (2005) and Silverstein (2015) for discussions of these critical but optimistic positions.
3. The literature making this argument is vast, but see especially the collective works coordinated by the Achac research group (Bancel et al. 2010; Blanchard & Bancel 2005; Blanchard et al. 2005). See also Hargreaves & McKinney (1997), Lebovics (2004), Lorcin (2006), Lyons (2013), Rosenberg (2006), Ross (1995), Silverstein (2004a), Smouts (2007), Stam & Shohat (2012), Stoler (2016), Stovall (2009), and Thomas (2013).
4. Moreover, France arguably maintains a colonial presence in its overseas departments and territories in the Caribbean, Indian Ocean, and southern Pacific. Anticolonial resistance remains particularly active in New Caledonia.
5. For an insightful discussion of the contested emergence and development of postcolonial critique in France, see Stam & Shohat (2012: 244–69). See also Diouf (2010) and Smouts (2007).
6. The *pieds-noirs* are the nearly 1 million European settlers of Algeria, often of Maltese, Spanish, Italian, and Jewish backgrounds, who were "repatriated" to France after the French–Algerian war. The *harkis* were the 200,000 or more Algerian Muslims engaged by the French army in some capacity during the war, up to 60,000 of whom were killed in the cycles of retributive violence following the 1962 armistice. On their memory work, see Crapanzano (2011), Hamoumou & Jordi (1999), Hureau (2001), and Smith (2006). On the specifically Berber war memories called forth during the Algerian civil war, see Silverstein (2000a) and Stora (1995).
7. See Robine (2006) for an early analysis of the PIR.
8. On the 2005 urban revolts and the state's reaction, see Lapeyronnie (2009), Le Goaziou & Mucchielli (2006), Mbembe (2009), and Silverstein & Tetreault (2006). Khiari analyzes the uprising as a specifically "anti-colonialist revolt" (Khiari 2009: 122).
9. Throughout the book, I follow Mayanthi Fernando's neologism "Muslim French" as a more accurate translation of "French citizens of Muslim faith," on which many insist (Fernando 2014: 15).
10. In some cases, as I will discuss in later chapters, these artists and activists have been brought to court on charges of "incitement to racial hatred" or "disturbing the public order," charges of which they have been largely

acquitted. The accusations nonetheless have effects on livelihoods. In December 2017, black journalist Rokhayo Diallo was dismissed from the national digital council after complaints from right-wing groups about her divisiveness because of past articles she had written about "institutional racism" in France.

11. On management and the reproduction of white nationhood, see Hage (1998).

12. For a similar discussion from the perspective of Réunion, an "old colony" like Haiti, but one that never achieved national liberation, see Vergès (1999, 2007).

13. For a theorization of friction as the condition of possibility for collaboration, see Tsing (2005).

14. On race/racism as a durable social formation, see Balibar & Wallerstein (1991), Gilroy (1987), Omi & Winant (1994), Sayad (2004), Silverstein (2005), and Winant (2004). For classic approaches to the phenomenology of race, see Du Bois (1989) and Fanon (1967). Khiari (2006: 89–95) has incorporated both sets of insights into his critical analysis of racism in France.

15. On Jewishness in colonial North Africa, see Arkin (2014), Schreier (2010), and Stein (2014).

16. The most notorious adoption of policy recommendations in the United States was the 1965 Moynihan Report, which treated the matrifocal African-American family as dysfunctional and at least partially responsible for enduring black poverty. See Lewis (1966).

1. MOBILE SUBJECTS

1. For a history of anti-immigrant racism in France, see Noiriel (1988, 2007). On Raspail and his broader influence, see Connelly & Kennedy (1994). Raspail was later revealed to be an inspiration for the American alt-right leader Steve Bannon.

2. "Beur" was a colloquial term for "second generation" Franco-Maghrebis, originally used by local activists but quickly appropriated in state discourse and subsequently disowned by those so referenced. It likely derives from the back slang (*verlan*) syllabic inversion of "Arab."

3. For political economic analyses of the *banlieue* (urban peripheries) and their policing, see Bouamama (2009), Dikeç (2007), Fassin (2013), Silverstein (2008b), and Wacquant (2008). I return to these issues in subsequent chapters.

4. Estimates of Muslims in France vary wildly from 2 to 5 million, depending on whether the counting is done based on ancestry or based on overt declarations in surveys. For general works on the subject, see Bowen (2006, 2010), Cesari (1994), Davidson (2012), Fernando (2014), Kepel (1987), Laurence & Vaisse (2006), and Roy (2004).

5. French Civil Code, art. 25.

6. The prime minister, Manuel Valls, echoing police officials, quickly denied such reports.

7. For a critical analysis of the *tournantes* scandal, see Mucchielli (2005); for a provocative discussion of "Arab" sexuality in France, see Mack (2017).

8. See the brilliant, critical review of Caldwell's book and other such tracts by Moroccan-American novelist Laila Lalami (2009).

9. Amelia Lyons (2013) has argued against the general portrayal of these migratory movements as exclusively masculine, given the large number of especially Algerian women and children in the metropole during the late colonial period.

10. For classic takes on how global cultural flows come to be indigenized, see Appadurai (1996), Sahlins (1988), and Tsing (2005).

11. On linguistic innovations and cultural crossings of young Muslim-French women in the peripheries of Paris, see Tetreault (2015). For a more general resource on the rich landscape of postcolonial artistic and literary forms, see Hargreaves & McKinney (1997).

12. See Beaman (2017) for a recent ethnographic study of middle-class and upwardly mobile Franco-Maghrebis.

13. Personal communication.

14. For a longer history of racial solidarity between French and American communities of color, see Keaton et al. (2012) and Stovall (1996).

15. For biographical discussions of Sayad's life, particularly in wartime Algeria, see Bourdieu & Wacquant (2000), Saint-Martin (1999), Sayad (2002), and Silverstein & Goodman (2009: 30–32).

16. "Immigration can only be with the precedent of colonization, and the situation of emigrants is that of the colonized; colonization survives, in a way, through the emigration that prolongs it" (Sayad 2006: 166).

17. Quoted from the CNHI website: http://www.histoire-immigration.fr/missions/le-projet-scientifique-et-culturel/le-projet (accessed December 15, 2017).

18. For discussions of the 1931 exposition and the various colonial museum projects since developed, see Aldrich (2005), Deleporte (2005), Lebovics (2004), Norindr (1996), and Sherman (2004). See Bancel & Lebovics (2010) and Thomas (2013: 41–58) for an insightful analysis of the CNHI in relation to broader public debates about immigration.

2. HOW DOES IT FEEL TO BE THE CRISIS?

1. For a provocative discussion of crisis as an analytical concept and mode of perception, see Roitman (2013).

2. The classic anthropological account of the relationship between history and structure is Lévi-Strauss (1966). See Sahlins (1981) for an application of structuralist methodology to the history of the Sandwich Islands.

3. On the broader issues of how to define Islam as an object of anthropological study, whether as a discursive tradition, a set of normative practices, an institutional structure, or a subjective belief system, see Asad (2009), Bowen (2012), Geertz (1968), and Gellner (1981).

4. On all of these points, see Scott (2006).

5. Treating submission, modesty, and the other work of pious Muslim female bodily discipline as agentive acts of ethical self-cultivation follows directly from the foundational work of Mahmood (2005) and Hirschkind (2006), who themselves draw on Foucault's approach to subjectivation through

Talal Asad. For a discussion of how older Muslim women born in North Africa—often taken to be cut off socially, culturally, and linguistically from mainstream French society—similarly actively adapt and transmit their religious practices in France, see Killian (2006). For an earlier set of revelatory interviews with a variety of covered women who express both aspects of choice and coercion, see Gaspard & Khosrokhavar (1995).

6. On "living together" (*vivre ensemble*) as a social expectation and basis for judgment in French multicultural urban environments, see Epstein (2011).

7. John Bowen (2006) has ethnographically unpacked the "public reasoning" behind the law. See also Winter (2008).

8. See Bowen (2010) for ethnographic details on the institutional arrangements and controversies around the regulation of these public aspects of Islamic practice in France.

9. Scholars of Christianity have underlined similar translation difficulties in other contexts. See Handman (2014) and Luhrmann (2012).

10. See Rosenberg (2006) for a history of the surveillance of migrants and the development of identification technologies.

11. Actress and animal-rights activist Brigitte Bardot has been convicted of multiple counts of incitement to racial hatred for her anti-Muslim public statements.

12. Some anti-Muslim hate groups have adopted the practice of offering free pork-based soup to homeless populations and asylum seekers.

13. Michel de Certeau discusses a parallel process, whereby residents of the Parisian *banlieue* of Sarcelles have taken on its general perception as a "total failure" as a source of symbolic value: "This extreme avatar provides its citizens with the 'prestige' of exceptional identity" (de Certeau 1984: 220).

3. THE MUSLIM AND THE JEW

1. Much French media and state attention regarding Muslim French has centered on French North Africans, considered the most susceptible to Islamist preaching (*da'wa*) and the most responsible for the reported rise in anti-Semitism.

2. For a critique of the discourse of the "new anti-Semitism" as a form of a "new Islamophobia," see Geisser (2003: 77–93); see also Balibar (2003), Hajjat & Mohammed (2013: 177–95), and Vidal (2003) for similar skepticism. Michel Wieviorka (2007) and his research team, in their comprehensive survey of anti-Semitic attitudes in France, attempt to formulate a balanced analysis that simultaneously recognizes the social challenge of increased anti-Semitism in France while warning against succumbing to the moral panic encouraged by authors like Brenner, Finkielkraut, Taguieff, and Trigano. See also Peace (2009).

3. Houria Bouteldja writes of French Jews as *dhimmis* of the Republic: "In the space of 50 years you have gone from being pariahs to *dhimmis of the Republic* in the service of the nation-state, and to *colonial troops* [*tirailleurs sénégalais*] in the service of Western imperialism" (Bouteldja 2016: 51, original emphasis).

4. For critical discussions of the appropriateness of the terminology "(new) anti-Semitism" and "Islamophobia" for denominating current racism against Jews and Muslims in France, see Bowen (2005: 524), Peace (2009: 118–21), and Wieviorka (2007: 62–68). "Anti-Semitism" technically references an older racial typology where Jews (as well as Arabs) were reviled as "Semites." "Islamophobia" registers a psychological fear of Islamic religion, rather than the structural discrimination and racialized discourse against Muslims which is at issue. See Hajjat & Mohammed (2013) for a genealogy of the category of "Islamophobia" in French scholarly and media discourse. Nonetheless, these are the terms in which the French debate has been addressed, and as such I continue to use them throughout this chapter. In this sense, I follow the lead of Marwan Muhammad, director of the Collective Against Islamophobia in France (CCIF), in focusing on its pragmatic, juridical definition: "illegal acts committed against individuals and institutions due to a presumption of belonging to the Muslim community" (Muhammad 2017: 69). This definition parallels precisely that of anti-Semitism as offered by Brian Klug (2003).

5. Indeed, during the early 2000s there were spates of anti-Arab and anti-Muslim attacks by North African Jews, whether taking place in the public spheres of pro-Israeli rallies, or "offline" in terms of street attacks and mosque burnings (Shatz 2005). On the more general rise of anti-Muslim attacks in France since the late 1990s, see Geisser (2003: 10–13).

6. See Partridge (2010) for a beautifully textured and revealing ethnography of a German class trip to Auschwitz with a group of Turkish and Palestinian schoolchildren.

7. Non-European Jews in Morocco and Tunisia did not have access to French nationality during the Protectorate period except through requested (and relatively rare) naturalization. They were nonetheless administered separately from Muslim populations, and subject to separate legal and educational regimes (Arkin 2014: 43–53). While Muslim Algerians gained nominal citizenship in the French Union after the World War II, they did not achieve French national citizenship until 1958.

8. For histories and analyses of North African immigration to France, see Gillette & Sayad (1976), Hargreaves (1995), Liauzu (1996), MacMaster (1997), Sayad (2004), Silverstein (2004a), Talha (1989), and Zehraoui (1994).

9. Bengharbit himself never supported anticolonial nationalism. On the historical debate over Bengharbit's role and his popular portrayal in recent films like *Les hommes libres/Free Men* (2011), directed by Ismaël Ferroukhi, see Aidi (2014: 293–97) and Katz (2012).

10. On the discourse of "lawless zones" in France, see Trémolet de Villiers (2002).

11. Originally conceived in 1978 and first introduced during the 1991 Gulf War, the plan operates according to a logic of armed deterrence, mobilizing the military to guard schools, transportation hubs, government buildings, and centers of tourism.

12. This is not to say that there actually is an Intifada in France, as some foreign journalists have implied (see Hussey 2014).

13. For an insightful analysis of the call for and moral panic over a European Jewish exodus, see Klug (2016a).

14. In one heavily reported and debated incident from 2004, a young women claimed to have been attacked on a Parisian commuter train by a group of youths who drew a swastika on her chest. The event elicited cries of outrage from Jewish and antiracist organizations, and public apologies, promises of redress, and stiffer penalties for anti-Semitic crimes from the government. When the woman later admitted that she had made up the attack, President Jacques Chirac publicly stated that what remained important was that such an attack could very well have occurred. In this sense, the attack, while purely imaginary, continued to function as a social fact with real-world effects (see Bernard 2004). The attack served as the basis for the feature film, *La fille du RER/The Girl on the Train* (2009).

15. In point of fact, Amazigh activists—like Berber speakers throughout North Africa and the diaspora—incorporate a wide variety of religious beliefs and practices into their everyday lives. While some militants engage in regular prayer and follow Islamic dietary restrictions, others go as far as to excise all references to God from their spoken language and harboring scarcely hidden contempt for believers amongst their ranks. However, even the most extreme atheists outwardly defend "traditional" forms of Berber Islamic practice that they claim to be flexible in application and perfectly integrated into larger cultural forms, and even the most pious Amazigh activists refuse to condone Islamist arguments for the priority of religion in political life. Such claims to Berber cultural-religious distinctiveness generally ignore movements of religious reformism and purification in which Berber groups themselves historically engaged, most particularly during the Almohad and Almoravid Berber empires of Andalusia, as well as the fact that Berber speakers number among the ranks of contemporary Al-Qaeda and Islamic State militants.

16. On the *convivencia* myth as a debate about European postcolonial identity, see Aidi (2006) and Shannon (2015: 163–76).

4. DANGEROUS SIGNS: *CHARLIE HEBDO* AND DIEUDONNÉ

1. Indeed, the name *Charlie Hebdo* derives in part from its first issue, which appeared in 1970 in the wake of the banning of the original publication, *Hara-Kiri*, for criticizing the public reverence for Charles de Gaulle when media reports of his passing overshadowed those of other tragic events occurring during the same period. The name also resonates with Charlie Brown, the protagonist of the *Peanuts* cartoons republished by *Hara-Kiri*.

2. In a 2012 interview in *Le Monde*, Charb famously channeled Mexican revolutionary Emiliano Zapata and others, claiming, "I'd rather die standing than live on my knees" (Santi 2015).

3. Note Rachida Dati, born in France to parents from Algeria and Morocco, who served as justice minister under Sarkozy. Sarkozy used affirmative-action hires within the government as a mode of rule. For a textured ethnographic study of the racial and religious dimensions of the French court system, see

Terrio (2009); on racializing taxonomies built into policing practices, see Fassin (2013).

4. Before taking hostages at the Hyper Cacher supermarket in Paris on January 9, Coulibaly shot a jogger in Fontenay-sous-Bois on January 7, and then a police officer and a sanitation worker in Montrouge on January 8.

5 "Visé par une enquête pour apologie du terrorisme, Dieudonné répond au parquet." *La Tribune*, January 12, 2015 (available at: https://www.latribune. fr/actualites/economie/france/20150112tribbf4e03a24/vise-par-enquete-pour-apologie-du-terrorisme-dieudonne-repond-au-parquet.html, accessed December 25, 2017).

6. Several French Jewish organizations, including the Union of Jewish Students of France and the International League against Racism and Anti-Semitism, took Dieudonné to court on charges of incitement to racial hatred, but he was judged not guilty.

7. See https://www.youtube.com/watch?v=15PcLLb6Olo (accessed December 25, 2017).

8. See http://www.youtube.com/watch?v=AtqXzrJlMZg (accessed February 16, 2014).

9. Note, however, that some have indeed performed *quenelles* at sites of anti-Jewish violence, including at the Toulouse Jewish school attacked by Mohamed Merah in 2012.

10. The show was banned in a number of cities, including Paris, and ultimately Dieudonné rewrote the show to expunge the controversial content.

5. ANXIOUS FOOTBALL

1. Some speculated that Anelka's gesture was directed at David Gold, the Jewish owner of the opposing team, West Ham United.

2. *Libération*, December 28, 2013 (available at: http://www.liberation.fr/societe/2013/12/28/football-anelka-fete-un-but-avec-une-quenelle-a-la-dieudonne_969444, accessed February 10, 2018).

3. National Front leader Jean-Marie Le Pen in particular had publicly questioned whether "there are too many blacks on the French team" (Forcari 2006: 10). Similar positions had been articulated as early as the late 1990s, and most notably in the wake of the urban violence of October and November 2005, by Alain Finkielkraut, who remarked in an interview with an Israeli newspaper that the French national soccer team was "composed almost exclusively of black players" and was the "ridicule" of Europe (Mishani & Smotriez 2005).

4. In thinking of football and national identification as empassioned practices, I am indebted to the work of Christian Bromberger (1995, 1998; Bromberger et al. 1995).

5. Durkheim had been publicly outspoken during the Dreyfus affair, writing in 1898 in support of Captain Alfred Dreyfus and against anti-Semitism. He lost his son André fighting in World War I and never psychologically or physically recovered.

6. The INSEP was originally founded in 1975 as the National Institute of Sport and Physical Education, inheriting its mission from numerous earlier

training facilities going back to the Joinville gymnastics teacher-training school founded in 1852.

7. The lion's share of the FFF's €200 million plus budget comes from corporate sponsorship and other commercial ventures.

8. Maple Razsa writes of Croatian anti-globalization activists who go to demonstrations so as to "feel the state on your own skin," to make sensible their otherwise abstract critique of the state as a violent institution (Razsa 2015: 138).

9. The exhibition catalogue (Boli et al. 2010), co-authored by over thirty scholars, contains a significantly more nuanced historical portrayal than the exhibit itself. Yet it still occasionally engages in hagiography. Zidane receives disproportionate treatment in multiple articles, but with only one of the concluding contributions even mentioning the 2006 headbutt (Dine 2010).

10. Before Algerian independence in 1962, the French national side included Algerian colonial subjects, and occasionally would play training matches against selections of North African Muslim players (Gastaut 2010a). In 1975, Algeria defeated an amateur French national team at the Mediterranean Games hosted in Algiers (Dubois 2010: 199), and the two teams met on several other occasions under that aegis. For other analyses of the 2001 match, see M. Amara (2006), Dine (2002), Gastaut (2008a, 2010b), and Lebovics (2004: 136–42).

11. Although President Hollande did acknowledge the "brutal" and "unjust" nature of French colonialism during a state visit to Algeria in 2012 to celebrate the fiftieth anniversary of independence, and although the then presidential candidate Emmanuel Macron declared that France should apologize, no formal state apology has yet occurred. See Stora (2010).

12. By comparison, of the Algerian team selected for the 1986 World Cup, only one player, Nordine Kourichi, was born and raised in France, and the vast majority of the side played their professional football in Algeria.

13. Indeed, former French national coach Aimé Jacquet later remarked that even as the match wore down toward penalty kicks, he remained absolutely convinced that Zidane would score the winning goal.

14. Much has been written about the incident and its aftermath (see Dubois 2010: 241–66). This section draws on my earlier discussion in Silverstein (2008a). For compelling analyses of Zidane and postcolonial corporeality more broadly, see Guénif-Souilamas (2009, 2010).

15. See Jaxel-Truer (2006). Materazzi and Zidane later revealed that the comments centered on Zidane's sister (and possibly his mother). Materazzi even claimed that he was too "uncultured" to even know what a "terrorist" was. Zidane nonetheless linked them to the broader racism the team had encountered. As Dubois notes, "racist insults are themselves often articulated, or cloaked, in the language of sexual violence or degradation" (Dubois 2010: 261).

16. Concern over the effect of Zidane's actions on the *banlieue* youth was repeated in the international press as well, most famously in Adam Gopnik's article in the *New Yorker* (Gopnik 2006).

17. See *Le Parisien*, July 14, 1998 (available at: http://www.leparisien.fr/une/la-zizoumania-sur-tous-les-fronts-14-07-1998-2000159227.php, accessed February 10, 2018).

6. TRACING PLACES: PARKOUR AND URBAN SPACE

1. On the history and spatial critique of *banlieue* cinema, see Austin (2009), Bloom (1999), Konstantarakos (1999), and Tarr (2005). The most emblematic film of the genre is Matthieu Kassovitz's *La haine* (1995), discussed in Chapter 3. One of the stars of the film, Hubert Koundé, originally suggested the name "parkour" to Belle (substituting a "k" for the "c" in *parcours*, meaning "course"). *La haine* was filmed on location in the Paris suburb of Chanteloup-les-Vignes using primarily local, non-professional actors. The film was loosely based on an actual anti-police demonstration that erupted in the wake of the 1993 point-blank shooting of *cité* youth Makome M'Bowole while in police custody. *La haine*, as well as Jean-François Richet's similar 1997 film *Ma 6-T va crack-er*, about gang warfare and anti-police hatred filmed in suburban Meaux, anticipated the 2005 "riots" that would occur in precisely these housing project locales. See Bloom (2009) for a discussion of *Banlieue 13*.

2. "Yamakasi" means "strong spirit" in the Congolese language Lingala, but was specifically adopted to invoke an Asian, martial arts style (Wilkinson 2007). For a history of parkour in France and beyond, see Atkinson (2009), Fuggle (2008), Thomson (2008), and Wilkinson (2007). The development of parkour by the teenagers Belle and Foucan functions as the origin myth for the sport, and Lisses (along with its now famous architectural features) has become a veritable pilgrimage destination for its global practitioners. See e.g. "The Lisses Trip" (available at: http: //www.worldwidejam.tv/buster. lisse.jam.parkour.html, accessed January 1, 2018).

3. Scholars have also analyzed parkour through the urban political theories of Alain Badiou (2005), Jacques Rancière (2004), and Henri Lefebvre (1991); see Mould (2009: 746), Thomson (2008: 255), and Savile (2008: 909) respectively.

4. Belle and Foucan split over the stylization, commercialization, and globalization of parkour. In contrast to Belle's ascetic ideology of bodily discipline and efficient movement, Foucan championed a more free-form bodily aesthetic and has marketed this brand of "freerunning" to an increasingly planetary audience (Atkinson 2009: 172–73).

5. Balibar (2004) promulgates the rights of all immigrants and those from a postcolonial immigrant background to full, active citizenship, and opposes this "right to belong" to French practices of "national preference" and what he sees as an encroaching European "apartheid." The original screenplay for Kassovitz's *La haine* was entitled *Droit de cité*, likewise playing on the multiple meanings of *cité* as citizenship, housing project, and citation.

6. Atkinson, referencing Brian Pronger (1998), argues that parkour defies the external goal orientation of "traditional sports": "Postsports are cooperative over competitive, socially inclusionary rather than hierarchical, process oriented, and holistic" (Atkinson 2009: 179). By situating parkour in its French postcolonial contexts of colonial violence, military discipline, and urban policing, I question this overly serene and liberatory perspective.

7. Both Belle and Foucan cite Hébert as an inspiration for their development of parkour, and parkour literature is filled with descriptions of his training

methods. See e.g. "Parkour history," Parkour Generations (available at: http://parkourgenerations.com/parkour-history/, accessed January 1, 2017).

8. Drawing on extant racial theories, Hébert differentiated between Anglo-Saxon and Mediterranean temperaments, characterizing the former as "cold" and in need of stimulation by sporting competition, while the latter (including the French) as susceptible to nervousness, irascibility, and aggression (Hébert 1946: 96–97). Interestingly, in the mid-2000s, parkour achieved notable success in Britain and the United States, with gyms dedicated to its training methods, organized demonstrations, "performance teams," and there were some highly controversial plans to organize televised competitions. Michael Atkinson, building on Eric Dunning (1999), characterizes this as a "sportization process" (Atkinson 2009: 173). Iain Borden (2001: 156–60), drawing on Lefebvre's theories of spatial politics and production, similarly recounts the commoditization of "skate culture" and the various ways skateboarders have sought to subvert—or personally profit from—such corporate capture of a subcultural style.

9. The stick-figure illustrations in Hébert's manual include racialized depictions of Africans and Polynesians alongside reproductions of classical figures. His earlier works also include seminude photographs of Africans and Polynesians taken during his travels. One series of photos from a 1907 trip to Africa depicts a man in a muscular pose with the caption: "Type of a natural athlete: A black from the Saracolés (Senegal) race who developed [his physique] through the instinctual practice of natural exercises useful for his way of life" (Hébert 1947: 8).

10. French colonial administrators and missionaries founded athletic clubs, sporting associations, and stadia across the imperial periphery, many of which would later provide the models for and sites of anticolonial nationalist movements (see Arnaud 1992; Deville-Danthu 1997; Dubois 2010; Silverstein 2002a). In the British Empire and turn-of-the-century America, sports were linked to a parallel movement of muscular Christianity, likewise concerned with racial strength and re-masculinization (see James 1993; MacAloon 2007; Mangan 1992; Putney 2001).

11. In an interview with Kassovitz, with whom Belle worked on the 2008 action film *Babylon A.D.*, Belle presents his practice of parkour as a way of reconnecting with his deceased father. He emphasizes parkour's instrumental (and potentially martial) logic—as a mode of overcoming obstacles—rather than the freestyle elements added to it (see the video available at: http://www.youtube.com/watch?v=Tv6Xj8tiDIQ, accessed January 2, 2018).

12. The notion of the colonial periphery as a laboratory, as an "experimental terrain" (*champ d'expérience*) of modernism, was elaborated in the early-twentieth century by the urban planners and architects engaged by the Moroccan resident general, Henri Lyautey (see Çelik 1997: 197; Wright 1997: 326–27).

13. The Casbah as a contested site of French modernist intervention, anti-colonial nationalism, and French counterinsurgency is brilliantly captured in the engaged writings of Frantz Fanon (1963, 1965), and in Gillo Ponte-

corvo's neorealist film *La battaglia de Algeri/The Battle of Algiers* (1965), based on a script by the revolutionary leader Yacef Saadi.

14. See Soulignac (1993) for a history of the construction of *banlieue* housing projects. There is a rich ethnographic literature on these lived spaces: see Bouamama (2009), Dubet & Lapeyronnie (1992), Duret (1996), Epstein (2011), Jazouli (1992), Lepoutre (1997), Silverstein (2004a, 2006), and Wacquant (2008).

15. For the history and key writings of the Situationists, see McDonough (2002).

16. On the notion of "unitary urbanism" as a critique of modernist urbanism, see McDonough (2002: 103–14).

17. Debord claimed that the very term "psychogeography" was coined by an "illiterate [Algerian] Kabyle" (Debord 1981a: 5), presumably an immigrant in Paris.

18. Tati was strongly influenced by Situationist writings (see Marie 2001). Contrast his ludic rendition of urban modernism to Jean-Luc Godard's bleak *Deux ou trois choses que je sais d'elle/Two or Three Things I Know About Her* (1967), where the ongoing construction of the suburban *cités* is linked to immobility and the degradation of human life.

19. The following draws on a longer discussion in Silverstein (2006) and Silverstein & Tetreault (2006).

20. *Le Monde*, June 21, 2005 (available at: http://www.lemonde.fr/societe/article/ 2005/06/21/les-propos-de-m-sarkozy-sur-le-nettoyage-de-la-courneuve-provoquent-l-indignation_664721_3224.html, accessed February 11, 2018).

21. Minister of the interior Eric Raoult first spoke of a "Marshall Plan for the banlieues" in 1995, and almost identical plans of state investment, using the same historical referent, were revived under the Sarkozy presidency in the wake of the 2005 uprising across the Parisian *banlieues*. But revitalization plans for these areas have been proposed repeatedly since at least 1977 (see Damon 2010; Pinard 2013).

22. On sports and Islam as putatively opposed models for postcolonial France, see Dubois (2010: 177–97) and Silverstein (2000b).

23. Borden (2001: 208–13) similarly discusses the ways skateboarders "mark territory" through scuffing, grinding, and gouging the architecture with their boards and wheels. Drawing on de Certeau (1984), he likens this to a "micro-spatial text" that might be read, according to the infamous graffito, as "skate and destroy."

24. See particularly Godard's *Week-end* (1967) and Tati's *Trafic* (1971).

25. In a poignant scene in the film *La haine*, a local police officer proposes helping one of the young protagonists procure funds to rebuild the boxing gym destroyed the night before in an antipolice riot. The boxer replies: "There's no point. Kids today prefer to fight in the streets."

26. In a much-watched interview with the French television channel TF1, David Belle gives viewers a tour of his hometown of Lisses, including the various architectural features where he developed his parkour skills. In addition to showing the routes less traveled up stairwells and off walls, Belle climbs the 75-foot tall sculpture known as the Dame du Lac—what Wilkinson (2007) calls the "shrine" of parkour—surrounded by a fence and a "keep out" (*acces interdit*) sign, and another declaring "no climbing" (*escalade*

interdite) twenty feet up and tagged by local youths. In the program, Belle and his running mates practice vaulting the fence, until at some point the interviewer remarks on the sign. With a wink and a chuckle, Belle replies, "Forbidden? Yeah, in principle." The footage can be seen at: https: //www. youtube.com/watch?v=cjibtmSLxQ4 (accessed January 2, 2018).

27. In their first public demonstrations for the *sapeur-pompiers*, they dressed as ninjas.

7. HIP-HOP NATIONS

1. All references to the songs and albums cited in this chapter are contained in the notes, with further details available in the discography section of the reference list.

2. The song appeared on an album of rap songs solicited to accompany the 1995 release of Matthieu Kassovitz's film *La haine*, which explicitly treated the subject of youth-police violence in the *cités* (Various artists, *La haine: Musiques inspirées du film*, 1995). The rappers were forced to pay a heavy fine, and subsequently the group concentrated their efforts on their individual careers and on establishing a musical production cooperative, Secteur Ä, in their native Sarcelles.

3. Monsieur R, "FranSSe," on *PolitiKment IncorreKt* (2004). The case was subsequently thrown out, as the court determined that deputy Mach had suffered no personal injury since his own children were no longer minors.

4. Suprême NTM were accused of "verbal abuse against public authority" for a 1995 Bastille Day performance of their 1993 hit "Police," in which the police are decried as a "veritable gang" of "brainless ones empowered by justice," and one of the characters' dreams of hunting down cops (*keufs*) in the subway. The incident occurred during a larger "liberty concert" held in the southern town of La Seyne-sur-Mer to protest against the National Front's recent mayoral victories in neighboring Toulon and Orange. During the performance the rappers called on the audience to "fuck the police," apparently indicating the security guards working at the concert. The group's two members were sentenced to six months in prison (reduced to two months suspended on appeal), plus a 50,000 franc fine and a six-month ban on all professional activity. For further discussion of the affair, see Hélénon (1998), Prévos (1998), and Silverstein (2002b).

5. Then interior minister Nicolas Sarkozy prosecuted Hamé for "defamation against the public administration" for an April 2002 article that appeared in La Rumeur's self-published fanzine that accompanied the release of their debut album. In the article, a sophisticated, hard-hitting analysis of the state production of "insecurity" in France's *cités*, Hamé maintained that, "The Ministry of Interior's reports never mention the hundreds of our brothers killed by the police force without any of the murderers investigated." After several rounds of prosecutorial appeal, the courts eventually dismissed the case on the grounds that the offending remarks did not refer to a single action or event that could be disproved. For a collection of documents related to the affair, as well as republication of Hamé's text, see: http://sitecon.

free.fr/rumeur.htm (last accessed December 31, 2017). For an analysis, see Tshimanga (2009: 258).

6. The interior minister Dominique de Villepin prosecuted the trio Sniper for having "incited the attacking and killing of police officers and state representatives" following a concert performance in Rouen on April 28, 2004 of their 2001 hit "La France," in which the rappers sang, in reference to the police, "You have to make them cry (*leur en faire baver*), that's all they deserve ... I have nothing to lose, I would like them to hang." The case and its appeal were both dismissed, with the judges opining that the lyrics merely expressed "the desolation and hopelessness (*mal de vivre*) of *banlieue* youth" (Kessous 2006).

7. Sarkozy's threats followed on from a series of complaints against Sniper from far-right militants, police unions, and the Jewish International League Against Racism and Anti-Semitism. The complaints referenced not only the song "La France" but also "Jetteur de pierres" ("Stone throwers"), a 2001 song about the Israeli–Palestinian conflict in which the Intifada is presented as justified resistance against a "colonizing power."

8. The "right to resemblance" should not be confused with the "right to indifference" avowed by many Muslim-French citizens interviewed by Mayanthi Fernando (2014: 70–71), that is, their desire to not be particularly remarked upon, to be "forgotten" as an object of attention and exclusion.

9. Throughout this chapter I use "hardcore" and "gangsta" interchangeably to reference a set of French hip-hop artists identifiable by their musical poetics (in particular their harshness of vocal flow and the complex layering of samples) and thematic content (their focus on racism and violence) that distinguish them from the more laid-back flows and less politically charged lyrics of artists like MC Solaar and TTC, as well as from the crossover styles of Zebda, FFF, and Raggasonic (which nonetheless may contain socio-political critiques). The distinction Krims (2000: 155) makes between "gangsta" and "conscious" genres in French hip-hop—which to a large extent replicate a prior US folk classification between West Coast and East Coast styles—no longer appears to apply, if it ever did. For a further discussion of the hardcore style, see Mucchielli (1999), Silverstein (2002b: 60), and Tshimanga (2009). Insofar as this chapter primarily addresses the period around the 2005 urban insurrection, I do not cover the innovative work and political engagements of contemporary hip-hop artists like Fianso (Sofiane Zermani), Nekfeu (Ken Samaras), or PNL (Peace 'N Lovés).

10. In borrowing the term "ghettocentricity," I am echoing rap artists' own deployment of the term "ghetto," as explicitly appropriated from the African-American hip-hop lexicon. As Wacquant (2008) argues, French *banlieues* should not be conflated with the relative ethno-racial homogeneity of American inner cities.

11. *Caillera* is back slang (*verlan*) for *racaille* or "scum," a term of insult that has been ambivalently appropriated by some young *cité* men, and particularly by gangsta rappers of the 1990s and early 2000s.

12. Rap group La Rumeur refer to the housing projects as a "concrete forest" ("Predateur isolé," on *L'ombre sur la mesure*, 2002), whereas Sinik terms those who live there "prisoners of the concrete" (*condamnés du béton*) ("Si

proche des miens," on *Sang froid*, 2006). For discussions of the Franco-Maghrebi ("Beur") fiction cited above, see Hargreaves (1997).

13. For discussions of the history and politics of hip-hop/rap in France, see Bazin (1995), Cannon (1997), Durand (2002), Gross et al. (1994), Molinero (2011), Prévos (1998), and Tshimanga (2009). This section draws on my longer discussion of "ghetto patrimony" in Silverstein (2012). Rap is certainly not the only musical form produced or consumed in the *cités*, with thriving Algerian *raï*, Moroccan *gnawa*, Berber *kabyle*, Antillean *zouk*, Congolese *soukous*, Jamaican reggae, Punjabi *bhangra*, and various other musical scenes connecting *banlieue* youth transnationally with listening publics in North Africa, sub-Saharan Africa, the Caribbean, the Indian Ocean, and beyond. But, since the late 1980s, it has been the single musical form that consistently unites *banlieue* youth across ethnic and racial lines, that is accessible to monolingual French speakers, that has minimal financial barriers to entry, and that is malleable to multiple, alternative musical styles. Indeed, rap–*raï*, rap–reggae, rap–*soukous*, and other fusions have become increasingly common over the past two decades.

14. The group's name refers to the building number in which the founding members grew up. As I discuss later, the names of rap groups, albums, and songs often reference the micro-spatial environments that animate their lives and musical sensibilities (see Silverstein 2002b).

15. 113, "Marginal," on *113 degrés* (2005).

16. 113, "Les evadés," on *Ni barreaux, ni barrières, ni frontières* (1998).

17. 113, "C'est ici que la vie commence," on *Ni barreaux, ni barrières, ni frontières* (1998).

18. Lunatic, "HLM3," on *Mauvais oeil* (2000).

19. La Clinique, "Est-ce aç la France?" on Various artists, *Sachons dire non* (1998).

20. 113, "Les évadés," on *Ni barreaux, ni barrières, ni frontières* (1998).

21. Assassin, "Kique ta merde," on *Le futur que nous réserve-t-il?* (1993). The "18th" mentioned in the lyrics is the *arrondissement* of Paris from which the group hails. See Cannon (1997: 162–63) for a discussion of this track.

22. Sniper, "La France," on *Du rire aux larmes* (2001). The word *bougnoules* is a derogatory term for North Africans, dating from the colonial era, that has been ambivalently appropriated by some rap artists.

23. See especially Assassin, "L'état assassine," on *L'homocide volontaire* (1995); Diam's, "Extrême miné," on Various artists, *Sachons dire non* (1998); Ministère AMER, "Sacrifice de poulets," on various artists, *La haine* (1995); Sniper, "Hommes de loi," on *Trait pour trait* (2006); and Suprême NTM, "Qu'est-ce qu'on attend," on *Paris sous les bombes* (1995).

24. See e.g. Monsieur R, "La FranSSe," on *Politikment incorrekt* (2004); and Sniper, "La France," on *Du rire aux larmes* (2001).

25. Sinistre, "Est-ce que ça vaut la peine?" on Various artists, *Sachons dire non* (1998). See also Expression Direkt, "Fin de Lutte," on the same album.

26. Kazkami, "Insurgé," on Mac Kregor, *Insurrection* (2006).

27. Monsieur R, "Revolutionaire," on *Black Album* (2006).

28. Sinik, "Un monde meilleur" and "Brûle," on *Sang froid* (2006).

29. Afrika Bambaataa, a DJ from the South Bronx, is credited as the "godfather" of hip-hop, having christened the artistic movement with its current name. He and his Zulu Nation crew of MCs, deejays, break-dancers, and grafitti artists spread hip-hop internationally on overseas tours, including to France. KRS-One (Lawrence Parker), an MC likewise from the South Bronx, was a member of the hardcore rap group Boogie Down Productions before embarking on a solo career and founding the Temple of Hip-Hop political movement.

30. See e.g. Suprême NTM, "Tout n'est pas si facile," on *Paris sous les bombes* (1995).

31. The al-Ahbash, with Ethiopian roots, are not a Sufi *tariqa* per se, but their connections to and the influence of from the Naqshbandiyya, Qadiriyya, and Rif'aiyya orders have been well documented. See Donahue (2008) and Hamzeh & Dekmejian (1996). On the Gülen movement, see Ebaugh (2010). On the 'Alawiyya, see Lings (1971). On the Boutshishiyya, see Ben Driss (2002), Haenni & Voix (2007), Kapchan (2009), Nabti (2007), and Zeghal (2008).

32. See the official websites: Boutshishiyya (http://www.saveurs-soufies.com), Gülen (http://fr.fgulen.com/), al-Ahbash (http://www.apbif.org/), and 'Alawiyya (http://aisa-net.com/).

33. Quoted from: https://www.institut-cultures-islam.org/ (accessed December 31, 2017).

34. See: http://www.apbif.org.

35. On the life, politics, and musical production of Abd al Malik, see Aidi (2014), Bourderionnet (2011), and Jouili (2013).

36. The film, *Qu'Allah bénisse la France!*, was titled after Malik's book and released in 2014.

37. Three of Malik's albums—*Gibraltar* (2006), *Dante* (2008), and *Château rouge* (2010)—won first prize in the "urban music" category of the French Victoire de la Musique awards.

38. NAP, *La racaille Sorte 1 Disque* (1996).

39. NAP, *A l'intérieur de nous* (2000).

40. Abd al Malik, *La face à face des coeurs* (2004).

41. Abd al Malik, "Noir & blanc," on *La face à face des coeurs* (2004).

42. Abd al Malik, "Céline," on *Gibraltar* (2006).

43. Abd al Malik, "C'est du lourd," on *Gibraltar* (2006).

44. See Médine, *Arabian Panther* (2008).

45. Médine, "Jihad," on *Jihad: Le plus grand combat est contre soi-même* (2005).

46. *11 septembre*.

47. For a discussion of Kery James and his Islamic project, see Molinero (2011: 112–14).

48. The concert was later released as a CD/DVD (Various artists, *Urban Peace*, 2002).

49. Kéry James, *Savoir & vivre ensemble* (2002).

50. Quoted from the sleeve notes for Kéry James, *Savoir & vivre ensemble* (2002).

CONCLUSION

1. Quoted from the program *On a tout essayé* ("We've tried it all"), broadcast on France 2 television on May 17, 2006.
2. Laurent Cantet's film, *Entre les Murs/The Class* (2008), based on a novel by former French school teacher François Bégaudeau (2006) built around his own classroom experiences, presents a particularly poignant, if at times ungenerous, portrayal of this dynamic.
3. Monsieur R, "Quoi ma gueule?" on *ANTICONstitutionellement* (2000).
4. The PIR was previously known as the Movement of the Indigènes of the Republic (MIR).
5. Bouteldja's book has recently been made available in English translation (Bouteldja 2017). All quotes in this chapter are from the original French edition. In September 2016, Sikh-American social-justice filmmaker and activist Valerie Kaur founded the Revolutionary Love Project, which has brought together faith leaders, activists, and academics from across different constituencies in the United States to fight against the reactionary populism of the Trump presidency. She draws on an ethic of love inspired by Gandhi and King, specifying that, "Love is not just a feeling, but an action." See: http://www.revolutionarylove.net/ (accessed January 4, 2018).

References

FILMOGRAPHY

Africa paradis, dir. Sylvestre Amoussou, 86 mins. France/Benin, 2006.

Babylon A.D., dir. Matthieu Kassovitz, 101 mins. France/UK/USA, 2008.

Banlieue 13/District 13, dir. Pierre Morel, 86 mins. France, 2004.

Banlieue 13: Ultimatum/District 13: Ultimatum, dir. Patrick Alessandrin, 106 mins. France, 2009.

La battaglia de Algeri/The Battle of Algiers, dir. Gillo Pontecorvo, 120 mins. Italy/ Algeria, 1965.

Deux ou trois choses que je sais d'elle/Two or Three Things I Know About Her, dir. Jean-Luc Godard, 87 mins. France, 1967.

Entre les murs/The Class, dir. Laurent Cantet, 128 mins. France, 2008.

La fille du RER/The Girl on the Train, dir. André Téchiné, 97/105 mins. France, 2009.

La haine, dir. Matthieu Kassovitz, 98 mins. France, 1995.

Les hommes libres/Free Men, dir. Ismaël Ferroukhi, 99 mins. France, 2011.

Ma 6-T va crack-er, dir. Jean-François Richet, 105 mins. France, 1997.

La petite Jérusalem, dir. Karin Albou, 96 mins. France, 2005.

Playtime, dir. Jacques Tati, 124 mins. France, 1967.

Qu'Allah bénisse la France!/May Allah bless France! dir. Abd al Malik, 95 mins. France, 2014.

Trafic, dir. Jacques Tati, 96 mins. France/Italy, 1971.

Week-end, dir. Jean-Luc Goddard, 105 mins. France, 1967.

Yamakasi: Les samouraïs des temps modernes, dir. Ariel Zeitoun and Julien Seri, 90 mins. France, 2001.

DISCOGRAPHY

113. 1998. *Ni barreaux, ni barrières, ni frontières*, compact disc, Invasion Records.

——2005. *113 degrés*, compact disc, Sony/BMG.

Assassin. 1993. *Le futur que nous réserve-t-il?* compact disc, Delabel.

——1995. *L'homocide volontaire*, compact disc, Delabel.

James, Kery. 2002. *Savoir & vivre ensemble*, compact disc, Naïve.

Lunatic. 2000. *Mauvais oeil*, compact disc, Warner.

Mac Kregor. 2006. *Insurrection*, compact disc, Hematom Concept.

Malik, Abd al. 2004. *La face à face des coeurs*, compact disc, Atmosphériques/ Universal.

——2006. *Gibraltar*, compact disc, Gibraltar/Atmosphériques.

——2008. *Dante*, compact disc, Polydor/Universal.

——2010. *Château rouge*, compact disc, Barclay/Universal.

11 *Septembre*.

—— 2005. *Jihad: Le plus grand combat est contre soi-même*, compact disc, Din Records.
—— 2008. *Arabian Panther*, compact disc, Because Music.
Monsieur R. 2000. *ANTICONstitutionellement*, compact disc, XIII Bis/Diamond.
—— 2004. *Politikment incorrekt*, compact disc, Diamond.
—— 2006. *Black Album*, compact disc, Diamond/Nocturne.
NAP. 1996. *La Racaille Sorte 1 Disque*, compact disc, High-Skills Records.
—— 2000. *A l'intérieur de nous*, compact disc, Sony.
La Rumeur. 2002. *L'ombre sur la mesure*, compact disc, EMI Music.
Sinik. 2006. *Sang froid*, compact disc, Six-O-Nine/Warner Music France.
Sniper. 2001. *Du rire aux larmes*, compact disc, Desh/Warner.
—— 2006. *Trait pour trait*, compact disc, Desh/Warner.
Suprême NTM. 1995. *Paris sous les bombes*, compact disc, Sony/Epic.
Various artists. 1995. *La haine: Musiques inspirées du film*, compact disc, Delabel.
—— 1998. *Sachons dire non*, compact disc, Untouchable/EMI.
—— 2002. *Urban Peace*, compact disc/DVD, Universal/Sony/EMI.

BIBLIOGRAPHY

Abderrahim, Kader. 2008. *L'indépendance comme seul but*. Paris: Méditerrannée.
Afghani, Massoud. 2009. Discours de Houria Boutledja à la Vème Marche des indigènes de la république. *Parti des Indigènes de la Republisque*, May 15. Available at: http://indigenes-republique.fr/discours-de-houria-bouteldja-a-la-veme-marche-des-indigenes-de-la-republique/, accessed February 10, 2018.
Agamben, Giorgio. 1999. *Remnants of Auschwitz: The Victim and the Archive*. New York: Zone Books.
—— 2005. *State of Exception*. Chicago: University of Chicago Press.
Aidi, Hisham. 2006. The interference of Al-Andalus: Spain, Islam, and the West. *Social Text* 24 (2): 67–88.
—— 2014. *Rebel Music: Race, Empire, and the New Muslim Youth Culture*. New York: Random House.
Aissaoui, Rabah. 2009. *Immigration and National Identity: North African Political Movements in Colonial and Postcolonial France*. New York: Palgrave Macmillan.
Aldrich, Robert. 2005. Le musée colonial impossible. In *Culture post-coloniale 1961–2006: Traces et mémoires coloniales en France*, ed. Pascal Blanchard and Nicolas Bancel. Paris: Autrement, pp. 83–101.
Allievi, Stefano. 1999. *Les convertis à l'Islam: Les nouveaux musulmans d'Europe*. Paris: L'Harmattan.
Amara, Fadela. 2006 [2003]. *Breaking the Silence: French Women's Voices from the Ghetto*. Berkeley: University of California Press.
Amara, Mahfoud. 2006. Soccer, post-colonial and post-conflict discourses in Algeria: Algérie–France, 6 october 2001, "ce n'était pas un simple match de foot". *International Review of Modern Sociology* 2: 217–39.
—— 2017. Sport labor migrant communities from the Maghreb in the GCC. In *Arab Migrant Communities in the GCC*, ed. Zahra Babar. London: Hurst, pp. 217–34.

Amselle, Jean-Loup. 2003. *Affirmative Exclusion: Cultural Pluralism and the Rule of Custom in France*. Ithaca, NY: Cornell University Press.

—— 2013. Dieudonné fair resurgir un antisémitisme postcolonial. *Le Monde*, December 31. Available at: http://www.lemonde.fr/idees/article/2013/12/31/affaire-dieudonne-un-antisemitisme-postcolonial_4341645_3232.html (accessed December 25, 2017).

Anderson, Benedict. 1991. *Imagined Communities*, rev. edn. London: Verso.

Andrès, Hervé. 2010. La nationalité dans le football, entre nationalisme et cosmopolitisme. In *Allez la France! Football et immigration*, ed. Claude Boli, Yvan Gastaut, and Fabrice Grognet. Paris: Gallimard, pp. 132–38.

Anidjar, Gil. 2003. *The Jew, the Arab: History of the Enemy*. Stanford: Stanford University Press.

Appadurai, Arjun. 1996. *Modernity at Large: Cultural Dimensions of Globalization*. Minneapolis: University of Minnesota Press.

Arab, Chadia. 2014. Parcours et nouvelles routes migratoires en Méditerranée: le cas des migrations marocaines. *Maghreb-Machrek* 220: 75–92.

Arkin, Kimberly A. 2014. *Rhinestones, Religion, and the Republic: Fashioning Jewishness in France*. Stanford: Stanford University Press.

Arnaud, Pierre (ed). 1992. *L'empire du sport*. Aix-en-Provence: Amaron.

Artiaga, Loïc. 2010. La politique des sentiments: Les migrations au prisme des autobiographies de footballeurs. In *Allez la France! Football et immigration*, ed. Claude Boli, Yvan Gastaut, and Fabrice Grognet. Paris: Gallimard, pp. 168–72.

Asad, Talal. 2003. *Formations of the Secular: Christianity, Islam, Modernity*. Stanford: Stanford University Press.

—— 2009 [1986]. The idea of an anthropology of Islam. *Qui Parle* 17(2): 1–30.

Atkinson, Michael. 2009. Parkour, anarcho-environmentalism, and poeisis. *Journal of Sport and Social Issues* 33(2): 169–94.

Austin, J.L. 1962. *How to Do Things with Words*. Oxford: Clarendon Press.

Austin, James F. 2009. Destroying the *banlieue*: Reconfigurations of suburban space in French film. *Yale French Studies* 115: 80–92.

Badiou, Alain. 2005. *Being and Event*. London: Continuum.

Bahloul, Joëlle. 1996. *The Architecture of Memory*. Cambridge: Cambridge University Press.

Balandier, Georges. 1951. La situation coloniale. *Cahiers Internationaux de Sociologie* 11: 44–79.

Balibar, Etienne. 1991. Is there a "neo-racism"? In *Race, Nation, Class: Ambiguous Identities*, ed. Etienne Balibar and Immanuel Wallerstein. New York: Verso, pp. 17–28.

—— 2003. Un nouvel antisémitisme? In *Antisémitisme: L'intolérable chantage. Israël–Palestine, une affaire française?* ed. Etienne Balibar et al. Paris: La Découverte, pp. 89–96.

—— 2004. *We the People of Europe? Reflections on Transnational Citizenship*. Princeton: Princeton University Press.

Balibar, Etienne, and Immanuel Wallerstein. 1991. *Race, Nation, Class: Ambiguous Identities*. London: Verso.

Bancel, Nicolas. 2005. L'histoire difficile: Esquisse d'une historiographie du fait colonial et postcolonial. In *La fracture coloniale*, ed. Pascal Blanchard, Nicolas Bancel, and Sandrine Lemaire. Paris: La Découverte, pp. 85–95.

Bancel, Nicolas, and Pascal Blanchard. 2005. Mémoire coloniale: Résistances à l'émergence d'un débat. In *Culture post-coloniale 1961–2006: Traces et mémoires coloniales en France*, ed. Pascal Blanchard and Nicolas Bancel. Paris: Autrement, pp. 22–41.

Bancel, Nicolas, and Herman Lebovics. 2011. Building the history museum to stop history: Nicolas Sarkozy's new presidential museum of French history. *French Cultural Studies* 22(4): 271–88.

Bancel, Nicolas, et al. 2002. *Zoos humains: Au temps des exhibitions humaines*. Paris: La Découverte.

—— 2010. *Ruptures postcoloniales: Les nouveaux visages de la société française*. Paris: La Découverte.

Barber, Benjamin. 1996. *Jihad vs. McWorld: Terrorism's Threat to Democracy*. New York: Ballantine.

Bayart, Jean-François. 2010. *Les études postcoloniales: Un carnival académique*. Paris: Karthala.

Bazin, Hugues. 1995. *La culture hip-hop*. Paris: Desclée de Brouwer.

Beaman, Jean. 2017. *Citizen Outsider: Children of North African Immigrants in Paris*. Berkeley: University of California Press.

Beaud, Stéphane, and Gérard Noiriel. 1990. L'immigration dans le football. *Vingtième Siècle* 26: 83–96.

Begag, Azouz. 1989. *Béni ou le paradis privé*. Paris: Seuil.

Bégaudeau, François. 2006. *Entre les murs*. Paris: Verticales.

Belguendouz, Abdelkrim. 1999. *Les Marocains à l'étranger: Citoyens et partenaires*. Kenitra: Boukili Impressions.

Bellil, Samira. 2002. *Dans l'enfer des tournantes*. Paris: Denoël.

Benbassa, Esther. 1999. *The Jews of France*. Princeton: Princeton University Press.

—— 2004. *La République face à ses minorities: Les juifs hier, les musulmans aujourd'hui*. Paris: Mille et Une Nuits.

—— 2006. Israéliens/Palestiniens, Juifs/Arabes: archéologie d'un conflit. In *Juifs et musulmans: Une histoire partagée, un dialogue à contraire*, ed. Esther Benbassa and Jean-Christophe Attias. Paris: La Découverte, pp. 61–75.

Benbassa, Esther, and Jean-Christophe Attias (eds). 2006. *Juifs et musulmans: Une histoire partagée, un dialogue à contraire*. Paris: La Découverte.

—— (eds). 2015. *Juifs et musulmans: Retisssons les liens!* Paris: CNRS.

Ben Driss, Karim. 2002. *Sidi Hamza al Qaâdiri Bouchich: Le renouveau du soufisme au Maroc*. Milan: Arché.

Benjamin, Walter. 1978 [1955]. Paris, capital of the nineteenth century. In *Reflections*. New York: Schocken, pp. 146–62.

Benlabbas, Mehdy. 2015. Contre la violence: Réetablir le dialogue. In *Juifs et musulmans: Retisssons les liens!* ed. Esther Benbassa and Jean-Christophe Attias. Paris: CNRS, pp. 21–27.

Ben-Yehoyada, Naor. 2017. *The Mediterranean Incarnate: Region Formation between Sicily and Tunisia since World War II*. Chicago: University of Chicago Press.

Berlant, Lauren. 1997. *The Queen of America Goes to Washington City: Essays on Sex and Citizenship*. Durham, NC: Duke University Press.

Berman, Marshall. 1982. *All That Is Solid Melts Into Air*. New York: Penguin.

Bernard, Ariane. 2004. Frenchwoman says she lied about anti-Semitic attack. *New York Times*, July 13. Available at: http://www.nytimes.com/2004/07/13/international/europe/frenchwoman-says-she-lied-about-antisemitic-attack.html (accessed February 17, 2018).

Blanchard, Pascal. 2010. Bleu-black-beur, l'équipe nationale aux "couleurs" de l'histoire. In *Allez la France! Football et immigration*, ed. Claude Boli, Yvan Gastaut, and Fabrice Grognet. Paris: Gallimard, pp. 122–31.

Blanchard, Pascal, and Nicolas Bancel (eds). 2005. *Culture post-coloniale 1961–2006: Traces et mémoires coloniales en France*. Paris: Autrement.

Blanchard, Pascal, Nicolas Bancel, and Sandrine Lemaire (eds). 2005. *La fracture coloniale: La société française au prisme de l'héritage colonial*. Paris: La Découverte.

Bloom, Peter. 1999. Beur cinema and the politics of location: French immigration politics and the naming of a film movement. *Social Identities* 5(4): 469–87.

—— 2009. The state of French cultural exceptionalism: The 2005 uprisings and the politics of visibility. In *Frenchness and the African Diaspora: Identity and Uprising in Contemporary France*, ed. Charles Tshimanga, Didier Gondola, and Peter J. Bloom. Bloomington: Indiana University Press, pp. 227–47.

Boli, Claude, Yvann Gastaut, and Fabrice Grognet. 2010. *Allez la France! Football et immigration*. Paris: Gallimard.

Boniface, Pascal. 2002. *La terre est ronde comme un ballon: Géopolitique et football*. Paris: Seuil.

Boniface, Pascal, and Médine. 2012. *Don't Panik: "N'ayez pas peur."* Paris: Desclée de Brouwer.

Borden, Iain. 2001. *Skateboarding, Space and the City: Architecture and the Body*. Oxford: Berg.

Bouamama, Saïd. 2009. *Les classes et quartiers populaires: Paupérisation, ethnicisation et discrimination*. Paris: Cygne.

Bouamama, Saïd, Hadjila Sad-Saoud, and Mokhtar Djerdoubi. 1994. *Contribution à la mémoire des banlieues*. Paris: Editions du Volga.

Boubekeur, Ahmed. 2010. Abdelmalek Sayad, pionnier d'une sociologie de l'immigration postcoloniale. In *Ruptures postcoloniales: Les nouveaux visages de la société française*, ed. Nicolas Bancel et al. Paris: La Découverte, pp. 37–48.

Bourderionnet, Olivier. 2011. A "picture-perfect" banlieue artist: Abd Al Malik or the perils of a conciliatory rap discourse. *French Cultural Studies* 22(2): 151–61.

Bourdieu, Pierre. 1958. *Sociologie de l'Algérie*. Paris: Presses Universitaires de France.

—— 1979 [1970]. The Kabyle house, or the world reversed. In *Algeria 1960*. Cambridge: Cambridge University Press, pp. 133–53.

—— 1988. *Homo Academicus*. Stanford: Stanford University Press.

—— 2000. *Pascalian Meditations*. Stanford: Stanford University Press.

Bourdieu, Pierre, and Abdelmalek Sayad. 1964. *Le déracinement: La crise de l'agriculture traditionnelle en Algérie*. Paris: Minuit.

Bourdieu, Pierre, and Loïc Wacquant. 1999. On the cunning of imperial reason. *Theory, Culture and Society* 16(1): 41–58.

—— 2000. The organic ethnologist of Algerian migration. *Ethnography* 1(2): 173–82.

Bouteldja, Houria. 2014. Dieudonné au prisme de la gauche blanche ou comment penser l'internationalisme domestique. Parti des Indigènes de la République. Available at: http://indigenes-republique.fr/dieudonne-au-prisme-de-la-gauche-blanche-ou-comment-penser-linternationalisme-domestique/ (accessed December 25, 2017).

—— 2016. *Les blancs, les juifs et nous: Vers une politique de l'amour révolutionnaire.* Paris: La Fabrique.

——2017. *The Whites, Jews, and Us: Toward a Revolutionary Politics of Love.* Los Angeles: Semiotext(e).

Bouteldja, Houria, and Sadri Khiari. 2012. *Nous sommes les indigènes de la République.* Paris: Amsterdam.

Bowen, John R. 2005. Commentary on Bunzl. *American Ethnologist* 32(4): 524–25.

—— 2006. *Why the French Don't Like Headscarves: Islam, the State, and Public Space.* Princeton: Princeton University Press.

——2010. *Can Islam Be French? Pluralism and Pragmatism in a Secularist State.* Princeton: Princeton University Press.

——2012. *A New Anthropology of Islam.* Cambridge: Cambridge University Press.

Boym, Svetlana. 2001. *The Future of Nostalgia.* New York: Basic Books.

Bozzo, Anna. 2005. Islam et la République: Une longue histoire de méfiance. In *La fracture coloniale,* ed. Pascal Blanchard, Nicolas Bancel, and Sandrine Lemaire. Paris: La Découverte, pp. 77–84.

Brand, Laurie. 2006. *Citizens Abroad: Emigration and the State in the Middle East and North Africa.* Cambridge: Cambridge University Press.

Braudel, Fernand. 1958. Histoire et sciences sociales: La longue durée. *Annales* 13(4): 725–53.

Brenner, Emmanuel. 2002. *Les territoires perdus de la République.* Paris: Mille et Une Nuits.

Bromberger, Christian. 1995. Football as world view and ritual. *French Cultural Studies* 6: 293–311.

——1998. *Football, la bagatelle la plus sérieuse du monde.* Paris: Bayard.

Bromberger, Christian, Alain Hayot, and Mario Mariotini. 1995. *Le match du football: Ethnologie d'une passion partisane à Marseille, Naples et Turin.* Paris: Maison des Sciences de l'Homme.

Brown, Wendy. 2006. *Regulating Aversion: Tolerance in the Age of Identity and Empire.* Princeton: Princeton University Press.

Bruckner, Pascal. 2006. *La tyrannie de la penitence: Essai sur le masochisme occidental.* Paris: Grasset.

Bunzl, Matti. 2005. Between anti-Semitism and Islamophobia: Some thoughts on the new Europe. *American Ethnologist* 32(4): 499–508.

Butler, Judith. 1990. *Gender Trouble: Feminism and the Subversion of Identity.* New York: Routledge.

Caillois, Roger. 2001 [1961]. *Man, Play, and Games,* trans. Meyer Barash. Urbana: University of Illinois Press.

Caldwell, Chris. 2009. *Reflections on Revolution in Europe: Immigration, Islam and the West.* New York: Anchor Books.

Camus, Albert. 2013 [1958]. *Algerian Chronicles,* ed. Alice Kaplan, trans. Arthur Goldhammer. Cambridge, MA: Belknap Press.

Cannon, Steven. 1997. "Panama City rapping: B-Boys in the banlieues and beyond." In *Post-Colonial Cultures in France*, ed. Alec G. Hargreaves and Mark McKinney. London: Routledge, pp. 150–66.

Cassely, Jean-Laurent. 2013. La dieudonnisation des esprits, une (grosse) quenelle qui vient d'en-bas. *Slate*, June 27. Available at: http://www.slate.fr/story/74429/dieudonne-quenelle (accessed December 25, 2017).

Castells, Manuel. 1983. *The City and the Grassroots: A Cross-Cultural Theory of Urban Social Movements*. Berkeley: University of California Press.

Caussé, Bruno. 2006. Zinédine Zidane, la legende térnie. *Le Monde*, July 11, p. 2.

Çelik, Zeynep. 1997. *Urban Forms and Colonial Confrontations: Algiers under French Rule*. Berkeley: University of California Press.

Cepel, Sylvain. 2014. A French clown's hateful gesture. *New York Times*, January 24, p. A25.

Césaire, Aimé. 2000 [1950]. *Discourse on Colonialism*. New York: Monthly Review Press.

Cesari, Jocelyne. 1994. *Etre musulman en France*. Paris: Karthala-IREMAM.

Chaker, Salem. 1990. *Imazighen ass-a (Berbères dans le Maghreb contemporain)*. Algiers: Editions Bouchene.

Chakrabarty, Dipesh. 2000. *Provincializing Europe: Postcolonial Thought and Historical Difference*. Princeton: Princeton University Press.

Chantelat, Pascal, Michel Fodimbi, and Jean Camy. 1996. *Sports de la cité: Anthopologie de la jeunesse sportive*. Paris: L'Harmattan.

Charef, Mehdi. 1983. *Le thé au harem d'Archi Ahmed*. Paris: Mercure de France.

Chtcheglov, Ivan. 1981 [1953]. Formulary for a new urbanism. In *Situationist International Anthology*, ed. Ken Knabb. Berkeley: Bureau of Public Secrets, pp. 1–4.

Cole, Joshua. 2010. Antisémitisme et situation coloniale pendant l'entre-deux-guerres en Algérie: Les émeutes antijuives de Constantine. *Vingtième Siècle* 108: 3–23.

Coller, Ian. 2010. *Arab France: Islam and the Making of Modern Europe, 1798–1831*. Berkeley: University of California Press.

Collyer, Michael. 2007. In-between places: Trans-Saharan transit migrants and the fragmented journey to Europe. *Antipode* 39(4): 668–90.

Colonna, Fanny, and Loïc Le Pape. 2010. *Traces, désirs et volonté d'être: L'après-colonie au Maghreb*. Arles: Sindbad/Actes Sud.

Comaroff, Jean, and John L. Comaroff. 2011. *Theory from the South: Or, How Euro-America is Evolving towards Africa*. New York: Routledge.

Connelly, Matthew, and Paul Kennedy. 1994. Must it be the Rest against the West? *Atlantic Monthly* 274(6): 61–84.

Crapanzano, Vincent. 2011. *The Harkis: The Wound That Never Heals*. Chicago: University of Chicago Press.

Crawford, David. 2013. Inventive articulation: How High Atlas farmers put the global to work. *Journal of North African Studies* 18(5): 639–51.

Damon, Julien. 2010. Les mots qui comptent: Plan Marshall pour les banlieues. *Sciences Humaines* 211. Available at: https://www.scienceshumaines.com/les-mots-qui-comptent-plan-marshall-pour-les-banlieues_fr_24909.html (accessed December 28, 2017).

Davidson, Naomi. 2012. *Only Muslim: Embodying Islam in Twentieth-Century France*. Ithaca, NY: Cornell University Press.

Davis, Mike. 2006. *Planet of Slums*. New York: Verso.

Daynes, Sarah. 1999. Processus de conversion et modes d'identification à l'Islam: l'exemple de la France et des Etats-Unis. *Social Compass* 46(3): 313–23.

De Boeck, Filip, and Sammy Baloji. 2016. *Suturing the City: Living Together in Congo's Urban Worlds*. London: Autograph.

Debord, Guy. 1981a [1955]. Introduction to a critique of urban geography. In *Situationist International Anthology*, ed. Ken Knabb. Berkeley: Bureau of Public Secrets, pp. 5–7.

—— 1981b [1956]. Theory of the dérive. In *Situationist International Anthology*, ed. Ken Knabb. Berkeley: Bureau of Public Secrets, pp. 50–54.

—— 1994 [1967]. *The Society of Spectacle*. New York: Zone Books.

De Certeau, Michel. 1984. *The Practice of Everyday Life*. Berkeley: University of California Press.

De Genova, Nicholas. 2001. Migrant "illegality" and deportability in everyday life. *Annual Review of Anthropology* 31: 419–47.

De Haas, Hein. 2006. Migration, remittances and regional development in southern Morocco. *Geoforum* 37(4): 565–80.

Deleporte, Susan Froning. 2005. Trois musées, une question, une République. In *La fracture coloniale*, ed. Pascal Blanchard, Nicolas Bancel, and Sandrine Lemaire. Paris: La Découverte, pp. 109–16.

Delerm, Philippe. 2006. Le Brésilien. *Le Figaro*, July 3, p. 15.

Deleuze, Gilles, and Félix Guattari. 1987. *A Thousand Plateaus: Capitalism and Schizophrenia*, trans. Brian Massumi. Minneapolis: University of Minnesota Press.

Deltombe, Thomas. 2005. *L'Islam imaginaire: La construction médiatique de l'islamophobie en France, 1975–2005*. Paris: La Découverte.

Denis, Jacques. 2008. Rap domestique, rap révolté. *Le Monde Diplomatique*, September, p. 38.

Derderian, Richard. 2004. *North Africans in Contemporary France: Becoming Visible*. New York: Palgrave Macmillan.

Désir, Harlem. 1985. *Touche pas à mon pote*. Paris: Grasset.

Deville-Danthu, Bernadette. 1997. *Le sport en noir et blanc: Du sport colonial au sport africain dans les anciens territoires français d'Afrique occidentale (1920–1965)*. Paris: L'Harmattan.

Dietschy, Paul. 2010. Le ballon migrateur. In *Allez la France! Football et immigration*, ed. Claude Boli, Yvan Gastaut, and Fabrice Grognet. Paris: Gallimard, pp. 25–28.

Dikeç, Mustafa. 2007. *Badlands of the Republic: Space, Politics, and Urban Policy*. Malden, MA: Blackwell.

Dine, Philip. 2002. France, Algeria and sport: From colonisation to globalisation. *Modern and Contemporary France* 10(4): 495–505.

—— 2010. Football et littérature. In *Allez la France! Football et immigration*, ed. Claude Boli, Yvan Gastaut, and Fabrice Grognet. Paris: Gallimard, pp. 162–67.

Diouf, Mamadou. 2010. Le *postcolonial studies* et leur réception dans le champ académique en France. In *Ruptures postcoloniales: Les nouveaux visages de la société française*, ed. Nicolas Bancel et al. Paris: La Découverte, pp. 149–58.

Djavann, Chahdortt. 2003. *Bas les voiles!* Paris: Gallimard.

Donahue, Katherine. 2008. The religious trajectories of the Moussaoui family. *ISIM Review* 21: 18–19.

Dorsey, James. 2016. *The Turbulent World of Middle East Soccer.* Oxford: Oxford University Press.

Douglas, Mary. 1966. *Purity and Danger.* London: Routledge.

Draï, Raphaël. 2001. *Sous le signe de Sion: L'antisémitisme nouveau est arrivé.* Paris: Michalon.

Droussent, Claude. 2006. L'édito. *L'Equipe,* July 10, p. 1.

Dubet, François. 1987. *La galère: Jeunes en survie.* Paris: Fayard.

Dubet, François, and Didier Lapeyronnie. 1992. *Les quartiers d'exil.* Paris: Seuil.

Dubois, Laurent. 2004a. *A Colony of Citizens: Revolution and Slave Emancipation in the French Caribbean, 1789–1804.* Chapel Hill: University of North Carolina Press.

—— 2004b. *Avengers of the New World: The Story of the Haitian Revolution.* Cambridge, MA: Harvard University Press.

—— 2010. *Soccer Empire: The World Cup and the Future of France.* Berkeley: University of California Press.

Du Bois, W.E.B. 1989 [1903]. *The Souls of Black Folk.* New York: Penguin.

Dunning, Eric. 1999. *Sport Matters: Sociological Studies of Sport, Violence and Civilization.* London: Routledge.

Durand, Alain-Philippe (ed.). 2002. *Black, Blanc, Beur: Rap Music and Hip-Hop Culture in the Francophone World.* Lanham, MD: Scarecrow Press.

Duret, Pascal. 1996. *Anthropologie de la fraternité dans les cités.* Paris: Presses Universitaires de France.

Durkheim, Emile. 1995 [1912]. *The Elementary Forms of Religious Life.* New York: Free Press.

Ebaugh, Helen. 2010. *The Gülen Movement: A Sociological Analysis of a Civic Movement Rooted in Moderate Islam.* Dordecht: Springer.

El Bachiri, Mohamed. 2017. *A Jihad for Love.* London: Head of Zeus.

Epstein, A.L. 1958. *Politics in an African Community.* Manchester: Manchester University Press.

Epstein, Beth S. 2011. *Collective Terms: Race, Culture and Community in a State-Planned City in France.* New York: Berghahn.

Evans, Martin. 1997. *The Memory of Resistance: French Opposition to the Algerian War (1954–1962).* Oxford: Berg.

Fadil, Nadia. 2009. Managing affects and sensibilities: The case of not-handshaking and not-fasting. *Social Anthropology* 17(4): 439–54.

Fanon, Frantz. 1963 [1961]. *The Wretched of the Earth.* New York: Grove Weidenfeld.

—— 1965. Algeria unveiled. In *A Dying Colonialism.* New York: Grove Press, pp. 35–67.

—— 1967 [1952]. *Black Skin, White Masks.* New York: Grove Weidenfeld.

Farred, Grant. 2008. *Long-Distance Love: A Passion for Football.* Philadelphia: Temple University Press.

Fassin, Didier. 2013. *Enforcing Order: An Ethnography of Urban Policing.* Cambridge: Polity Press.

Fatès, Youcef. 1994. *Sport et tiers monde.* Paris: Presses Universitaires de France.

Feldman, Greg. 2012. *The Migration Apparatus: Security, Labor and Policymaking in the European Union*. Stanford: Stanford University Press.

Ferguson, James. 1992. The country and the city on the Copperbelt. *Cultural Anthropology* 7(1): 80–92.

Fernando, Mayanthi L. 2014. *The Republic Unsettled: Muslim French and the Contradictions of Secularism*. Durham, NC: Duke University Press.

Finkielkraut, Alain. 2003. *Au nom de l'autre: Réflexions sur l'antisémitisme qui vient*. Paris: Gallimard.

Foer, Franklin. 2004. *How Soccer Explains the World: An (Unlikely) Theory of Globalization*. New York: HarperCollins.

Forcari, Christophe. 2006. L'extrême droit célèbre la défaite de Bleus trop noirs. *Libération*, July 12, p. 10.

Foucault, Michel. 1997. *Il faut défendre la société*. Paris: Gallimard.

——2002 [1969]. *The Archaeology of Knowledge*. New York: Routledge.

Fourest, Caroline. 2010 [2004]. *Frère Tariq: Le double discours de Tariq Ramadan*. Paris: Grasset.

——2015. *Eloge du blasphème*. Paris: Grasset.

Frenkiel, Stanislas. 2010. Quand les footballeurs algériens partent "à l'aventure" (1976–1980). In *Allez la France! Football et immigration*, ed. Claude Boli, Yvan Gastaut, and Fabrice Grognet. Paris: Gallimard, pp. 110–13.

Friedman, Thomas. 1999. *The Lexus and the Olive Tree: Understanding Globalization*. New York: Farrar, Straus, and Giroux.

Fuggle, Sophie. 2008. Discourses of subversion: The ethics and aesthetics of capoeira and parkour. *Dance Research* 26(2): 204–22.

Gallissot, René. 1985. *Misère de l'antiracisme: Racisme et identité nationale: Le défi de l'immigration*. Paris: Editions Acantère.

Gallo, Max. 2006. *Fier d'être français*. Paris: Fayard.

Gans, Herbert J. 1979. Symbolic ethnicity: The future of ethnic groups and cultures in America. *Ethnic and Racial Studies* 2(1): 9–17.

Gaspard, Françoise, and Farhad Khosrokhavar. 1995. *Le foulard et la République*. Paris: La Découverte.

Gasparini, William. 2008. L'intégration par le sport: Genèse d'une croyance collective. *Sociétés Contemporaines* 69(1): 7–23.

Gastaut, Yvan. 2008a. Le sport comme révélateur des ambiguïtés du processus d'intégration des populations immigrées: Le cas du match de football France–Algérie. *Sociétés Contemporaines* 69: 49–73.

——2008b. *Le métissage par le foot: L'intégration, mais jusqu'où*. Paris: Autrement.

—— 2010a. Une victoire prémontoire: Le match France–Afrique du Nord d'octobre 1954. In *Allez la France! Football et immigration*, ed. Claude Boli, Yvan Gastaut, and Fabrice Grognet. Paris: Gallimard, p. 97.

—— 2010b. La Marseillaise sera sifflée trois fois. In *Allez la France! Football et immigration*, ed. Claude Boli, Yvan Gastaut, and Fabrice Grognet. Paris: Gallimard, p. 119.

Geertz, Clifford. 1968. *Islam Observed: Religious Development in Morocco and Indonesia*. Chicago: University of Chicago Press.

——1973. Notes on the Balinese cockfight. In *The Interpretation of Cultures*. New York: Basic Books, pp. 412–53.

Geisser, Vincent. 2003. *La nouvelle islamophobie*. Paris: La Découverte.

Gellner, Ernest. 1981. *Muslim Society*. Cambridge: Cambridge University Press.

Gillette, Alain, and Abdelmalek Sayad. 1976. *L'immigration algérienne en France*. Paris: Editions Entente.

Gilroy, Paul. 1987. *There Ain't No Black in the Union Jack: The Cultural Politics of Race and Nation*. London: Hutchinson.

—— 1993. *The Black Atlantic: Double Consciousness and Modernity*. Cambridge, MA: Harvard University Press.

Glick Schiller, Nina, Linda Basch, and Cristina Szanton Blanc. 1995. From immigrant to transmigrant: Theorizing transnational migration. *Anthropological Quarterly* 68(1): 48–63.

Gluckman, Max. 1961. Anthropological problems arising from the African industrial revolution. In *Social Change in Modern Africa*, ed. Aidan Southall. London: Oxford University Press, pp. 67–82.

Goodman, Jane E. 2005. *Berber Culture on the World Stage: From Village to Video*. Bloomington: Indiana University Press.

Gopnik, Adam. 2006. Rules of the game: Can we forgive him? *New Yorker*, July 24, pp. 22–23.

Graebner, Seth. 2007. *History's Place: Nostalgia and the City in French Algerian Literature*. Lanham, MD: Lexington Books.

Grandmaison, Olivier Le Cour. 2005. *Coloniser, exterminer: Sur la guerre et l'état colonial*. Paris: Fayard.

Gross, Joan, David McMurray, and Ted Swedenburg. 1994. Arab noise and Ramadan nights: Rai, rap, and Franco-Maghrebi identity. *Diaspora* 3(1): 3–39.

Guénif-Souilamas, Nacira. 2006. La Française voilée, la beurette, le garçon arabe et le musulman laic: Les figures assignées du racisme vertueux. In *La République mise à nu par son immigration*, ed. Nacira Guénif-Souilamas. Paris: La Fabrique, pp. 109–32.

—— 2009. Zidane: Portrait of the artist as political avatar. In *Frenchness and the African Diaspora: Identity and Uprising in Contemporary France*, ed. Charles Tshimanga, Didier Gondola, and Peter J. Bloom. Bloomington: Indiana University Press, pp. 205–26.

—— 2010. Le corps-frontière, traces et trajets postcoloniaux. In *Ruptures postcoloniales: Les nouveaux visages de la société française*, ed. Nicolas Bancel et al. Paris: La Découverte, pp. 217–29.

Guénif-Souilamas, Nacira, and Eric Macé. 2004. *Les féministes et le garçon arabe*. Paris: Editions de l'Aube.

Guénif-Souilamas, Nacira, et al. 2015. Qu'est-ce que ça fait d'être un problème. *Mediapart*, January 21. Available at: https://blogs.mediapart.fr/edition/les-in-vites-de-mediapart/article/210115/qu-est-ce-que-ca-fait-d-etre-un-probleme (accessed December 25, 2017).

Haenni, Patrick, and Raphaël Voix. 2007. God by all means: Eclectic faith and Sufi resurgence among the Moroccan bourgeoisie. In *Sufism and the "Modern" in Islam*, ed. Martin van Bruinessen and Julia Day Howell. London: I.B. Tauris, pp. 241–56.

Hage, Ghassan. 1998. *White Nation: Fantasies of White Supremacy in Multicultural Society*. Annandale: Pluto Press Australia.

Hajjat, Abdellali. 2013. *La marche pour l'égalité et contre le racisme*. Paris: Amsterdam.

Hajjat, Abdellali, and Marwan Mohammed. 2013. *Islamophobie: Comment les élites françaises fabriquent le "problème musulman"*. Paris: La Découverte.

Hamzeh, A. Nizar, and Hrair R. Dekmejian. 1996. A Sufi response to political Islamism: Al-Ahbash of Lebanon. *International Journal of Middle Eastern Studies* 28: 217–29.

Handman, Courtney. 2014. *Critical Christianity: Translation and Denominational Conflict in Papua New Guinea*. Berkeley: University of California Press.

Hannerz, Ulf. 1991. *Cultural Complexity*. New York: Columbia University Press.

Hamoumou, Mohand, and Jean-Jacques Jordi. 1999. *Les Harkis, une mémoire enfouie*. Paris: Autrement.

Hare, Geoff. 2003. *Football in France: A Cultural History*. Oxford: Berg.

Hargreaves, Alec. 1995. *Immigration, "Race," and Ethnicity in Contemporary France*. London: Routledge.

——1997. *Immigration and Identity in Beur Fiction: Voices from the North African Immigrant Community in France*, 2nd edn. Oxford: Berg.

Hargreaves, Alec G., and Mark McKinney (eds). 1997. *Post-Colonial Cultures in France*. New York: Routledge.

Haroun, Ali. 1986. *Le septième wilaya*. Paris: Seuil.

Harvey, David. 2000. *Spaces of Hope*. Berkeley: University of California Press.

——2001. Globalization and the "spatial fix". *Geographische Revue* 3(2): 23–30.

Hébert, Georges. 1946 [1925]. *Le sport contre l'éducation physique*, 4th edn. Paris: Vuibert.

——1947 [1912]. *L'éducation physique ou l'entrainement complet par la méthode naturelle*, 12th edn. Paris: Vuibert.

——1949 [1942]. *L'éducation physique, virile et morale par la méthode naturelle*, Vol. 2, 3rd edn. Paris: Vuibert.

Hélénon, Véronique. 1998. Rap music in the land of human rights: The prosecution of Supreme NTM. *Black Renaissance/Renaissance Noire* 3: 233–40.

Herzfeld, Michael. 1997. *Cultural Intimacy: Social Poetics in the Nation-State*. New York: Routledge.

Hirschkind, Charles. 2006. *The Ethical Soundscape: Cassette Sermons and Islamic Counterpublics*. New York: Columbia University Press.

Hirschman, Albert O. 1970. *Exit, Voice, and Loyalty: Responses to Decline in Firms, Organizations, and States*. Cambridge, MA: Harvard University Press.

Hobsbawm, Eric. 1959. *Primitive Rebels*. New York: Praeger.

——2000 [1969]. *Bandits*. New York: New Press.

Hoffman, Katherine. 2002. Moving and dwelling: Building the Moroccan Ashelhi homeland. *American Ethnologist* 29(4): 928–62.

Hollis-Touré, Isabel. 2016. The multidirectional memory of *Charlie Hebdo*. *French Cultural Studies* 27(3): 293–302.

Holmes, Douglas R. 2000. *Integral Europe: Fast-Capitalism, Multiculturalism, Neofascism*. Princeton: Princeton University Press.

Holt, Richard. 1981. *Sport and Society in Modern France*. London: Palgrave Macmillan.

Houellebecq, Michel. 2015. *La soumission*. Paris: Flammarion.

House, Jim, and Neil MacMaster. 2009. *Paris 1961: Algerians, State Terror, and Memory*. Oxford: Oxford University Press.

Huntington, Samuel. 1996. *The Clash of Civilizations and the Remaking of the World Order*. New York: Simon and Schuster.

Hureau, Joëlle. 2001. *La mémoire des pieds-noirs*. Paris: Perrin.

Hussey, Andrew. 2014. *The French Intifada: The Long War between France and Its Arabs*. New York: Farrar, Straus and Giroux.

Hyman, Paula E. 1998. *The Jews of Modern France*. Berkeley: University of California Press.

Ilahiane, Hsain. 2004. *Ethnicities, Community Making, and Agrarian Change: The Political Ecology of a Moroccan Oasis*. Lanham, MD: University Press of America.

James, C.L.R. 1993 [1963]. *Beyond a Boundary*. Durham, NC: Duke University Press.

James, Stuart. 2014. Nicolas Anelka banned for five matches and fined £80,000 for quenelle. *Guardian*, February 27. Available at: https://www.theguardian.com/football/2014/feb/27/nicola-anelka-suspended-five-matches-fa-quenelle (accessed February 10, 2018).

Jaxel-Truer, Pierre. 2006. Mais qu'a bien pu dire Materazzi à Zidane? *Le Monde*, July 12, p. 10.

Jazouli, Adil. 1992. *Les années banlieues*. Paris: Seuil.

Jobard, Fabien, and René Lévy. 2009. *Police et minorités visibles: Les contrôles d'identité à Paris*. New York: Open Society Justice Initiative.

Jouili, Jeanette. 2013. Rapping the Republic: Utopia, critique, and Muslim role models in secular France. *French Politics, Culture and Society* 31(2): 58–80.

——2015. *Pious Practice and Secular Constraints: Women in the Islamic Revival in Europe*. Stanford: Stanford University Press.

Kane, Abdoulaye. 2008. Senegalese Sufi orders in the transnational space: Moving religious activities from home to host countries and creating diasporic identities. In *Migration and Creative Expressions in Africa and the African Diasporas*, ed. Toyin Falola, Niyi Afolabi and Aderonke Adesanya. Durham, NC: Carolina Academic Press, pp. 471–81.

Kapchan, Deborah. 2007. *Traveling Spirit Masters: Gnawa Trance and Music in the Global Marketplace*. Middletown, CT: Wesleyan University Press.

——2009. Learning to listen: The sound of Sufism in France. *World of Music* 51(2): 65–89.

——2013. The aesthetics of the invisible: Sacred music in secular (French) places. *TDR: The Drama Review* 57(3): 132–47.

Kastoryano, Riva. 2002. *Negotiating Identities: States and Immigrants in France and Germany*. Princeton: Princeton University Press.

Katz, Ethan B. 2012. Did the Paris mosque save the Jews? A mystery and its memory. *Jewish Quarterly Review* 102(2): 256–87.

——2015. *The Burdens of Brotherhood: Jews and Muslims from North Africa to France*. Cambridge, MA: Harvard University Press.

Keaton, Trica. 2006. *Muslim Girls and the Other France: Race, Identity Politics, and Social Exclusion*. Bloomington: Indiana University Press.

Keaton, Trica, T.D. Sharpley-Whiting, and Tyler Stovall. 2012. *Black France/France Noire: The History and Politics of Blackness*. Durham, NC: Duke University Press.

Kelley, Robin D.G. 1996. Kickin' reality, kickin' ballistics: Gangsta rap and postindustrial Los Angeles. In *Droppin' Science: Critical Essays on Rap Music and Hip Hop Culture*, ed. William Eric Perkins. Philadelphia: Temple University Press, pp. 183–227.

Kepel, Gilles. 1987. *Les banlieues de l'Islam: Naissance d'une religion en France*. Paris: Seuil.

Kessous, Mustapha. 2005. Des parlementaires réclament des poursuites contre les rappeurs. *Le Monde*, November 24. Available at: http://www.lemonde.fr/societe/article/2005/11/24/des-parlementaires-reclament-des-poursuites-contre-des-rappeurs_713789_3224.html (accessed February 13, 2018).

—— 2006. Les poursuites contre le rappeur Monsieur R jugées irrecevables. *Le Monde*, June 27. Available at: http://www.lemonde.fr/societe/article/2006/06/27/les-poursuites-contre-le-rappeur-monsieur-r-jugees-irrecevables_788717_3224.html (accessed February 13, 2018).

Kettane, Nacer. 1985. *Le sourire de Brahim*. Paris: Denoël.

Khatib, Abdelhafid. 1958. Essai de description psychogéographique des Halles. *Internationale Situationniste* 2. Available at: http://isituationniste.blogspot.com/2007/04/essai-de-description-psychogeographique.html (accessed January 1, 2018).

Khellil, Mohand. 1979. *L'exil kabyle: Essai d'analyse du vécu des migrants*. Paris: L'Harmattan.

Khiari, Sadri. 2006. *Pour une politique de la racaille: Immigré-e-s, indigènes et jeunes de banlieues*. Paris: Textuel.

—— 2009. *La contre-révolution coloniale en France: De de Gaulle à Sarkozy*. Paris: La Fabrique.

Killian, Caitlin. 2006. *North African Women in France: Gender, Culture, and Identity*. Stanford: Stanford University Press.

Kiwan, Nadia. 2016. Freedom of thought in the aftermath of the *Charlie Hebdo* attacks. *French Cultural Studies* 27(3): 233–44.

Kleinman, Julie. 2016. "All sons and daughters of the Republic": Producing difference in French education. *Journal of the Royal Anthropological Institute* 22(2): 261–78.

Klug, Brian. 2003. The collective Jew: Israel and the new anti-Semitism. *Patterns of Prejudice* 37(2): 117–38.

—— 2016a. To flee or not to flee: Is that the question? *International Journal of Public Theology* 10: 338–53.

—— 2016b. In the heat of the moment: Bringing "Je suis Charlie" into focus. *French Cultural Studies* 27(3): 223–32.

Konstantarakos, Myrto. 1999. Which mapping of the city? *La Haine* and the *cinéma de banlieue*. In *French Cinema in the 1990s: Continuity and Difference*, ed. Phil Powrie. Oxford: Oxford University Press, pp. xx–xx.

Koselleck, Reinhart. 2004 [1979]. *Futures Past: On the Semantics of Historical Time*. New York: Columbia University Press.

Krims, Adam. 2000. *Rap Music and the Poetics of Identity*. Cambridge: Cambridge University Press.

Kuper, Simon. 2006 [1994]. *Soccer Against the Enemy: How the World's Most Popular Sport Starts and Fuels Revolutions and Keeps Dictators in Power*. New York: Nation Books.

Lakhdar, Mounia, Geneviève Vinsonneau, Michael Apter, and Etienne Mullet. 2007. Conversion to Islam among French adolescents and adults: A systematic inventory of motives. *International Journal for the Psychology of Religion* 17(1): 1–15.

Lalami, Leila. 2009. The new Inquisition. *The Nation*, November 24. Available at: https://www.thenation.com/article/new-inquisition/ (accessed December 18, 2017).

Lallaoui, Mehdi. 1993. *Du bidonville aux HLM*. Paris: Syros.

Lapeyronnie, Didier. 2005. La banlieue comme théâtre colonial, ou la fracture coloniale dans les quartiers. In *La fracture coloniale*, ed. Pascal Blanchard, Nicolas Bancel, and Sandrine Lemaire. Paris: La Découverte, pp. 213–22.

——— 2009. Primitive rebellion in the French banlieues: On the fall 2005 riots. In *Frenchness and the African Diaspora: Identity and Uprising in Contemporary France*, ed. Charles Tshimanga, Didier Gondola, and Peter J. Bloom. Bloomington: Indiana University Press, pp. 21–46.

Laurence, Jonathan. 2012. *The Emancipation of Europe's Muslims*. Princeton: Princeton University Press.

Laurence, Jonathan, and Justin Vaisse. 2006. *Integrating Islam: Political and Religious Challenges in Contemporary France*. Washington, DC: Brookings Institute Press.

Lebegue, Thomas, Dominique Simonnot, and Patricia Tourancheau. 2005. "Je connais mieux ce qui se passe en banlieue que Thuram". *Libération*, December 23. Available at: http:// www.liberation.fr/evenement/2005/12/23/je-connais-mieux-ce-qui-se-passe-en-banlieue-que-thuram_542670 (accessed February 10, 2018).

Lebovics, Henri. 1994. *True France: The Wars over Cultural Identity, 1900–1945*. Ithaca, NY: Cornell University Press.

——— 2004. *Bringing the Empire Back Home: France in the Global Age*. Durham, NC: Duke University Press.

Leclercq, Florent. 1995. Banlieues: Plan et arrière-plan. *L'Express*, November 9. Available at: https://www.lexpress.fr/informations/banlieues-plan-et-arriere-plan_610675.html (accessed February 10, 2018).

Lefebvre, Henri. 1991 [1974]. *The Production of Space*. Oxford: Blackwell.

——— 1996 [1968]. Right to the city. In *Writings on Cities*. Oxford: Blackwell, pp. 63–183.

Lefeuvre, Daniel. 2006. *Pour en finir avec la répentence coloniale*. Paris: Flammarion.

Le Goaziou, Véronique, and Laurent Mucchielli. 2006. *Quand les banlieues brûlent: Retour sur les émeutes de novembre 2005*. Paris: La Découverte.

Lepoutre, David. 1997. *Coeur de banlieue: Codes, rites et langage*. Paris: Odile Jacob.

Lesprit, Bruno. 2009. Equipe de France: Les raisons du désamour. *Le Monde*, November 30. Available at: http://www.lemonde.fr/sport/article/2009/11/30/equipe-de-france-les-raisons-du-desamour_1274058_3242.html (accessed December 26, 2017).

Le Sueur, James D. 2005. *Uncivil War: Intellectuals and Identity Politics during the Decolonization of Algeria*, 2nd edn. Lincoln: University of Nebraska Press.

Lévi-Strauss, Claude. 1966. *The Savage Mind*. Chicago: University of Chicago Press.

Levitt, Peggy. 2001. *The Transnational Villagers*. Berkeley: University of California Press.

Lévy-Willard, Annette. 2006. Les juifs et l'argent, rapprochement nauseux. *Libération*, February 23. Available at: http://www.liberation.fr/societe/2006/02/23/les-juifs-et-l-argent-rapprochement-nauseeux_30947 (accessed February 18, 2018).

Lewis, Bernard. 1990. The roots of Muslim rage. *Atlantic Monthly* 266(3): 47–60.

Lewis, Oscar. 1966. The culture of poverty. *Scientific American* 215(4): 19–25.

Liauzu, Claude. 1996. *Histoire des migrations en Méditerranée occidentale*. Brussels: Complexe.

Lings, Martin. 1971. *A Sufi Saint in the Twentieth Century: Shaikh Ahmad Al-ʿAlawi: His Spiritual Heritage and Legacy*. Berkeley: University of California Press.

Liogier, Raphaël. 2012. *Le mythe de l'islamisation*. Paris: Seuil.

Lorcin, Patricia M.E. 1995. *Imperial Identities. Stereotyping, Prejudice and Race in Colonial Algeria*. London: I.B. Tauris.

—— (ed.). 2006. *Algeria and France, 1800–2000: Identity, Memory, Nostalgia*. Syracuse, NY: Syracuse University Press.

Luhrmann, Tanya. 2012. *When God Talks Back: Understanding the American Evangelical Relationship with God*. New York: Vintage.

Lyons, Amelia H. 2013. *The Civilizing Mission in the Metropole: Algerian Families and the French Welfare State during Decolonization*. Stanford: Stanford University Press.

MacAloon, John J. 1981. *This Great Symbol: Pierre de Coubertin and the Origins of the Modern Olympic Games*. Chicago: University of Chicago Press.

—— 1984. Olympic Games and the theory of spectacle in modern societies. In *Rite, Drama, Festival, Spectacle: Rehearsals Towards a Theory of Cultural Performance*, ed. John J. MacAloon. Philadelphia: Institute for the Study of Human Issues, pp. 241–80.

—— (ed.). 2007. *Muscular Christianity in Colonial and Post-Colonial Worlds*. London: Routledge.

McDonough, Tom. 2002. *Guy Debord and the Situationist International*. Cambridge, MA: MIT Press.

Mack, Mehammed Amadeus. 2017. *Sexagon: Muslims, France, and the Sexualization of National Culture*. New York: Fordham University Press.

MacMaster, Neil. 1991. The "seuil de tolérance": The uses of a "scientific" racist concept. In *Race, Discourse and Power in France*, ed. Maxim Silverman. Brookfield, VT: Grower Publishing, pp. 14–28.

—— 1997. *Colonial Migrants and Racism: Algerians in France, 1900–1962*. New York: St. Martin's Press.

McMurray, David. 2001. *In and Out of Morocco: Smuggling and Migration in a Frontier Boomtown*. Minneapolis: University of Minnesota Press.

Maddy-Weitzman, Bruce. 2011. *The Berber Identity Movement and the Challenge to North African States*. Austin: University of Texas Press.

Mahmood, Saba. 2005. *Politics of Piety: The Islamic Revival and the Feminist Subject*. Princeton: Princeton University Press.

—— 2016. *Religious Difference in a Secular Age: A Minority Report*. Princeton: Princeton University Press.

Makdisi, Ussama. 2007. *Artillery of Heaven: American Missionaries and the Failed Conversion of the Middle East*. Ithaca, NY: Cornell University Press.

Malik, Abd al. 2004. *Qu'Allah bénisse la France!* Paris: Albin Michel.

—— 2010. *La guerre des banlieues n'aura pas lieu*. Paris: Le Cherche Midi.

—— 2012. *Le dernier Français*. Paris: Cherche Midi.

Malkki, Liisa. 1992. National geographic: The rooting of peoples and the territorialization of national identity among scholars and refugees. *Cultural Anthropology* 7(1): 24–44.

Mamdani, Mahmood. 2004. *Good Muslim, Bad Muslim: America, the Cold War, and the Roots of Terror*. New York: Doubleday.

Mandard, Stéphane. 2006. Zinédine Zidane présente des excuses mais se dit sans regrets. *Le Monde*, July 13. Available at: http://www.lemonde.fr/sport/article/2006/07/13/zinedine-zidane-presente-des-excuses-mais-se-dit-sans-regrets_795038_3242.html (accessed February 10, 2018).

Mandel, Maud S. 2014. *Muslims and Jews in France: History of Conflict*. Princeton: Princeton University Press.

Mangan, J.A. (ed.). 1992. *The Cultural Bond: Sport, Empire, Society*. London: Frank Cass.

Marie, Laurent. 2001. Jacques Tati's *Play Time* as New Babylon. In *Cinema and the City: Film and Urban Societies in Global Context*, ed. Mark Shiel and Tony Fitzmaurice. New York: Blackwell, pp. 257–69.

Marx, Karl. 1978 [1853]. On imperialism in India. In *The Marx–Engels Reader*, ed. Robert Tucker. New York: Norton, pp. 653–64.

Marx, Karl, and Friedrich Engels. 1978 [1848]. Manifesto of the Communist Party. In *The Marx–Engels Reader*, ed. Robert Tucker. New York: Norton, pp. 469–500.

Mbembe, Achille. 2009. The Republic and its beasts: On the riots in the French *banlieues*. In *Frenchness and the African Diaspora: Identity and Uprising in Contemporary France*, ed. Charles Tshimanga, Didier Gondola, and Peter J. Bloom. Bloomington: Indiana University Press, pp. 47–54.

Médioni, Gilles. 2004. Les rappeurs d'Allah. *L'Express*, June 7. Available at: https://www.lexpress.fr/culture/musique/les-rappeurs-d-allah_489437.html (accessed January 1, 2018).

Memmi, Albert. 1991 [1957]. *The Colonizer and the Colonized*, trans. Howard Greenfeld. Boston: Beacon Press.

—— 2006 [2004]. *Decolonization and the Decolonized*, trans. Robert Bononno. Minneapolis: University of Minnesota Press.

Mishani, Dror, and Aurelia Smotriez. 2005. What sort of Frenchmen are they? Interview with Alain Finkielkraut. *Haaretz*, November 25. Available at: https://www.haaretz.com/1.4882406 (accessed February 10, 2018).

Mitchell, J. Clyde. 1956. *The Kalela Dance: Aspects of Social Relationships among Urban Africans in Northern Rhodesia*. Manchester: Manchester University Press.

Mohammed, Marwan, and Laurent Mucchielli. 2006. La police dans les "quartiers sensibles": Un profond malaise. In *Quand les banlieues brûlent: Retour sur les émeutes de novembre 2005*, ed. Véronique Le Goaziou and Laurent Mucchielli. Paris: La Découverte, pp. 98–119.

Molinero, Stéphanie. 2011. The meanings of religious talk in French rap music. In *Religion and Popular Music in Europe*, ed. Thomas Bossius, Andreas Häger, and Keith Kahn-Harris. London: I.B. Tauris, pp. 105–23.

Mouillard, Sylvain. 2010. Les bleus: "petits merdeux" de banlieue ou boucs émissaires? *Libération*, June 24. Available at: http://www.liberation.fr/sports/2010/06/24/les-bleus-petits-merdeux-de-banlieue-ou-boucs-emissaires_661532 (accessed December 26, 2017).

Mould, Oli. 2009. Parkour, the city, the event. *Environment and Planning D: Society and Space* 27: 738–50.

Mucchielli, Laurent. 1999. Le rap, tentative d'expression politique et de mobilisation collective des jeunes des quartiers relegués. *Mouvements, Sociétés, Politique et Culture* 3: 60–66.

—— 2005. *Le scandale des "tournantes": Dérives médiatiques, contre-enquête sociologique*. Paris: La Découverte.

Muhammad, Marwan. 2017. *Nous (aussi) sommes la nation: Pourquoi il faut lutter contre l'islamophobie*. Paris: La Découverte.

Nabti, Mehdi. 2007. Des soufis en banlieue parisienne: Mise en scène d'une spiritualité musulmane. *Archives de Sciences Sociales des Religions* 140: 49–68.

Nait-Challal, Michel. 2008. *Dribbleurs de l'indépendance: L'incroyable histoire de l'équipe de football du FLN algérien*. Paris: Prolongations.

Ndiaye, Pap. 2008. *La condition noire: Essai sur une minorité française*. Paris: Calmann-Lévy.

Noiriel, Gérard. 1988. *Le creuset français: Histoire de l'immigration (XIXe–XXe siècles)*. Paris: Seuil.

—— 2007. *Immigration, antisémitisme et racisme en France (XIXe–XXe siècles): Discours publics, humiliations privées*. Paris: Fayard.

Norindr, Panivong. 1996. *Phantasmic Indochina: French Colonial Ideology in Architecture, Film, and Literature*. Durham, NC: Duke University Press.

Omi, Michael, and Howard Winant. 1994. *Racial Formations in the United States*. New York: Routledge.

Ortuzar, Jimena. 2009. Parkour or l'art du déplacement. *TDR: The Dance Review* 53(3): 54–66.

Oujibou, Fatima. 2009. *Converties de l'Islam: Témoignages*. Paris: Editions de Paris.

Özyürek, Esra. 2015. *Being German, Becoming Muslim: Race, Religion, and Conversion in the New Europe*. Princeton: Princeton University Press.

Pandolfo, Stefania. 2007. The burning. *Anthropological Theory* 7(3): 329–63.

Paoli, Paul-François. 2006. *Nous ne sommes pas coupables*. Paris: La Table Ronde.

Parti Socialiste. 1981. *La France au pluriel*. Paris: Editions Entente.

Partridge, Damani. 2010. Holocaust *Mahnmal* (memorial): Monumental memory amidst contemporary race. *Comparative Studies in Society and History* 52(4): 820–50.

—— 2012. *Hypersexuality and Headscarves: Race, Sex, and Citizenship in the New Germany*. Bloomington: Indiana University Press.

Paxton, Robert. 1972. *Vichy France: Old Guard and New Order, 1940–1944*. New York: Knopf.

Peace, Timothy. 2009. *Un antisémitisme nouveau?* The debate about a "new anti-Semitism" in France. *Patterns of Prejudice* 43(2): 103–21.

PEN America. 2015. "French laws against hate speech are bad news for free speech," July 14. Available at: https://pen.org/frances-laws-against-hate-speech-are-bad-news-for-free-speech/ (accessed December 23, 2017).

Penketh, Anne. 2015. Policeman Ahmed Merabet mourned after death in Charlie Hebdo attack. *Guardian*, January 8. Available at: https://www.theguardian.com/world/2015/jan/08/ahmed-merabet-mourned-charlie-hebdo-paris-attack (accessed February 11, 2018).

Pinard, Sarah. 2013. 40 ans de "plan banlieue". *Le Figaro*, February 20. Available at: http://www.lefigaro.fr/actualite-france/2013/02/20/01016-20130220ARTFIG00388-40-ans-de-plan-banlieue.php (accessed January 2, 2018).

Plenel, Edwy. 2016. *For the Muslims: Islamophobia in France*, trans. David Fernbach. London: Verso.

Prakash, Gyan (ed.). 1995. *After Colonialism: Imperial Histories and Postcolonial Displacements*. Princeton: Princeton University Press.

Prévos, André. 1998. Hip hop, rap, and repression in France and the United States. *Popular Music and Society* 22(2): 67–78.

Pronger, Brian. 1998. Post-sport: Transgressing boundaries in physical culture. In *Sport and Postmodern Times*, ed. G. Rail. Albany: State University of New York Press, pp. 277–300.

Prost, Antoine. 2002. *Republican Identities in War and Peace: Representations of France in the Nineteenth and Twentieth Centuries*. Oxford: Berg.

Pujadas, David, and Ahmed Salam. 1995. *La tentation du jihad*. Paris: J.C. Lattès.

Putney, Clifford. 2001. *Muscular Christianity: Manhood and Sports in Protestant America, 1880–1920*. Cambridge, MA: Harvard University Press.

Rabinow, Paul. 1989. *French Modern: Norms and Forms of the Social Environment*. Cambridge, MA: MIT Press.

Ramadan, Tariq. 2004. *Western Muslims and the Future of Islam*. Oxford: Oxford University Press.

Rancière, Jacques. 2004. *The Politics of Aesthetics*. London: Continuum.

Raspail, Jean. 1973. *Le camp des saints*. Paris: Robert Laffont.

Razsa, Maple. 2015. *Bastards of Utopia: Living Radical Politics after Socialism*. Bloomington: Indiana University Press.

Redeker, Robert. 2002. *Le sport contre les peuples*. Paris: Berg International Editeurs.

Renan, Ernst. 1990 [1882]. What is a nation? In *Nation and Narration*, ed. Homi Bhabha. London: Routledge, pp. 10–20.

Rimet, Jules. 1954. *Football et rapprochement des peuples*. Zurich: FIFA.

Robine, Jérémy. 2006. Les "indigènes de la République": Nation et question postcoloniale. *Hérodote* 120: 118–48.

Rogozen-Soltar, Mikaela H. 2017. *Spain Unmoored: Migration, Conversion, and the Politics of Islam*. Bloomington: Indiana University Press.

Roitman, Janet. 2013. *Anti-Crisis*. Durham, NC: Duke University Press.

Rosello, Mireille. 1998. *Declining the Stereotype: Ethnicity and Representation in French Cultures*. Hanover: University Press of New Hampshire.

Rosenberg, Clifford. 2006. *Policing Paris: The Origins of Modern Immigration Control Between the Wars*. Ithaca, NY: Cornell University Press.

Ross, Kristin. 1995. *Fast Cars, Clean Bodies: Decolonization and the Reordering of French Culture*. Cambridge, MA: MIT Press.

Rothberg, Michael. 2009. *Multidirectional Memory: Remembering the Holocaust in the Age of Decolonization*. Stanford: Stanford University Press.

Rousso, Henri. 1991. *The Vichy Syndrome: History and Memory in France since 1944*. Cambridge, MA: Harvard University Press.

Roy, Olivier. 2004. *Globalized Islam: The Search for a New Ummah*. New York: Columbia University Press.

Saada, Emmanuelle. 2006. Un racisme de l'expansion: Les discriminations raciales au regard des situations coloniales. In *De la question sociale à la question raciale? Répresenter la société française*, ed. Didier Fassin and Eric Fassin. Paris: La Découverte, pp. 55–71.

Sahlins, Marshall. 1981. *Historical Metaphors and Mythical Realities: Structure in the Early History of the Sandwich Islands Kingdom*. Ann Arbor: University of Michigan Press.

—— 1988. Cosmologies of capitalism: The trans-Pacific sector of the "world system". *Proceedings of the British Academy* 74: 1–51.

—— 2004. *Apologies to Thucydides: Understanding History as Culture and Vice Versa*. Chicago: University of Chicago Press.

Saint-Martin, Monique de. 1999. Un sociologue critique. *Migrance* 14: 36–39.

Sakhoui, Fethi. 1996. L'insertion par le sport des jeunes d'origine maghrébine des banlieues en difficulté. *Migrations Société* 8(45): 81–100.

Salzbrunn, Monika. 2002. Transnational Senegalese politics in France. *ISIM Newsletter* 10: 29.

Sandberg, Sheryl. 2013. *Lean In: Women, Work, and the Will to Lead*. New York: Knopf.

Santi, Pascale. 2015. Charb, le rire d'abord. *Le Monde*, January 7. Available at: http://www.lemonde.fr/actualite-medias/article/2015/01/07/charb-je-prefere-mourir-debout-que-vivre-a-genoux_4550759_3236.html (accessed February 11, 2018).

Savile, Stephen John. 2008. Playing with fear: Parkour and the mobility of emotion. *Social and Cultural Geography* 9(8): 891–914.

Sayad, Abdelmalek. 1990. Les maux-à-mots de l'immigration: Entretien avec Jean Leca. *Politix: Revue des Sciences Sociales du Politique* 3(12): 7–24.

—— 2002. Entretien avec Hassan Afraoui. In *Histoire et recherche identitaire*. Algiers: Bouchene, pp. 45–105.

—— 2004. *The Suffering of the Immigrant*. Cambridge: Polity Press.

—— 2006. *L'immigration, ou les paradoxes de l'altérité*. Paris: Raisons d'Agir.

Sayad, Abdelmalek, and Eliane Dupuy. 1995. *Un Nanterre algérien, terre de bidonvilles*. Paris: Autrement.

Schreier, Joshua. 2010. *Arabs of Jewish Faith: The Civilizing Mission in Colonial Algeria*. New Brunswick, NJ: Rutgers University Press.

Scott, Joan. 2006. *The Politics of the Veil*. Princeton: Princeton University Press.

Sedgwick, Mark J. 2004. In search of a counter-Reformation: Anti-Sufi stereotypes and the Budshishiyya's response. In *An Islamic Reformation?* ed. Michelle Browers and Charles Kurzman. Lanham, MD: Lexington Books, pp. 125–46.

Shahid, Leila, Michel Warschawski, and Dominique Vidal. 2006. *Les banlieues, le proche-orient et nous*. Paris: Editions de l'Atelier.

Shannon, Jonathan. 2015. *Performing Al-Andalus: Music and Nostalgia across the Mediterranean*. Bloomington: Indiana University Press.

Shatz, Adam. 2005. The Jewish question. *New York Review of Books*, September 22. Available at: http://www.nybooks.com/articles/2005/09/22/the-jewish-question/ (accessed February 13, 2018).

Shepard, Todd. 2006. *The Invention of Decolonization: The Algerian War and the Remaking of France*. Ithaca, NY: Cornell University Press.

Sherman, Daniel. 2004. "Peoples ethnographic": Objects, museums, and the colonial inheritance of French ethnography. *French Historical Studies* 27(3): 669–703.

Silverstein, Paul A. 2000a. Franco–Algerian war and remembrance: Discourse, nationalism, and post-coloniality. In *Francophone Studies: Discourse and Multiplicity*, ed. Kamal Salhi. Exeter: Elm Bank Publications, pp. 147–72.

——— 2000b. Sporting faith: Islam, soccer, and the French nation-state. *Social Text* 18(4): 25–53.

——— 2002a. Stadium politics: Sport, Islam, and Amazigh consciousness in France and North Africa. In *With God on their Side: Sport in the Service of Religion*, ed. Tara Magdalinski and Timothy Chandler. London: Routledge, pp. 37–70.

——— 2002b. "Why are we waiting to start the fire?": French gangsta rap and the critique of state capitalism. In *Black, Blanc, Beur: Rap Music and Hip Hop Culture in the Francophone World*, ed. Alain-Philippe Durand. Lanham, MD: Scarecrow Press, pp. 45–67.

——— 2002c. France's *Mare Nostrum*: Colonial and postcolonial constructions of the French Mediterranean. *Journal of North African Studies* 7(4): 1–22.

——— 2003. Martyrs and patriots: Ethnic, national, and transnational dimensions of Kabyle politics. *Journal of North African Studies* 8(1): 87–111.

——— 2004a. *Algeria in France: Transpolitics, Race, and Nation*. Bloomington: Indiana University Press.

——— 2004b. On rooting and uprooting: Kabyle *habitus*, domesticity, and structural nostalgia. *Ethnography* 5(4): 553–78.

——— 2005. Immigrant racialization and the new savage slot: Race, migration, and immigration in the New Europe. *Annual Review of Anthropology* 34: 363–84.

——— 2006. Guerilla capitalism and ghettocentric cosmopolitanism in the French urban periphery. In *Frontiers of Capital: Ethnographic Reflections on the New Economy*, ed. Melissa Fisher and Gregory Downey. Durham, NC: Duke University Press, pp. 282–304.

——— 2007a. The Maghrib abroad: Immigrant transpolitics and cultural involution in France. In *The Maghrib in the New Century: Identity, Religion, and Politics*, ed. Bruce Maddy-Weitzman and Daniel Zissenwine. Gainesville: University of Florida Press, pp. 235–64.

——— 2007b. Islam, *laïcité*, and Amazigh activism in France and North Africa. In *North African Mosaic: A Cultural Reappraisal of Ethnic and Religious Minorities*, ed. Nabil Boudraa and Joseph Krause. Newcastle: Cambridge Scholars Press, pp. 104–18.

——— 2008a. Kabyle immigrant politics and racialized citizenship in France. In *Citizenship, Political Engagement, and Belonging: Immigrants in Europe and the United States*, ed. Deborah Reed-Danahay and Caroline B. Brettell. New Brunswick: Rutgers University Press, pp. 23–42.

—— 2008b. Thin lines on the pavement: The racialization and spatialization of violence in postcolonial (sub)urban France. In *Gendering Urban Space in the Middle East, South Asia, and Africa*, ed. Kamran Ali and Martina Rieker. New York: Palgrave Macmillan, pp. 169–205.

—— 2010. The local dimensions of transnational Berberism: Racial politics, land rights, and cultural activism in southeastern Morocco. In *Berbers and Others: Shifting Parameters of Ethnicity in the Contemporary Maghrib*, ed. Katherine Hoffman and Susan Gilson Miller. Bloomington: Indiana University Press, pp. 83–102.

—— 2011. Masquerade politics: Race, Islam, and the scales of Amazigh activism in southeastern Morocco. *Nations and Nationalism* 17(1): 65–84.

—— 2012. Le patrimoine du ghetto: Rap et racialisation de la violence dans les banlieues françaises. In *L'Atlantique multiracial: Discours, politiques, dénis*, ed. James Cohen, Andrew J. Diamond, and Philippe Vervaecke. Paris: Karthala, pp. 95–118.

—— 2015. Rethinking colonialism and decolonisation in Algeria, sixty years later: On Bourdieu's *Algerian Sketches* and Camus' *Algerian Chronicles*. *European Journal of Cultural and Political Sociology* 2(2): 89–121.

—— 2018. The Amazigh movement in a changing North Africa. In *Social Currents in North Africa: Culture and Governance after the Arab Spring*, ed. Osama Abi-Mershed. London: Hurst, pp. 73–91.

Silverstein, Paul, and Jane Goodman. 2009. Introduction: Bourdieu in Algeria. In *Bourdieu in Algeria: Colonial Politics, Ethnographic Practices, Theoretical Developments*, ed. Jane Goodman and Paul Silverstein. Lincoln: University of Nebraska Press, pp. 1–64.

Silverstein, Paul, and Chantal Tetreault. 2006. Postcolonial urban apartheid. *Items and Issues* 5(4): 8–15.

Simone, AbdouMaliq. 2004. *For the City Yet to Come: Changing African Life in Four Cities*. Durham, NC: Duke University Press.

Skali, Faouzi. 1999. *La face à face des coeurs: Le soufisme aujourd'hui*. Gordes: Editions du Relié.

Slezhkine, Yuri. 2006. *The Jewish Century*. Princeton: Princeton University Press.

Smith, Andrea. 2006. *Colonial Memory and Postcolonial Europe: Maltese Settlers in Algeria and France*. Bloomington: Indiana University Press.

Smouts, Marie-Claude (ed.). 2007. *La situation postcoloniale*. Paris: Presses de la Fondation Nationale des Sciences Politiques.

Soulignac, Françoise. 1993. *La banlieue parisienne: Cent cinquante ans de transformations*. Paris: La Documentation Française.

Spengler, Oswald. 1926 [1918]. *The Decline of the West*. New York: Knopf.

Spivak, Gayatri. 1999. *A Critique of Postcolonial Reason: Toward a History of the Vanishing Point*. Cambridge, MA: Harvard University Press.

Stam, Robert, and Ella Shohat. 2012. *Race in Translation: Culture Wars around the Postcolonial Atlantic*. New York: New York University Press.

Stein, Sarah Abrevaya. 2014. *Saharan Jews and the Fate of French Algeria*. Chicago: University of Chicago Press.

Sternhell, Zeev. 1983. *Ni droite ni gauche: L'idéologie fasciste en France*. Paris: Seuil.

Stoler, Ann Laura. 2016. *Duress: Imperial Durabilities in Our Times*. Durham, NC: Duke University Press.

Stora, Benjamin. 1991. *La gangrène et l'oubli. La mémoire de la guerre d'Algérie*. Paris: La Découverte.

—— 1995a. Algérie: Absence et surabondance de mémoire. *Esprit* 208: 62–67.

—— 1995b. *L'Algérie en 1995: La guerre, l'histoire, la politique*. Paris: Michalon.

—— 2010. Entre la France et l'Algérie, le traumatisme (post)colonial des années 2000. In *Ruptures postcoloniales: Les nouveaux visages de la société française*, ed. Nicolas Bancel et al. Paris: La Découverte, pp. 328–43.

Stovall, Tyler. 1996. *Paris Noir: African Americans in the City of Lights*. New York: Houghton Mifflin.

—— 2009. Diversity and difference in postcolonial France. In *Postcolonial Thought in the French-Speaking World*, ed. Charles Forsdick and David Murphy. Liverpool: Liverpool University Press, pp. 259–70.

Sveinsson, Kjartan Páll. 2009. *Who Cares About the White Working Class*. London: Runnymede Trust.

Swedenburg, Ted. 2015. Beur/Maghribi musical interventions in France: Rai and rap. *Journal of North African Studies* 20(1): 109–26.

Taguieff, Pierre-André. 1991. *Face au racisme*. Paris: La Découverte.

—— 2004. *Rising from the Muck: The New Anti-Semitism in Europe*. Chicago: Ivan R. Dee.

—— 2005. *La République enlisée*. Paris: Syrtes.

Taïeb, Eric. 2010. Les publics immigrés du football. In *Allez la France! Football et immigration*, ed. Claude Boli, Yvan Gastaut, and Fabrice Grognet. Paris: Gallimard, pp. 181–85.

Talha, Larbi. 1989. *Le salariat immigré devant la crise*. Paris: Editions du Centre National de la Recherche Scientifique.

Tarlo, Emma, and Annelies Moors (eds). 2013. *Islamic Fashion and Anti-Fashion: New Perspectives from Europe and North America*. London: Bloomsbury.

Tarr, Carrie. 2005. *Reframing Difference: Beur and Banlieue Filmmaking in France*. Manchester: Manchester University Press.

Temime, Emile. 1990. *Migrance: Histoire des migrations à Marseille*. Aix-en-Provence: Edisud.

Terrio, Susan. 2009. *Judging Mohammed: Juvenile Delinquency, Immigration, and Exclusion at the Paris Palais de Justice*. Stanford: Stanford University Press.

Tetreault, Chantal. 2015. *Transcultural Teens: Performing Youth Identities in French Cités*. Malden, MA: Wiley-Blackwell.

Thomas, Dominic. 2013. *Africa and France: Postcolonial Cultures, Migration, and Racism*. Bloomington: Indiana University Press.

Thomson, David. 2008. Jump City: Parkour and the Traces. *South Atlantic Quarterly* 107(2): 251–63.

Tillion, Germaine. 1958 [1957]. *Algeria: The Realities*, trans. Ronald Matthews. New York: Knopf.

—— 1961 [1960]. *France and Algeria: Complementary Enemies*. New York: Knopf.

Tilly, Charles. 1999. *Durable Inequality*. Berkeley: University of California Press.

Todd, Emmanuel. 2015. *Qui est Charlie? Sociologie d'une crise religieuse*. Paris: Seuil.

Topolski, Anya. 2016. A Genealogy of the "Judeo-Christian" Signifier: A Tale of Europe's Identity Crisis. In *Is There a Judeo-Christian Tradition? A European Perspective*, ed. Emmanuel Nathan and Anya Topolski. Berlin: De Gruyter, pp. 267–84.

Trémolet de Villiers, Vincent. 2002. "Les zones de non-droit" dans la République française, mythe ou réalité, PhD thesis. Paris: Université de Paris II.

Trigano, Shmuel. 2003. *La démission de la République: Juifs et musulmans en France*. Paris: Presses Universitaires de France.

Trotsky, Leon. 1968 [1936]. *Whither France?* New York: Merit Publishers.

Trouillot, Michel-Rolph. 1995. *Silencing the Past: Power and the Production of History*. Boston: Beacon Press.

Truong, Nicolas. 2016. Elisabeth Badinter appelle au boycott des marques qui se lancent dans la mode islamique. *Le Monde*, April 2. Available at: http://www.lemonde.fr/idees/article/2016/04/02/elisabeth-badinter-une-partie-de-la-gauche-a-baisse-la-garde-devant-le-communautarisme_4894360_3232.html (accessed January 2, 2018).

Tshimanga, Charles. 2009. Let the music play: The African diaspora, popular culture, and national identity in contemporary France. In *Frenchness and the African Diaspora: Identity and Uprising in Contemporary France*, ed. Charles Tshimanga, Didier Gondola, and Peter J. Bloom. Bloomington: Indiana University Press, pp. 248–76.

Tsing, Anna. 2005. *Friction: An Ethnography of Global Connection*. Princeton: Princeton University Press.

Turner, Terence. 1995. Response to Verena Stolcke. *Current Anthropology* 36: 16–18.

Turner, Victor. 1974. *Dramas, Fields, and Metaphors: Symbolic Action in Human Society*. Ithaca, NY: Cornell University Press.

Vergès, Françoise. 1999. *Monsters and Revolutionaries: Colonial Family Romance and "Métissage"*. Durham, NC: Duke University Press.

——2007. *La mémoire enchaînée: Questions sur l'esclavage*. Paris: Albin Michel.

Vertovec, Steven. 2007. Super-diversity and its implications. *Ethnic and Racial Studies* 30(6): 1024–54.

Vidal, Dominique. 2003. *Le mal-être juif: Entre repli, assimilation et manipulations*. Marseille: Agone.

Vigarello, Georges. 1978. *Le corps redressé: Histoire d'un pouvoir pédagogique*. Paris: Armand Colin.

Wacquant, Loïc. 2008. *Urban Outcasts: A Comparative Sociology of Advanced Marginality*. Cambridge: Polity Press.

Warner, Michael. 2002. *Publics and Counterpublics*. Cambridge, MA: MIT Press.

Weber, Eugen. 1976. *Peasants into Frenchmen*. Stanford: Stanford University Press.

Weil, Simone. 2003 [1943]. *Simone Weil on Colonialism: An Ethic of the Other*. Lanham, MD: Rowman and Littlefield.

Welch, Edward, and John Periovolaris. 2016. The place of the republic: Space, territory and identity around and after *Charlie Hebdo*. *French Cultural Studies* 27(3): 279–92.

Wieviorka, Michel. 2007. *The Lure of Anti-Semitism: Hatred of Jews in Present-Day France*, trans. Kristin Couper Lobel and Anna Declerck. Leiden: Brill.

——2013. Derrière l'affaire Dieudonné, l'essor d'un public "antisystème". *Le Monde*, December 31. Available at: http://www.lemonde.fr/idees/article/2013/12/31/affaire-dieudonne-l-essor-d-un-public-antisysteme_4341646_3232.html (accessed December 25, 2017).

Wilder, Gary. 2005. *The French Imperial Nation-State: Négritude and Colonial Humanism between the Two World Wars*. Chicago: University of Chicago Press.

——2015. *Freedom Time: Négritude, Decolonization and the Future of the World*. Durham, NC: Duke University Press.

Wilkinson, Alec. 2007. No obstacles: Navigating the world by leaps and bounds. *New Yorker*, April 16. Available at: https://www.newyorker.com/magazine/2007/04/16/no-obstacles (accessed January 3, 2018).

Winant, Howard. 2004. *The New Politics of Race*. Minneapolis: University of Minnesota Press.

Winter, Bronwyn. 2008. *Hijab and the Republic: Uncovering the French Headscarf Debate*. Syracuse, NY: Syracuse University Press.

Wright, Gwendolyn. 1997. Tradition in the service of modernity: Architecture and urbanism in French colonial policy, 1900–1930. In *Tensions of Empire: Colonial Cultures in a Bourgeois World*, ed. Frederick Cooper and Ann Laura Stoler. Berkeley: University of California Press, pp. 322–45.

Yahi, Naïma. 2010. Le "onze du FLN", un lieu de mémoire. In *Allez la France! Football et immigration*, ed. Claude Boli, Yvan Gastaut, and Fabrice Grognet. Paris: Gallimard, pp. 105–9.

Ye'or, Bat. 2002. *Islam and Dhimmitude: Where Civilizations Collide*. Madison, NJ: Farleigh Dickinson University Press.

——2005. *Eurabia: The Euro-Arab Axis*. Madison, NJ: Farleigh Dickinson University Press.

Zeghal, Malika. 2008. *Islamism in Morocco: Religion, Authoritarianism and Electoral Politics*. Princeton: Markus Wiener.

Zehraoui, Ahsène. 1994. *L'immigration: De l'homme seul à la famille*. Paris: CIEMI/L'Harmattan.

Zemmour, Eric. 2014. *Le suicide français*. Paris: Albin Michel.

Index